BASEBALL: 1862 TO 2003

JOHN SHIFFERT

PublishAmerica
Baltimore

First printing

ISBN: 1-4137-4276-9
PUBLISHED BY PUBLISHAMERICA, LLLP
www.publishamerica.com
Baltimore

Printed in the United States of America

*For the man who taught me about baseball,
my father, John A. Shiffert, Sr.*

Acknowledgements

After some 45 years as a baseball fan, it is impossible to accurately recall all the people whose input, knowledge, advice, criticism, opinions and information have gone into making *Baseball: 1862 to 2003* possible. Since they all have, in one way or another, had a hand in making this book possible, I owe you all a debt of gratitude. (Just don't come asking for a cut of the profits…)

Certainly, the first person on the list is my father, also John Shiffert, who took me to my first game at Connie Mack Stadium in 1957, where the Phillies lost to the Reds and Joe Nuxhall… although we did get a foul ball in batting practice, courtesy of Phillies' shortstop, Chico Fernandez. Second, is my grandfather, Ralph Milo Shiffert, who not only taught my father about baseball, but who was the source of many great stories about the National Pastime, stories about Eddie Plank, Stuffy McInnis and other baseball greats in the Philadelphia pantheon. Granddad and I also went to two especially memorable Phillies games that added to my sense of history: the final home opener at Connie Mack Stadium in 1970 (when Chris Short shut out the Cubs, 2-0) and Steve Carlton's only win for the Phillies in 1985 (my dad made it a threesome that night… it was the last game my grandfather attended), when the great Lefty was clearly at the end of an historic career.

After that, it gets sort of complicated, as many, many subscribers to my 19 to 21 e-zine, and visitors to my website (www.baseball19to21.com—look, Ma, I'm a Dot Com!) have offered information, opinions and advice over the past year. While I will take this opportunity to thank all of you, this is also the place to specifically acknowledge the electronic contributions (in some cases e-mail, in some cases e-columns) of 10 individuals whose words have found their way onto these pages… Jim Baker, Bill Deane, Rob Neyer, Lee Sinins, Bill Chuck, Joe Ptak, Kevin Warren, Ron Cobb, Brian Walton, Rich Lally and my dad. Thank you, one and all, and thank you for your permission to use your thoughts in this work. Of particular note are the three "My Favorite Team Essays" that make Chapter 34 one of my personal favorites (along with the 1993 Phillies). Baker's and my father's essays therein are originals, however, it is only right and proper to acknowledge that Bill Deane's piece on the 1976 Cincinnati Reds originally appeared in the August 2, 2003 edition of a fine small town daily, the Oneonta, NY *Daily Star*. When you're in Cooperstown, the *Daily Star* is the paper to read. In addition to the above-named individuals, several more of my e-mail correspondents have provided insight and experience that have influenced the contents of this book and its eventual publication. So, to… Ken Hirdt, Cecilia Tan, Bob Gordon, Bruce Brown, T. Scott Brandon, Darren Viola, Howard Garson, Matthew Coyne, Rod Nelson, Vic Debs and Maxwell Kates, take a bow.

On another level, I'd like to acknowledge the indirect contributions of several quite notably baseball writers, none of whom I have ever met (and all but two of whom are now dead), but whose work made this book, and many, many like it, possible. They are… Henry Chadwick, O.P. Caylor, Francis Richter, Hugh Fullerton, Ernest Lanigan, Fred Lieb, Lee Allen, Allen Lewis, Jayson Stark, and, of course, Bill James. (Richter, Lieb, Lewis and Stark all being fellow Philadelphians as well.)

Finally, several friends have also contributed in one way or another, notably… Ted Taylor, Jim Hardy, Pete DeCoursey, Peter Zolja, Harry Gratwick and Dr. Larry Levine.

Table of Contents

INTRODUCTION

If you put together Bruce Chen and the Chinese cyclical philosophy of history with the Mad Russian personality of Lou Novikoff, what do you get? Baseball, of course. Where just about everything that happens has some sort of historical precedent, and, well, you never know what might happen. Let's take a couple of examples from the 2003 season…

Under the Chinese theory of history… the Chicago Cubs have a seemingly safe lead, and their pitcher has a shutout going in the late innings of a key post-season game. Then, thanks in part to some inexplicable happenings, the roof falls in, and the Cubbies get blown out in nothing flat. The Steve Bartman-fueled debacle in game six of the 2003 NLCS? Yes… and that's also a perfectly good description of the biggest meltdown in World Series history, in 1929, when the Athletics dropped a 10-spot on those very same Cubs to erase an 8-0 lead in game four.

As to the Mad Russian part… did anyone expect that one of the big stories around the 2003 All-Star Game would be the first-ever Sausage Slashing in major league history, wherein a young woman, dressed up as an Italian Sausage and running in a smoked meat footrace, would be bopped by an overweight Pirate dressed like a bottle of mustard? Of course, there have been previous incidents of mascots or other costumed figures running afoul of players and/or managers (notably the long-standing feud between the Phillie Phanatic and Tommy Lasorda), but who expected Randall Simon to take a bat to one of the participants in the Milwaukee Brewers' nightly Sausage Race. Is baseball a great game, or what?

That's what *Baseball: 1862 to 2003* is about… the past and the present of baseball. Baseball books typically come in three varieties… books about baseball history, books about baseball's current events, and books about baseball statistics. But, here's something new – you're holding a book on baseball history that also includes a weekly review of the 2003 season, and uses some familiar statistical tools.

Along the way, we'll introduce three new metrics – three new means of measuring offensive performance… Isolated Discipline, The Ordonez Line and The Rule of 10. Isolated Discipline, or ID, is a means of gauging how willing a batter is to take a walk. By subtracting a hitter's batting average from his on-base average (OBA), ID gives us a better measure than OBA alone, of a player's relative ability to get on base. The Ordonez Line "replaces" (at least in this work) the now-outdated Mendoza Line. Since OPS (on base + slugging percentage) is a far better measure of a player's offensive value, why not have a means of expressing a really bad hitter in terms of his OPS failing to clear a minimum standard? In this case, that would be Rey Ordonez… quite possibly the worst regular offensive player of the Rocketball Era. With Ole Ray now sulking at home after the Padres had the nerve to make him compete for their shortstop job, his career OPS is currently stuck at .602. Hence, The Ordonez Line is pegged at .600. Finally, The Rule of 10 is a simple way, at a glance, to tell if a current player is above average in the two most important offensive skills – extra base hits, and walks. In both leagues, over the past 10 years or so, both extra base hits and walks have averaged out to roughly 10 percent of "at bats." Hence, if your favorite player has a ratio of less than 10 to 1 for at bats to extra base hits, and at bats to walks, you know he's above average… despite what the BBWAA types and the manager of your favorite team may tell you.

In addition to Isolated Discipline, The Ordonez Line and The Rule of 10, several hopefully familiar stats and methods – most of which were originally devised by Bill James -- are used throughout this book. These include…

OPS – On base average plus slugging percentage. A mark of .800 is around average, 1.000 will usually put you up around the league leaders, and .600 is The Ordonez Line.

Isolated Power (or IP) – The slugging percentage version of ID. Subtract a player's batting average from his slugging percentage, and you have a pretty good idea how much power he has. An IP over .200

is pretty good.

Adjusted ERA (or ERA+) – An ERA of 3.00 is a lot better today than it was back in 1908. Adjusted ERA takes into account both how many runs were scored in an individual year or era, as well as the home parks for the pitcher. It's expressed as a three-digit figure percentage. In other words, an ERA+ of 110 is 10 percent above the league average for that year, taking into account the park factor for the pitcher in question. Similarly, an ERA+ of 80 is 20 percent worse than the league average.

The Black Ink Test – A Jamesian device that allows comparison of a player's accomplishments across different eras. The various baseball encyclopedias list league-leading totals in **bold face** (or black ink, if you will), making tabulating this stat fairly easy. Varying point totals are given for leading a league in different offensive and defensive categories. Hence, if you lead your league in doubles in 1908 (the Deadball Era), it's just as valuable in this test if you lead in doubles in 1999 (the Rocketball Era)… making an automatic period adjustment.

The Favorite Toy – Another Jamesian trick, now called Career Assessment (boring… let's stick with The Favorite Toy). This is a means of calculating a player's chance of reaching a specific statistical goal and is based on the player's productivity over the past three years in that statistic, his age and how many wins, or home runs or anything else he needs to reach the specific goal.

Game Scores – Yet another James invention… it's a means of accurately rating every single performance by a starting pitcher. Theoretically, it's a scale of 1-100, although once every blue moon someone will top 100, and there are sometimes some really bad starts that go below zero. Usually, there are about 10 scores of 90 or better in each league each year.

Runs Created – James invented this one back in the 1980s as a means of better measuring a player's offensive contribution… in other words, using a mathematical formula (in some version pretty simple, in others very complicated) how many of the games most basic currency – runs – did he create each year?

Range Factor – Another means of gauging defensive skill. Anyone can have a high fielding percentage… this measures how many balls per game a player got to as well.

The National Pastime's rich history provides a wide variety of instructive examples that illuminate the events of 2003 through a weekly review of the just-finished season, written as the events of 2003 were happening, and looking at them through the lens of baseball history to show how events from baseball's past resonate in today's game.

In every weekly chapter, we'll look at a timely historical event – usually, something that happened in the same week or month in the past, and ranging from birthdays, to players' debuts and other milestones, to events on the field – from baseball's history and tie it to a event or news story from 2003's headlines, sometimes comparing the past and the present, sometimes contrasting the two, sometimes using an event from the past as a jumping off point to look at what's happening in 2003. In some chapters, the main focus is on the historical event. In others, the current event takes center stage. Either way, it's meant to be entertaining, to be fun, because, after all, baseball IS a game, and games are to be enjoyed. Enjoy!

CHAPTER 1

December 16, 2002

Item: December 5, 1978 – The Philadelphia Phillies sign one Peter Edward Rose, Sr., to what is then the largest contract in baseball history – $3.2 million over four years.

Let's take a look at two remarkably similar players, one whose career was centered on the 60s and 70s, and one whose career ran through the 70s and into the 80s. Both were lead-off men. The first was a second baseman who converted to the outfield in mid-career, and the other a third baseman who moved, as many do, across the diamond to first as he grew older. Player "A" (the earlier lead-off man) had a 12-year major league career, made eight All-Star teams and won two Gold Gloves in the outfield. Player "B" didn't win any Gold Gloves, but did make nine All-Star teams in his 12-year career in the majors.

Remarkably enough, these two players posted almost totally identical batting records:

	G	AB	R	H	2B	3B	HR	RBI	SB	BB	SO	BA	OBP	SLG	OPS
A	1781	7026	1082	2128	373	67	80	657	99	783	571	.303	375	.409	.784
B	1781	7027	1083	2128	373	68	80	657	99	783	572	.303	375	.409	.784

You can't get much closer than that, can you? In addition, these two each scored 32 on the Black Ink Test, between them leading the league at one time or another in batting average, on base average, games played, at bats, runs, hits, doubles and even hit by pitch. About the only significant difference – other than playing different positions, is that Player "A" made the top 10 in the MVP voting seven times, and Player "B" only made it three times.

Now, the question before the house is… are these two players Hall of Fame candidates?

Well, 12 years and 1781 games is a pretty short career. However, they do meet the minimum (10 years) requirement for the HOF, and, indeed plenty of Hall of Famers have had shorter careers… for instance, Ralph Kiner (1472G), Ross Youngs (1211G), Sam Thompson (1407G), Chuck Klein (1753G), King Kelly (1455G) and Freddie Lindstrom (1438G). Of course, most of these were mistakes by the Veterans Committee or 19th Century stars playing under significantly different conditions (including a much shorter schedule), so maybe that's not a good indicator.

Certainly, their league leadership totals (the average HOFer scores 27 in black ink – the type face used to denote league leadership in the record books) and their multiple appearances in the All-Star Game speak well for their chances. Player "A" also has a strong MVP voting record, including winning the award once. And, a .303 BA with a .375 OBP isn't bad for a lead-off man in the offensively-challenged 60s, 70s and 80s.

So, what you have are a couple of players who were clearly considered stars during their relatively short careers. They hit for a good average, got on base and controlled the strike zone pretty well, and had some doubles power, although mostly they piled up a lot of singles. Hall of Famers? Maybe, maybe not, except for the next round of mistakes by the Veterans Committee. (Hopefully, with the Committee's new configuration, the mistakes of the past are less likely to happen.)

Of course, as you have undoubtedly figured out by now, Player "A" and Player "B" don't exist, and they never did. They are the two halves of Pete Rose's career. Add them together, and you have the player we called "The Original Jack" when I was in college in Indiana. (For those of you unfamiliar with Midwestern terminology, a "hilljack" is a somewhat, shall we say, unsophisticated, resident of southwestern Ohio.)

Now, Pete's certainly been in the news a lot recently, what with his "secret" meeting with Bud.Com. As to whether or not Pete should be reinstated in the good graces of baseball, well that's another story. Without going into ad nauseam detail, suffice it to say that, A) the most careful baseball researcher and thinker on the planet says in *The New Bill James Historical Baseball Abstract* that the actual evidence that Rose is extremely weak.[1] And, B) yes, gambling and betting in baseball was the sport's biggest problem from the mid 1860s (throwing a game was called "hippodroming" then) until maybe the mid 1920s. But that was almost 80 years ago. There's been one baseball gambling scandal (outside of Pete) since then, in the Evangeline League (of all places), right after World War II. I mean, let's get some perspective here... Cesar Cedeno shot and killed Altagracia De La Cruz... is that worse than gambling?

Anyway, whether or not you think Pete should be back in baseball's good graces, there's no denying the man could play a little baseball... especially when you can divide him up into two players and still have two possible Hall of Famers.

CHAPTER 2

December 23, 2002

Item: December 25, 1958 – Rickey Henley Henderson is born in Chicago, Il.

Word has it that Rickey stole the pillow off his mom's bed when he was six months old… it was the closest thing in the house to second base… and he hasn't stopped stealing since. At the moment, it's an astounding total of 1403 bases to date for the greatest lead-off man in baseball history.

To try and put that into some kind of meaningful perspective… possibly the finest base stealer of the years (1963 to 1984) immediately preceding Mr. Henderson was little Joe Morgan, who is 11th all-time in stolen bases with 689 – less than half of Henderson's total. Tim Raines, Henderson's exact contemporary, and the second-greatest lead-off man, is in fifth place with 808… less than 58% of Henderson's total. Willie Wilson and Bert Campaneris, combined, are almost 100 steals behind Rickey. Maury Wills and Otis Nixon are 200 in arrears. For goodness sakes, at the age of 43, the man successfully stole eight out of 10 bases for the 2002 Red Sox. (Wonder if Bill James, a major Henderson supporter, will persuade the Sox to keep him around in 2003?)

Add in 3040 hits, 870 extra base hits and the career records for runs scored (2288 – a far more significant accomplishment than he's given credit for) and walks (2179), and that's a pretty fair lead-off man… even if he has offended a lot of people during his 24-year career.

His offenses (as opposed to his offense) notwithstanding … in honor of Rickey Henderson, and in light of the holiday season, here is the All-Time Players Born on a Holiday Team:

1B – Hank Greenberg (January 1)
2B – Nellie Fox (December 25)
3B – Pie Traynor (November 11)
SS – Joe Cronin (October 12)
C – Rick Ferrell (October 12)
OF – Rickey Henderson (December 25)
OF – Manny Ramirez (May 30)
OF – Pepper Martin (February 29)
P – Tim Keefe (January 1)
P – Mickey Welch (July 4)
P – Pud Galvin (December 25)
P – Amos Rusie (May 30)
RP – Roberto Hernandez (November 11)
PH – Don Newcombe (June 14)
Mgr. – Chuck Tanner (July 4)

Among those who didn't make the cut were Red Schoendienst (February 2), Rabbit Maranville (November 11), George Mullin (July 4), George Case (November 11), Ken Keltner (October 31) and Al Rosen (February 29).

(What are the odds that, out of the dozen men who have played major league baseball and who were born on Leap Year Day, that two of them would be stars of the magnitude of Martin and Rosen? Is this a great game, or what?)

That's not a bad lineup – an all-Hall of Fame infield, catcher and 19th Century starting rotation. And, you don't really have to apologize for an outfield of Henderson, Ramirez (a sure HOFer and a probable) and Martin.

CHAPTER 3

ITEM: November 1914, December 1914, January 1915–Connie Mack breaks up the American League's first great dynasty, disposing of future Hall of Famers for filthy lucre, over-the-hill talent and never-got-to-the-hill talent

Well, there was a war on… two wars, for that matter. "The Great War" in Europe (not that it had much effect on baseball until 1918) and, right here at home, the Federal League War, wherein the well-capitalized "Feds" had been throwing large and vulgar sums of cash money at National and American League players since early 1914 in an attempt to become a third major league.

And, while war may well be all that General Sherman said it was, it is also very expensive. Maybe not as expensive as free agency, but costly nonetheless. It cost Philadelphia a great team; perhaps in a fashion similar to what rising salaries, luxury taxes and shrinking budgets may end up costing Atlanta. In baseball, as in almost everything else, there's nothing new under the sun.

Following the 1914 World Series, Connie Mack sold the reigning American League MVP, second baseman Eddie Collins, to the White Sox, and released pitchers Chief Bender, Eddie Plank and Jack Coombs. The first three would one day enter the Hall of Fame, and Coombs had been the Athletics' ace as recently as the 1910 and 1911 seasons. Meanwhile, during the 1915 season, Mack was bringing in (among others) the immortal "Squiz" Pillion and Bruno Haas to take their places.

The other big loss between the 1914 and 1915 seasons was another future Hall of Famer, J. Franklin "Home Run" Baker, who sat out the entire 1915 season in what was either a salary dispute, or a fit of pique because Mack had disposed of the other four players. Supporting the latter theory, author Fred Lieb quotes Mack in his bio, *Grand Old Man of Baseball*, that the Athletics had torn up Collins', Baker's and "other key players" contracts in the middle of the 1914 season, and had presented them with new, three-year deals... the Federal League War equivalent of trying to keep them out of the free agent market.[2]

In either case, Baker spent 1915 on his Maryland farm, and the A's did a first to worst, going from dynasty to just plain nasty, falling from 99-53 in 1914 to 43-109, a horrendous drop of 56 games.

Of course, even before the start of the 1915 season, Mack faced financial problems. During the 1914 season, while the A's were winning their fourth pennant in five years (and sixth in the AL's first 14 seasons), attendance was down at Shibe Park. From 571,896 in 1913 (second in the league) to 346,641 (fifth in the league) in 1914. In other words, like the AOL-Time Warner Braves of 2002, their cash flow was drying up and under capitalization was facing Mack square in the catcher's mask.

So, in November 1914, Coombs goes to Brooklyn. In December, Collins is sold outright to the White Sox for $50,000. In January 1915, in an attempt to fill Collins' spot, Mack picks up an over-the-hill Napoleon Lajoie from Cleveland for the waiver price. (Can you say, "Vinny Castilla?") And, before the 1915 season started, Plank and Bender did indeed sign with the Federal League.

Interestingly Mack – unlike John Schuerholz – was always reluctant to admit the reason for the break-up was money. The Federal League war was dramatically raising expenses – most notably in the area of salaries of the stars. An instructive example was Washington Senators' ace, Walter Johnson, who received a $10,000 bonus from tight-fisted White Sox owner Charlie Comiskey... to keep him out of the hands of the Federals' Chicago Whales.

Mack, on the other hand, seems not to have had options like that, possibly because he had been beating up on the league for the past six years, and his fellow owners (and perhaps league president, Ban

Johnson – with whom Mack spent Thanksgiving Week 1914 in Philadelphia) wanted to restore a little parity to the circuit.

Now, fast forward to the fall of 2002. Despite 11 first place finishes in 12 years, attendance has been steadily dropping at Turner Field (from 3.4 million in 1997 to 2.6 million in 2002), while, at the same time, the Braves have changed hands, from the profligate Ted Turner to the staggering corporate giant, AOL-Time Warner.

So, what do the Braves do? They essentially grant their long-time ace, Tom Glavine, free agency, after first picking up the faded Mike Hampton in a trade. And, they let two of their key relievers, Chris Hammond and Mike Remlinger, take the same route out of the South as Glavine. Then, they sign the never-got-to-the-hill Paul Byrd to a contract.

Finally, just in time for Christmas, the capper. They trade arguably their best pitcher, Kevin Millwood, to their closest pursuer -- the Philadelphia Phillies – for a backup catcher (Johnny Estrada) who likewise will probably never make the hill. At least Schuerholz is more honest than Mack, branding the trade as necessary due to the economics of baseball which, he also says, stink.

(Hey… why didn't the economics of baseball stink a few years ago when the Braves had the money to pay Glavine and Greg Maddux big bucks?)

Let's see. That's three pitchers who were allowed to walk, and another key player given away for practically nothing, plus a few has-beens or never-weres brought in to take their places. Sound familiar? Maybe Chipper Jones will sit out the 2003 season in a fit of pique.

Or maybe it's Philadelphia's turn to be repaid for the events of the winter of 1914/15.

CHAPTER 4

January 6, 2003

Item: Dec. 11, 1917–The Phillies trade Grover Cleveland Alexander and his catcher, Reindeer Bill Killefer, to the Cubs for catcher Bill "Pickles" Dillhoefer, pitcher Mike Prendergast and $55,000.

Dumb trades. What can you say about dumb trades? Having briefly touched upon the Kevin Millwood for Johnny Estrada deal last chapter, the time is ripe to look further into the subject of "what were they thinking of?" trades.

Generally speaking, really bad trades fall into one of two categories… deals wherein some financial consideration is really the determining factor (call them Money Trades), and deals where somebody made an egregious mistake in evaluating talent (call them Bonehead Trades). Clearly, the Braves trading a 27-year-old power pitcher coming off an 18-win season to a division rival for a 26-year-old catcher who played 10 games in the majors in 2002 is, as John Schuerholz admitted, a money deal.

At first glance, the 1917 Phillies trading a three-time, 30-game winner and their starting catcher for a second-year receiver who would play a total of eight games for the Phillies (but who does make the All-Nickname Team) and a pitcher who would win fewer games in his entire career than Alex had won in 1916 and 1917 alone is inexplicable. Even the $55,000 doesn't balance it out. After all, just two years later the Red Sox would get $125,000 cash and a $300,000 loan for another young star pitcher.

(If The Curse of the Bambino has indeed doomed the Sox to

baseball purgatory for the past 82 years, what is to be made of the Trade of Alex? After finishing second, sixth, first, second and second from 1913 to 1917, the Phillies finished above .500 exactly once in the next 31 years following their gift to the Windy City.)

On the surface, the reason for the Alexander trade was unique – Phillies owner, William Baker, claimed that he traded Alex because the future Hall of Famer had been drafted into the military for service in World War I, and that there were no guarantees that Old Pete would come back from France in one piece. Ironically, Baker was right… although the actual causes of Alexander's epilepsy cannot be stated with absolute certainty (among other things, he suffered a severe beaning in the minors, while there is also evidence that he was shell-shocked as well as accidentally gassed in France), it seems certain that his war experience did him no good. Clearly, WW I must have exacerbated his already-present alcoholism.

However, whatever Alex may have suffered during and after the war, it didn't make much difference in his pitching. He would go on to win another 183 games from 1918 to 1929 (having won 190 for the Phillies) and election to the Hall of Fame.

Of course Baker, a former New York police commissioner who ran possibly the most undercapitalized major league operation in history, did admit years later that he made the deal for the money… something the Phillies would repeat time and again until the Carpenter family took over the team in the 1940s.

Other famous Money Trades include most of the deals Connie Mack made in breaking up his two great teams, the Boston Braves dealing Rogers Hornsby to the Cubs for five stiffs and $200,000, and several St. Louis Browns' (who were also traditionally undercapitalized) deals, including shipping Ellis Kinder and Junior Stephens off to the Red Sox for NINE stiffs and $375,000. Of course, Money Trades are being made now, even as we speak, not because the team in question needs money, but because they can't afford to pay the going salary rates. Bye-bye, Bartolo. We'll miss ya, Millwood.

Bonehead Trades, on the other hand, are always good for a laugh after the fact… at least, for one of the parties involved. The Cubs' famous deal sending Lou Brock to the Cards for Ernie Broglio, Bitsy Bobby Shantz and Doug Clemens is one that comes to mind. Of course, they balanced that out by getting Fergie Jenkins and Adolfo Phillips from the Phillies for Larry Jackson and Bob Buhl. And one would suspect that the Reds would like to have revoked the Frank Robinson (he was an old 30, said Bill DeWitt) for Milt Pappas, Jack Baldschun and Dick Simpson deal following the 1966 season. It's also possible that the Mets might have won a few more pennants if they had held on to Nolan Ryan instead of trading him for Jim Fregosi.

For some time the Giants specialized in these faux pas, trading away George Foster, Gaylord Perry, Garry Maddox, Gary Mathews, Orlando Cepeda, Bill White, Bobby Bonds, all three Alou Brothers and all five Marx Brothers for very little return.

The worst of the Giants' trades was dealing Foster for Frank Duffy (who they desperately needed as a backup for Chris Speier) and Vern Geishert (who?). Seems the Giants saw Foster's Selective Service physical, which said he was 4-F because of a back injury, and they were afraid it would recur. So they gave Foster to the Reds instead of Bernie Williams. Shades of Pete Alexander!

CHAPTER 5

January 13, 2003

ITEM: Jan. 27, 1982–The Cubs acquire shortstop, Larry Bowa, and a minor league infielder from the Phillies for shortstop, Ivan DeJesus.

Talk about a Bonehead Trade… The Phillies traded a shortstop that had been a cornerstone of their team since 1970. A five-time All-Star and a two-time Gold Glove winner who had finished third in the MVP voting in 1978. A team leader who would go on to accumulate career totals 2191 hits and 318 stolen bases, and who was coming off a year when he hit .283. A shortstop who, at the age of 38 (in 1984), was still good enough in the field to keep the Cubs' best prospect (Shawn Dunston) on the bench. And they threw in a minor league infielder as well. And they got…

Another shortstop, coming off a .194 season, who would total 1167 hits and 194 steals (although he did walk a little more than Bowa) in his career and who would never be confused with a Gold Glove winner. What were they (i.e. Phillies' boss Bill Giles) thinking of? Especially since that minor league infielder was Ryne Sandberg.

After his first year of eligibility, Sandberg may not be a Hall of Famer, but he was a far site better ballplayer then Ivan DeJesus.

Former Phillies manager Dallas Green was Cubs' general manager at that time. And, he knew something. He wanted Bowa, and he knew the Phillies' personnel inside and out. And he knew he wanted Ryne Sandberg. In fact, he actually called Bowa (this was long before the days of e-mail), first to see if he would go along with the deal, and secondly, to tell him he wanted Sandberg as well. Talk about your insider trading...

Now, as many of the Phillies past and present will probably tell you, dealing with Larry Bowa isn't necessarily the easiest thing in the world. In fact, when Phillies' scout Eddie Bockman first went to see Bowa play in college, he didn't see much, because Bowa was tossed out of both games of a doubleheader in the first inning.

Skip ahead to the end of the 1981 season. Bowa has truly ticked off Giles in a contract dispute. And he's determined to get rid of the skinny, hyper kid who broke in on the last Opening Day in Connie Mack Stadium history – Apr. 7, 1970. (I was there with my grandfather. The Phils won 2-0 behind Chris Short.) However, there's one little problem. To paraphrase Casey Stengel, you have to have a shortstop, or you'll have a lot of ground balls roll into left field. So, Giles wants to get a major league shortstop in the worst way in exchange for Bowa. And that's what he gets... a shortstop in the worst way. And Giles (along with chief scout Hugh Alexander, who should have known better) throws Sandberg into the trade. Does that explain it a little better? Well, maybe yes, maybe no.

On the one hand, the Phillies had another hot prospect coming up at second base – Juan Samuel – who would take over that spot in 1984. So maybe the felt they didn't need Sandberg at second, and he certainly wasn't needed at third base (which is where he played in his first season for the Cubs), Mike Schmidt was there. On the other hand, Giles could have kept Sandberg, and made him the shortstop in 1982. He played short for five of the six games he got into during his late season call-up in 1981. You have to think anyone who would win nine Gold Gloves at second and was able to play 133 games at third might have been a capable shortstop.

But, was he a Hall of Famer?

CHAPTER 6

Item–January 15, 1929: Michael King is born in Atlanta.

Michael King? Who did he play for?

In many ways, he played for us all. Specifically, one person who comes to mind is another native Georgian, Jack Roosevelt Robinson, because Michael King became Martin Luther King, Jr. on his sixth birthday. Or, maybe, Jackie Robinson played for Martin Luther King.

Either way, if there ever was a ballplayer that defined "Hall of Famer," it was Jackie Robinson.

But, what about another pretty fair second baseman? Ryne Sandberg? The results of the recent Hall of Fame election, wherein Sandberg drew less than 50% of the vote, has caused more than a fair amount of gnashing of literary teeth throughout the land… and not just in the Land of the Skunk (the Indian translation of Shee-caw-go). Does "Ryno" deserve to be in the Hall? Let's compare him to Robinson, first in raw numbers, and then on averages per 162 games…

	G	AB	R	H	2B	3B	HR	RBI
Robinson	1382	4877	947	1518	273	54	137	734
Sandberg	2164	8385	1318	2386	403	76	282	1061

	SB	BB	SO	BA	OBP	SLG	OPS
Robinson	197	740	291	.311	.409	.474	.883
Sandberg	344	761	1260	.285	.344	.452	.796

	AB	R	H	2B	3B	HR	RBI	SB	BB	SO
Robinson	572	111	178	32	6	16	86	23	87	34
Sandberg	628	99	179	30	6	21	79	26	57	94

Their career figures don't really have much in common. For obvious reasons, Sandberg's major league career was much longer (a plus factor in his HOF argument) and he piles up far more impressive counting stats than Robinson. However, Jackie's plate discipline (his K/W ratio) is far better, as is his OPS and its components, although Sandberg does show slightly better isolated power (slugging minus batting average, for the uninitiated.)

On a seasonal basis, they do look more similar, with Robinson still getting a big edge in runs scored and K/W ratio and Sandberg having a little more home run power, but using up far more (56) outs per season.

Let's also add a comparison of Sandberg and Robinson taking Sandberg's stats starting at the age of 28 – which is, of course, when Jackie was first allowed to showcase his talents in the major leagues.

	G	AB	R	H	2B	3B	HR	RBI
Robinson	1382	4877	947	1518	273	54	137	734
Sandberg	1242	4716	743	1330	225	35	192	657
	SB	BB	SO	BA	OBP	SLG	OPS	
Robinson	197	740	291	.311	.409	.474	.883	
Sandberg	134	460	734	.282	.346	.467	.813	

Ouch! At least if you're a Ryne Sandberg fan. Except for home runs and isolated power, Robinson blows him away on totals AND percentages.

It's probably safe to say that each player enjoyed the best offensive home park of his era, although Robinson did have the benefit of playing in a higher scoring era… but not by much. During Jackie's 10-year career, National League teams averaged 4.49 runs per game. Sandberg, who retired just as the Rocketball Era was coming in – a factor that undoubtedly had a negative effect on his HOF vote total – played when teams averaged 4.23 runs per game, a difference of only 6%. Even if we give Ryno a 6% boost in his output, that still only bumps his career OPS to .844, still almost 40 points below Robinson.

However, Sandberg's raw totals are nonetheless pretty good, most notably the career record for home runs (277) by a second baseman.

Now, what about defense? Sandberg has those nine Gold Gloves, and Robinson's reputation wasn't built on his defense, was it? Well, according to Bill James' Win Shares system, Robinson ranks fifth all-time for defensive excellence among second basemen that played more than 3,000 innings at the position.[3]

Well, having spent several graphs being patently unfair to Mr. Sandberg by comparing him to a player James ranks as the fourth greatest second baseman in history, it is time to give the throw-in in the Bowa/DeJesus trade his due. After all, Sandberg is ranked as the seventh greatest ever to play his position by James, who also assumes, in the *New Historical Baseball Abstract* that Ryno will have a plaque in Cooperstown.[4] Furthermore, the esteemed Rob Neyer of ESPN.com now has Sandberg at the top of his list of deserving candidates for the Hall.

Nevertheless, there actually were some arguments made against Sandberg's candidacy over the past month, notably that he only drove in more than 80 runs six times.

Well, excuuuuuuse me, but that's a classical fallacy in Hall of Fame arguments. Like saying Reggie Jackson doesn't belong because he didn't hit for average, or that Honus Wagner should be kicked out because he barely hit 100 home runs, or that Jackie Robinson doesn't belong because he didn't drive in runs either. Sandberg, like Robinson, didn't typically hit in an RBI spot in the lineup. They were both top-of-the-order hitters.

Another strike against Sandberg seems to be that his heyday – 1983 to 1993 – was a lousy era for second basemen. However, during those 11 years, there can be no doubt who the top dog was at second, and that may be Sandberg's strongest argument – he was the best at his position in the major leagues for more than 10 years… longer than the minimum time required to be eligible for the Hall of Fame. Let's look at Top 20 finishes among the MVP voters by second basemen for the period 1983 to 1993.

Ryne Sandberg – 6
Robbie Alomar – 3
Bill Doran – 2
Steve Sax – 2
Carlos Baerga – 2

Not a perfect measure, but, realistically, Robbie Alomar is the only candidate who can challenge Sandberg's title as Best Second Baseman of His Era. And, although Alomar didn't come up until 1988, Sandberg still had more Top 20 finishes among the MVP voters from 1989 to 1993 (four to three). So, while Alomar was clearly taking over at second when Sandberg made his ill-advised first retirement in 1994, Ryne Sandberg was the best second baseman in baseball looking at the period 1983 (when he took over from Joe Morgan) to 1993 as a whole.

And that, my friends, is a Hall of Famer.

CHAPTER 7

January 27, 2003

Item–January 22, 1962: Jackie Jensen retires for the final time.

Jackie Jensen, like Michael Jordan, retired several times. You see, Jackie had this problem with flying. He didn't like it.

And, he had the misfortune of coming into baseball right about the time teams started flying from series-to-series, instead of staying on the ground like we were all intended. (I mean, even Rickey Henderson doesn't have wings… of course, he's no angel, either.) So, Jensen retired… several times… when the fear of flying (hmmm… there's a good title for a book in there somewhere) got to be too much. Some of his retirements were brief. One lasted an entire season – he missed the 1960 campaign with his feet on the ground. And that brings up an interesting question… what effect does missing an entire season have on the production of a top-flight hitter?

Just for purposes of comparison, let's look at eight pretty fair batsmen who, for one reason or another, missed full seasons during their major league careers. In chronological order they are: Harry "Old Jasper" Davis, J. Franklin "Home Run" Baker, George Sisler, Stan Musial (without a doubt, "The Man"), the aforementioned Mr. Jensen, Dave "Mr. May" Winfield, the much-discussed Ryne Sandberg and Andres Gallaraga. Baker, Sisler, Musial and Winfield all reside in Cooperstown. Assuming the Veterans Committee and the BBWAA get their acts together, Davis and Sandberg will join them some day, while Gallaraga would seem to have a chance at some point, and Jensen will always be a "what if?"

For this study, we'll look at their batting average, on-base percentage, slugging percentage and OPS (on-base + slugging) for the year before they sat out, and the two years after they came back. Note a couple of exceptions… both Davis and Sandberg played very little in the year before they sat out, so we've also included the year before that. And, Jensen only played one more year after coming back from his 1960 retirement.

	Age	Year	BA	OBP	Slg	OPS
Davis						
	24	1898	.262	.300	.399	.699
	25	1899	.188	.288	.312	.600 (18 games)
	27	1901	.306	.340	.452	.792
	28	1902	.307	.343	.444	.787
Baker						
	28	1914	.319	.380	.442	.822
	30	1916	.269	.344	.428	.772
	31	1917	.282	.345	.365	.710
	33	1919	.293	.346	.388	.734
	35	1921	.294	.353	.436	.789
	36	1922	.278	.327	.444	.771
Sisler						
	29	1922	.420	.467	.594	1.061
	31	1924	.305	.340	.421	.761
	32	1925	.345	.371	.479	.850
Musial						
	23	1944	.347	.440	.549	.989
	25	1946	.365	.434	.587	.921
	26	1947	.312	.398	.504	.902

Jensen

32	1959	.277	.372	.492	.864
34	1961	.263	.350	.392	.742

Winfield

36	1988	.322	.398	.530	.928
38	1990	.267	.338	.453	.791
39	1991	.262	.326	.472	.798

Sandberg

33	1993	.309	.359	.412	.771
34	1994	.238	.312	.390	.702 (57 games)
36	1996	.244	.316	.444	.760
37	1997	.264	.308	.403	.711

Gallaraga

37	1998	.305	.397	.595	.992
39	2000	.302	.369	.526	.895
40	2001	.256	.326	.459	.785

Hmmm… looks like the moral of the story is: If you sit out a year, you better not plan on coming back, unless you're willing to take a pay cut. (Oops, they don't do pay cuts anymore. Well, you get the idea.) In every case, except for Harry Davis and Home Run Baker's second "retirement," the numbers of some pretty good hitters declined in the two seasons following their sabbaticals. Even the 25 and 26-year-old Stan Musial couldn't match his pre-war 1944 season – although there would be reason to believe that the level of competition in baseball was somewhat higher in 1946 than it was in 1944. Still, it took him another full year to come all the way back and become a full-fledged superstar (in 1948).

Furthermore, there is good reason to at least partially discount Davis' and Baker's figures. Davis was going from the long-established National League of 1898 and 1899 to the first two years of what was, in effect, an expansion league, the American League in 1901 and 1902.

And Baker, when he came back after sitting out 1920 after his wife's death, was just a part-time player for the Yankees.

Now, these declines could be blamed on physical ailments. Certainly the cases of Sisler, Winfield and Gallaraga could fall into that category. Sisler missed the 1923 season with a severe sinus problem that was said to have damaged his eyesight for the rest of his life. Winfield (injury) and Gallaraga (cancer) both had back problems.

But, what of Davis, Baker, Musial and Sandberg? Davis sat out 1900 working as a clerk for the Pennsy (the late, lamented Pennsylvania Railroad). Baker sat during 1915 in a fit of pique (and played semi-pro ball back in Maryland, by the way) because Connie Mack was breaking up his first great dynasty. Musial enlisted in World War II and Sandberg just decided he didn't want to play… a decision (along with his decision to come back and play below his previous level) that may well have cost him mucho votes in this year's Hall of Fame balloting.

So, if you're hurting late in your career, and you miss a season… better think twice about returning. And, if you do decide to retire, especially in your 30s, better you should stay retired than sully your reputation. Right Ryno?

CHAPTER 8

February 3, 2003

Item: January 27, 1927 – Commissioner Kenesaw Mountain Landis clears Ty Cobb, Tris Speaker, Smoky Joe Wood, Pancho Villa, Prester John, Bull Craver, Attila the Hun, Dick Higham, Robin Hood, Mark Van Hoose, Mark Dicken, Hal Chase, Kaiser Wilhelm (the German monarch, not the pitcher), Jim Devlin, the Duke of Earl and everyone else involved in an alleged attempt to fix the Detroit Tigers/Cleveland Indians game of Sept. 25, 1919.

Well, guess who's back in the news. That's right, it's Pete. (No last name needed – just like the mis-spelled Kenesaw) Actually, it's probably fair to assume that Pete Rose won't be out of the news any time soon, at least until this little matter of his status with major league baseball is resolved.

Funny, isn't it, how Ty Cobb and Pete Rose seemed to be continually brought together by fate, or bad judgment, or character flaws, or whatever. The only two players to top 4,000 hits. Pete's youngest son is named "Tyler" (his wife at the time wouldn't let him use Tyrus). A couple of fighters who couldn't stay out of the news, even if they wanted to. Singles and doubles hitters who played like their knickers were on fire and got every ounce of accomplishment out of their ability. Pete's third-closest comp (in similarity scores for hitters) among all players is Cobb. Cobb's fourth-closest comp is Pete. And both tied to betting on baseball.

First, let's run the numbers from the field…

	G	AB	R	H	2B	3B	HR	RBI	SB	BB	BA	OBP	SA	OPS
Rose	3562	14053	2165	4256	746	135	160	1314	198	1566	.303	.375	.409	.784
Cobb	3035	11434	2246	4189	724	295	117	1937	892	1249	.366	.433	.512	.945

No, they're not really good comps – only close in runs, hits and doubles… but, considering just how extreme their numbers are compared to everyone else who ever played baseball, they match up to each other pretty well.

They may, or may not, match up in betting as well. Let's play pretend… and assume that John Dowd's investigation had turned up a letter from Rose that read (in part) like this…

Dear (Name of a pitcher – call him #1 – who was active in 1986):
(Name of another then-current player – call him #2) and myself were considerably disappointed in our business proposition… we completely fell down and of course felt badly over it.

Rose then goes on to say that the whole matter had been, "quite a responsibility, and I don't care for it again, I can assure you."

Sound harmless? Well, there's another letter, this one from player #2 to player #1, and this includes a certified check for $1650 and reads (in part)…

Rose did not get up a cent. He told us that and I believed him… If we ever get another chance like this we will know enough to try and get down early.

As my father would say, UH-OH! Especially since the second letter also explains that the bookie in question, a Cincinnati park attendant, had been able to bet only $600 for each of them (Rose, and players #1 and 2.)

Think there would be any talk of reinstating Pete if those two letters really existed?

And yet, they do exist. Just change Pete Rose to Ty Cobb, #1 to Dutch Leonard and #2 to Smoky Joe Wood. While it's true that Leonard hated Cobb's guts (gee, that really made him unique, didn't it?), he really did present two such letters to Landis, along with a story that must have curled the judge's white mane, in October 1926. Here's Dutch's tale…

Then-Tigers Leonard and Cobb met with then-Indians Speaker and Wood after the Tigers-Indians game of Sept. 24, 1919. Speaker, noting that his Indians had already clinched second place (behind the Black Sox) and that the Tigers were still battling for third (a slice of the World Series money) with the Yankees, suggested that the Tigers didn't have to worry about their next day's game with the Indians… in other words, the Tigers were sure to win. Then, Leonard says, the four of them agreed that, since the outcome was pre-determined, they might as well make some extra money on the deal.[5]

Again, according to Leonard (who also claimed that Cobb ran him out of baseball in 1925, and that Speaker helped by not signing him after the Tigers let him go), Cobb suggested that a Navin Field attendant, Fred West, act as the bag man for them and get the bets down. Because the bets were so close to the game, and the odds so prohibitive, West was only able to get $600 down – hence, the reference to completely falling down. The Tigers won the game in question, 9-5.

Leonard's story may have been taken with a grain of salt, except that he had these two letters, one written by Cobb from his home in Augusta in October 1919, and the other from Wood.[6]

Leonard first tried to show the letters to American League President, Ban Johnson, in May 1926, and Johnson, in cahoots with Tigers owner Frank Navin, bought Leonard off to the tune of $20,000! However, the letters eventually came to Landis' attention and ended up as the lynchpin in the seven-year-old war for control of baseball that he was fighting with Johnson.[7]

In the end, Landis won, Johnson's power was broken, and both Cobb and Speaker (Wood and Leonard were out of baseball by this point) were exonerated – as a means of showing Johnson (who had previously "banned" them from the American League) who was boss. However, that doesn't make Cobb innocent of, at the very least, having insider knowledge of a possible fix, and possibly using same to bet on a game. Landis, who had previously banned Buck Weaver for knowledge of the Black Sox scandal (even though he played the 1919 Series honestly), had the gall to say this about the Cobb/Speaker affair…

"These players have not been, nor are they now, found guilty of fixing a ball game. By no decent system of justice could such a finding be made."[8]

Notice that all Landis said was "fixing a ball game." He didn't say anything about betting on the game or talking about a fix. Landis was able to base this statement on the fact that Leonard refused to appear at a hearing in front of him (Landis) to personally face Cobb – because Leonard was afraid Cobb would try to kill him (a distinct possibility.)[9] Nevertheless, Landis, who had made his "reputation" as a federal judge on showy cases that were later overturned, clearly continued his rather questionable "legal" practices once he was off the bench. Assuming Landis could read, there's no denying the implications of the Cobb and Wood letters when they're put together.

Especially since Cobb himself admitted to Landis that he wrote the letter to Leonard,[10] but claimed he wasn't part of the conspiracy, he was just an intermediary, passing information from Wood to Leonard and suggesting West as the bag man. Furthermore, he admitted that he had bet on the first two games of the 1919 World Series[11] (a statement he took back later in his life.)[12] Buck Weaver – who was banned for just listening to talk about a fix -- must have spun in his grave at that one – and he wasn't even dead yet!

So, to recap… Ty Cobb admitted he bet on baseball and admitted he was part of, at the very least, a betting deal on a game that he played in. And he was one of the first five people voted into the Hall of Fame. Clearly, betting on baseball has not always been the peche mortal that it has become.

And, you have to think that there's one other thing Rose and Cobb have in common… they badly wanted to regain baseball's good graces. Baseball was/is their life. Pete was clearly no Angel (just a Red, Phillie and Expo), but, it seems he's no Ty Cobb, either, in more ways than one.

CHAPTER 9

February 10, 2003

Item: January 24, 1980 – Fred Wilpon and Nelson Doubleday buy the Mets (and, for the first time, a Doubleday is actually involved with baseball).

The Mets, the Mets… when Wilpon's and Doubleday's money came to the rescue of the Payson Estate, there was some speculation that the Mets' glory day of 1969 would return. It did. In 1986. And now, both those days are long gone. The Mets are now solidly Number Two in the New York market, even when their owners have a knock down, drag out buyout fight, such as just concluded in Mr. Wilpon's favor. What can be said about the Mets going into the 2003 season?

Well, Mike Piazza says the Mets are the team to beat in the National League East in 2003…

Love ya, Mike… and us Montgomery County, Pennsylvania boys should stick together, but you should be in a minority of one on this one. (At least outside of New York.)

OK, I'll give you that Tom Glavine and Mike Stanton are an upgrade to the pitching staff, and Cliff Floyd can hit a little bit. But, they're not the problem, Mike, YOU are, along with your holdover buddies Mo Vaughn, Roger Cedeno, Jeromy Burnitz and maybe even Robbie Alomar. Sorry, Mike, but it's still an old and overpaid team, and hence, likely to go nowhere.

Considering that the Mets were 13th in runs scored in the National League last year, we might want to ask, who on this team is likely to have a better offensive year in 2003 than they did in 2002?

Assuming the immortal Ty Wigginton is their third baseman (or is he a second baseman, or an outfielder… he played all over the place in September), let's look at the Mets' probable Opening Day lineup. This chart shows the present age of the Mets' eight prospective regulars, plus their OPS for their last three active seasons (skipping a year in Vaughn's case.)

Name **(Not changed to** **protect the innocent)**	**Position**	**Age**	**Last 3 OPS**
Mike Piazza	C	34	1012, 957, 903
Mo "Hippo" Vaughn	1B	35	866, 863, 805
Robbie Alomar	2B	34	853, 956, 707
Rey "At Least I'm Not Ordonez" Sanchez	SS	31	636, 636, 663
Ty Wigginton	3B	25	880
Cliff Floyd	LF	30	907, 968, 921
Roger Cedeno	CF	28	781, 733, 664
Jeromy Burnitz	RF	33	812, 851, 676

Hmmm... not a pretty sight. All past their peak except Wigginton and Cedeno (who never got to the peak … his career OPS is .721.) Noted offensive powerhouse Rey Sanchez is the only one whose OPS went up from 2001 to 2002. At least he's consistent, consistently bad, that is. In his favor though, he is an upgrade from Rey Ordonez. Maybe phenom, Jose Reyes, will come up and save the day.

Yes, my boy Piazza (we grew up about 10 miles from each other, though 15 years apart) is still an offensive threat. But, even he seems to be going downhill, as do most catchers – usually due to injuries – when they get to their mid-30s.

Mighty (Big) Mo – I think we can conclude that he will still continue to carry the entire symphony orchestra (along with Elton John and Billy Joel) on his back. If he slips below .800 he becomes Travis Lee without the defense.

Robbie Alomar is the best bet among 2002's underachievers to bounce back, assuming his fragile psyche (remember, this is the guy who went off so badly at an umpire that he spit at him) can handle the pressure of playing in New York. However, like Vaughn, Burnitz and Piazza, he is moving into his mid-30s.

While he's unlikely to be mistaken for Cobb, and his 116 ML at bats aren't enough to base many predictions on, the word seems to be that Wigginton should be an offensive or defensive match for… maybe The Fonz, but not Edgardo Alfonzo.

Roger Cedeno… a Henry Cotto clone with more speed. Whoop-de-doo!

As for Burnitz, yes, he may be better, but it's taking a chance to assume improvement at age 33. And, who is the REAL Jeromy Burnitz, the guy who had four good years with the Brewers, or the guy the Mets got rid of the first time around?

In summary… yes, it is possible that Piazza, Vaughn, Alomar or Burnitz may bounce back. However, remember that any group of players at their age will decline as a group. So that leaves only Cliff Floyd (plus two zeros and a rookie) to pick up the offensive slack, and he may find that pitcher's paradise Shea Stadium and its deep gaps in the power alleys are not well-suited to gap hitters. (Hello, Mr. Alomar.)

As for the pitchers, it's true, a Glavine/Leiter/Astacio/Trachsel rotation looks pretty good. However, they are, respectively, 37/37/33/32. Let's see what sort of trends there might be for the starters: (*That first column is Adjusted ERA.)

Glavine

Year	ERA*	IP	K	K/9	BB	K/BB
2000	136	241	152	5.7	65	2.3:1
2001	123	219	116	4.8	97	1.2:1
2002	139	224	127	5.1	78	1.6:1

Leiter

Year	ERA*	IP	K	K/9	BB	K/BB
2000	136	208	200	8.7	76	2.6:1
2001	124	188	142	6.8	46	3.1:1
2002	112	205	172	7.5	69	2.5:1

Astacio

Year	ERA*	IP	K	K/9	BB	K/BB
2000	113	197	193	8.8	77	2.5:1
2001	100	170	144	7.6	54	2.7:1
2002	82	192	152	7.1	63	2.4:1

Trachsel

Year	ERA*	IP	K	K/9	BB	K/BB
2000	103	201	110	4.9	74	1.5:1
2001	92	174	144	7.5	47	3.1:1
2002	116	174	105	5.4	69	1.5:1

Hmmm… mixed messages at best.

Glavine is still a pretty good pitcher… however, his strikeout rate and strikeout to walk ratio aren't as good as Leiter's and Astacio's, and are about the same as Steve Trachsel's! Has Glavine been living on the Braves' defense? And, does he know that the Mets made something like 90 infield errors last year (with Ordonez and Alfonzo)? While Glavine's not likely to go from Cy Young to Sayonara, he's likely to find he had a better shot at 300 wins with Atlanta OR Philadelphia. And, in addition to a questionable infield, he may wonder where Andruw Jones is when fly balls start falling in Shea's power alleys. We'll have to wait and see.

Leiter, the Mets' other ace, presents a mixed bag of worsening ERAs and varying strikeout and walk data. And, as for Astacio, I wouldn't bet the ranch on a pitcher with a weak rotator cuff (who threw 192 innings with same last year), progressively poorer adjusted ERAs and decreasing (though still pretty good) strikeouts. Trachsel? An innings eater at best. Number five starter Mike Bacsik? Gag me with a spoon… as they used to say back in the 80s.

Finally, yes, Benitez, Stanton, Strickland, et al make up a pretty good bullpen (plus Franco, if he's able to come back), but, you need more than a good pen to contend. They had that last year, and finished 26 ½ games out. It's hard to see that Cliff Floyd and Tom Glavine will make up that big of a difference especially since, as Spring Training was getting rolling, the Mets signed the following players ("Position" denotes that spot the Mets hope they'll play) to bolster that old and overpaid team.

Name	Age	Position	2002 Stats
David Cone	40	P	Retired
Jay Bell	37	3B	.163/.250/.306
Tsuyoshi Shinjo	31	OF	.238/.294/.370
Tony Clark	30	OF	.207/.265/.291
Donovan Osborne	33	P	0-1, 6.19

When Tsuyoshi (.664 OPS) Shinjo is your best chance offensively to bolster the team, and a 40-year-old retiree is your best pitching pick-up… you have a problem… or, maybe Phillips sees they have a problem and is frantically casting around for someone, anyone, to pull a miracle out of the hat and become a productive fill-in for one of their holes.

(One other note... there is a pattern here. Phillips is clearly enamored with players who boast a .556 OPS, since both Clark... who, by the way, has NEVER played the outfield in the major leagues... and Bell racked up that number last year.)

Looks like third place to me, unless Steve Phillips can pull off a miracle (which is what it will take with all those big contracts) to really beef up the offense.

CHAPTER 10

February 17, 2003

Item: February 1905 – The Cleveland Blues are renamed the Cleveland Naps in honor of their player-manager, Napoleon Lajoie.

What a concept… naming a team after someone. Nowadays, they're not even naming stadiums after people. Despite the PR disaster that was Enron Field, it appears as if Jacobs Field and Turner Field are the last two of that breed.

But, what of team names? It's a subject that's going to come up within the next year, when the Expos are unceremoniously ushered out of Montreal to… somewhere, anywhere. Wherever it is, it not only has to be better than Montreal, but, they'll have to change their name as well. After all, the current team was named after Expo '67, held in the Canadian city two years before the first major league (sort of) team outside the U.S. lost 110 games despite having Gene Mauch as the manager and Coco Laboy as the third baseman. (How can you not root for a player named Coco Laboy? It would be the same as booing Bombo Rivera.) Calling a Washington-based team the Expos makes about as much sense as calling a Los Angeles-based team the Lakers or the Trolley Dodgers.

However, it seems unlikely that the Expos will become the Vancouver Vlads or the DC Duques. Naming teams after people, or coming up with names that have a connection to some prominent member of the organization, is surely passé at this point.

And yet, it was quite common up until about World War I. The team now known as the Chicago Cubs were the Colts for several years, named after their player-manager Cap Anson, who starred in a stage play called *The Runaway Colt.* And, when long-time Colt Anson finally left Chicago, the team became the Orphans, in recognition of the loss of their "Cap." The Dodgers, in their early years in Brooklyn (c. 1900) were called the Superbas, after manager Ned Hanlon and a well-known troupe of entertainers called Hanlon's Superbas. Prior to that, they were the Bridegrooms, after a bunch of their players got married in the off-season. And, when Lajoie left to go back to the Athletics, and a new name was needed for Cleveland's American League team, a newspaper poll came up with "Indians," in honor of the late 19th Century Cleveland Spider pheenom Louis Sockalexis, the first American Indian to make a splash in baseball.

The team that now plays in Turner Field holds the record for "Most Names Connected to Different People" with three. When George Dovey bought the Boston Nationals in 1906, the team was renamed the Doves in his honor. By the time the 1911 season started, William Russell owned the team, and they were the Rustlers. Then, when Russell died after a year, future Hall of Famer John Montgomery Ward put together a three-man syndicate with most of the money coming from New York millionaire James Gaffney. No, they didn't change the name to the Gaffers (although that might not be a bad name for the current Arizona or New York National League teams), the Boston NL team became the Braves.

You see, Gaffney was a member of the infamous Tammany Hall political machine that had run New York City since back in the days of Bosses Croker and Tweed. And the Tammany Hall symbol (or logo, if you will) was an Indian brave. And a member of the Tammany Hall machine was known as a "brave of Tammany Hall." And so, except for a detour as the Bees in the 1930s, they've been the Braves ever since.

(Ironic, isn't it? The two teams whose names now draw the most flak are named in honor of an Indian, and in context with someone who had nothing to do with Native Americans.)

It's sort of a shame that the quaint practice of naming teams after people has gone by the books. Imagine the possibilities…

For players:

-Arizona Units
-San Francisco Bonds (Barry's probably suggested this already)
-Texas A-Rods
-Colorado Walkers (would this help their plate discipline?)

For managers:

-Tampa Bay Sweet Loosers
-New York Howes
-Philadelphia Bowa Constrictors
-Cincinnati Monkeys (say "BobBoone" real fast)

And for owners:

-Baltimore (hmmm… better not, he's a lawyer, and lawyers sue)
-Anaheim Mickey Mouses (why not, ever hear of the Anaheim Mighty Ducks?)
-Detroit Pizzas
-New York Bosses (the very first Rotisserie League in New York had a team called the "Stein Brenners")

Ahhh, for the good old days…

CHAPTER 11

February 24, 2003

Item: February 24, 1874 – John Peter Wagner is born in Mansfield, Pa.

Happy 129th birthday, you big Honus (a German term of endearment, and also a German nickname for Johannes… John, in English).

One of the really fine subjects for debate in baseball is when you talk about the greatest (fill in the blank) ever. And, traditionally, you'll get a real debate when you talk about every position in the field, except two. One of the outfield spots pretty commonly goes to that Ruth fella. And the shortstop is pretty sure to be the aforementioned Mr. Wagner. (Some misguided souls actually think George Brett was the greatest third baseman ever... but that's a discussion for another chapter.)

Now, the subject of who's the Greatest Shortstop has come up before. Back around 1983 and 1984, there was speculation that Robin Yount might be on his way to becoming the Number One Short fielder. Oops, he became an outfielder in 1985, and never set foot in the infield again, except for a dozen games at first. Similar rumblings probably came out of Chicago after the 1960 season, when Mr. Cub was coming off back-to-back MVP seasons, and even picked up a Gold Glove. Nope, Ernie Banks went to first base in 1962, and never looked back across the diamond except for 11 games at third.

But, with the recent accomplishments of the 240 Million Dollar Man – born a little over 101 years after the Big Honus – is Wagner still deserving of the crown, "The Greatest Shortstop of All Time?" The answer is, "yes." And here's why…

There can be no doubt that Alex Rodriguez is a remarkable and unique talent. A power-hitting shortstop. I mean, the man hit 57 home runs last year and also won the AL Gold Glove at the most important defensive position. (Would someone please explain why he wasn't the MVP in 2002?)

Here's how his offensive stats stack up against Wagner on a per/162 game basis.

	AB	R	H	2B	3B	HR	RBI	SB	W	BA	OBP	SA	OPS
Wagner	605	101	198	37	15	6	100	42	56	.327	.391	.466	.857
Rodriguez	637	129	197	37	2	43	127	23	69	.309	.380	.579	.959

Did I mention that A-Rod can hit a little?

However, the thing is, so could Honus. And, there are two other factors to take into consideration… 1) the offensive eras they played in, and, 2) A-Rod is, even as we speak, right at his peak. He turned 27 last July, and has yet to experience the "downside" of his career, which, unless he becomes Shoeless Joe Jackson or Ed Delahanty, will lead to a gradual eroding of his impressive averages.

First, what are the respective values of their offensive contributions? During A-Rod's seven seasons as a regular, American League teams have scored 5.07 runs per game. During Wagner's 19 seasons as a regular, National League teams scored 4.15 runs per game, or 81.9% as much. Converting A-Rod's and Honus' numbers into Runs Created per 162 games, we find Rodriguez at 139.8 and Wagner at 109.3. (This is using the 1987 Bill James "Stolen Base" version of the Runs Created Formula,[13] and giving Wagner credit for being a 70% success as a base stealer. Caught Stealing numbers were only kept for one year of his career, and he was a 59% successful base stealer at age 40.)

But, suppose we multiply A-Rod's number by .819, hence making the adjustment for his playing in the Rocketball Era and Wagner playing in the Deadball Era? Then A-Rod's figure is 114.4 runs per 162 games.

Another way to look at this is… given the 81.9% adjustment, A-Rod has created, on the average, as many runs in a season as a team would score in 27.6 games. For Wagner, it's as many runs as an NL team in his era would have scored in 26.3 games.

If you want to try another measurement, let's use James' "Black Ink Test," which measures how many times a player led his league in offensive categories – a nice metric across eras, since you're comparing players with their contemporaries, providing an automatic adjustment between big hitting and low hitting eras. A-Rod has already racked up 30 points in Black Ink – an excellent total. But, Wagner's total is 109! If A-Rod plays another 18 years (until he's 44, or about the age Wagner retired) at the same level of excellence, he'll still only get to 90 in Black Ink.

An aside at this point. Wagner didn't devote most of his playing time to shortstop until 1903, when he was 29 years old. Just in case you're interested, and you want to compare "pure" shortstops to shortstops, note that Wagner's offensive numbers per 162 games for his entire career are essentially the same as his numbers for the period from 1903 to 1916 (he played first base in his last season – 1917.)

	AB	R	H	2B	3B	HR	RBI	SB	W	BA	OBP	SA	OPS
Wagner (all)	605	101	198	37	15	6	100	42	56	.327	.391	.466	.857
Wagner (03-16)	599	99	194	36	15	6	94	42	60	.324	.385	.464	.849

Any way you look at it, Wagner's and Rodriguez's offensive contributions are pretty close… for now.

However, it is well-established that field players, as a whole, tend to peak around the age of 27, and, as a whole, begin a gradual decline after that age. That's not to say A-Rod is going to fall off the face of the earth this year, but it is pretty safe to state that, when his final totals are established after his retirement, he will not have averaged 139.8 runs created per 162 games. Unless he stops playing at a relatively young age (as did Ed Delahanty and Joe Jackson – though for much different reasons) he will experience a decline phase to his career, and that will bring down his averages (even as he builds on his totals.)

But, let's say that A-Rod drinks out of whatever Fountain of Youth that Barry Bonds uses, and his offensive numbers fade very little until he retires. What about Wagner's and Rodriguez's respective defensive accomplishments?

I will not pretend to be an expert on judging defensive statistics. I'm not sure anyone is for a certainty. However, it is interesting to note that last year's Gold Glove was A-Rod's first, and that a source as distinguished as Mr. James has proclaimed Wagner "among the greatest defensive players in the history of baseball."[14]

A simple metric of defensive ability is range factor – in other words, how many balls did they get to per game? Thus far, A-Rod's range factor at short is 4.44, approximately 2% above the American League average (during his career to date) of 4.35.

On the other hand, Wagner's range factor as a shortstop (remembering that he played every other position except catcher) was 5.63, or 8.7% better than the National League average of 5.18 during his career. And that's counting the 356 games he played at short after the age of 40 – when his range factor was still above the league average.

To close the argument, we'll mention one other metric. In *The New Bill James Historical Baseball Abstract* the author ranks Babe Ruth as the number one player of all time, and Honus Wagner as number two.[15] If that is indeed an accurate assessment of baseball history (and I believe it is), then A-Rod will have to become the second greatest baseball player overall to supplant Honus as the number one shortstop.

And that will take some doing…

CHAPTER 12

March 4, 2003

Item: February 29, 1976 –Terrence Long is born in Montgomery, Alabama… and to think, he's only had six birthdays since then.

Let's play pretend.

Let's say you're the best General Manager in baseball. For want of a better name, we'll call you Billy Beane.

You're so good, the Boston Red Sox tried to lure you out of Oakland, and then "settled" on hiring Bill James instead to provide the sabrmetric approach for the Olde Towne Team.

You're so good, you have a sabrmetric statistic named after you… Rob Neyer's Beane Count.

You're so good, you've brought home three straight playoff teams despite typical Bay Area fan disinterest and a budget that looks like the per capita GNP of Kazakhstan (it's not very high.)

As usual, the 2003 season presents you with a number of problems in terms of trying to cobble together your type of offense… a high on base percentage crew that features plate discipline as its outstanding characteristic. Among these problems are the aforementioned lack of money, lack on fans to provide more money, and only having one outfield position set – right fielder Jermaine Dye – after David Justice (a Beane type of guy – good walks, good power) retires on you. Here are some potential outfielders you can try to choose from, along with some key 2002 statistics…

	BA	W	K	OBP	SLG	OPS
Player A	.240	48	96	.298	.390	.689
Player B	.262	21	83	.296	.410	.706
Player C	.223	38	47	.369	.352	.721
Player D	.262	36	59	.338	.489	.827

Hmmm… Well, Player A looks like a refugee from Tampa Bay. Player B, with a 4 to 1 strikeout to walk ratio, clearly has never seen a pitch he didn't like. He's hardly a Beane-type player. C clearly has the best plate discipline, although he does have a little less power than the other three. D has the best power and, thanks to that power that actually boosts his OPS above .800, is the best offensive player. If you were Billy Beane, who would you keep, and who would you send to Tampa Bay in a trade?

Oddly enough, at this point, it appears as if Oakland is going with A, B and D. Which seems sort of strange… wouldn't you think Billy Beane would want to have C and D get most of the at bats in the outfield? I mean, what do you want with two guys with a sub-.300 on base average who also don't have much power and who are clearly breakfast cereal players (they're Special K).

Now, who are our mystery men?

Well, Player A is the Leap Year Birthday Boy himself, Terence Long. And Player B is a refugee from the Baltimore Orioles (where the days of walks and three run homers are loooong gone) who you've picked up for some inexplicable reason… Chris Singleton. Player D is a pretty fair 37-year-old returnee to the fold who you've just added, Ron Gant.

And Player C is an Oakland fan favorite (who might even draw some fans to the park) who is so anxious to play for the Athletics (for the fifth time, it should be noted) that he's willing to play for the major league minimum (which saves you a bundle, as well.) That's right, he's a future Hall of Famer who happens to hold the major league records for stolen bases, runs scored and walks. He's Rickey Henderson. However, Beane doesn't seem to be interested in him. Maybe he thinks perennial prospect Adam Piatt (at least his career OPS is .748) will ride to the rescue and save the day.

Now, Terrence Long is a pretty good player for a six-year-old. However, the A's attraction to him is even more inexplicable than their acquisition of Singleton. He's managed to have his OPS decrease in both of the past two years, and he's hardly Garry Maddox in the field… he has 12 assists, 25 errors and a sub-average range factor for his three years in Oakland. Maybe he's holding Beane's mother for ransom. The 30-year-old Singleton is at least a good fielder, but both the White Sox and Orioles have discovered he doesn't get on base enough to justify making him a regular. So what do the A's want with him? On the other hand, Gant is a classic Beane pickup… or, at least he's worth a one-year trial… he still has some power, and will take a walk.

The real question is, why won't Beane even consider Henderson? If only as a minimum salary pinchrunner/pinchhitter/gate attraction? Is he THAT much of a pain in the clubhouse? Does Beane expect his legs to fall off and his eyes to go bad this year? Or is this just a case of age discrimination? Should the AARP get involved? Call 1-800-OLDFOLKS now to register your complaint.

CHAPTER 13

Item: March 8, 1895 – Jack Bentley born in Sandy Spring, Maryland.

Spring Training regularly produces a slew of interesting stories… George Steinbrenner blasting one of his players… an unknown hitting over .500 during the exhibition season (back in the early 70s in Clearwater, his name was Ron "Palm Trees" Stone)… maybe a manager getting fired or a Hall of Famer trying to make a comeback five years too late… that sort of stuff.

However, for Spring Training 2003, there's a truly unique story unfolding, and, yes, it has something to do with Mr. Bentley.

For the first time since Robin Yount reached 3000 hits, the Milwaukee Brewers are making news for something other than the foibles of their erstwhile used car dealer owner. In this case, his name is Brooks Kieschnick and he's attempting something that's hardly ever been done since Bentley's days – he's trying to make the Brewers roster as a two-way player… a pitcher AND a hitter. He's an unusual enough story that Peter Gammons of ESPN.com stopped agonizing over the Red Sox long enough to write a column on the subject. Ditto, fellow ESPNer Rob Neyer, who asked (albeit indirectly) a very interesting question as part of his column on Kieschnick… who was the last two-way player? The player that comes immediately to mind is the one-and-only Babe, who went 9-5 with a 2.97 ERA and set a major league record with 29 home runs back in 1919. But, surely, someone has pulled double duty in the majors since then?

Well, if you use at least five games on the mound and at least 25 games in the field (not just pinch hitting… there have been plenty of pitcher/pinch hitters over the years) during the course of a season as a fair standard for a two-way player, then, yes, there were not one, but two of them in the 1960s. We'll let the suspense build for a minute at this point…

One early such player was Jack Bentley, who was also the first player ever known as "the next Babe Ruth." Like the Babe, Bentley came from Jack Dunn's minor league Baltimore Oriole powerhouse, and like the Babe, he was a pitcher who could hit. A pitcher and a first basemen for the Orioles, Bentley actually began his major league career as an 18-year-old pitcher in 1913 with the Senators. (For our younger readers… there actually used to be a major league baseball team in our nation's capitol.)

Between 1917 and 1922 (with a year out for WWI) he toiled for Dunn, who converted him into a first sacker and spot starter. And he tore up the International League, ringing up won-loss records like 16-3, 12-1 and 13-2 while leading the league in home runs in 1921 and hitting a tidy .412 in the process. Following the 1922 season, he was sold to John McGraw – who already had some experience with two-way players – for a tidy chunk of change ($65,000). Interestingly, McGraw used him primarily as a pitcher, although he did play a fair amount at first for the Phillies in 1926. For his major league career, Bentley went 46-33 with a slightly higher than average ERA in 138 games on the mound. At the plate, he hit .291/.316/.406, (batting/on-base/slugging) playing 59 games at first and three in the outfield in addition to his pitching duties. OK, but not Babe Ruth.

However, he was better than Mel Queen, Jr. and Wonderful Willie Smith… the last two major leaguers to go both ways in the same season. Return with us now to those thrilling days of 1966. Mel Queen has already had two cups of coffee as an outfielder with the Cincinnati Reds, and he's hit under the Mendoza Line. Cincy figures he has a good arm, so he switches to pitching **at the major league level** during the 1966 season. The results in '66 aren't too good – for 32 games in the outfield and seven on the mound, he hits .127. Pitching, he's 0-0 with a save and a 6.43 ERA. However, as a full-time pitcher in 1967, he racks up a fine 14-8 record with a 2.76 ERA… and, thanks partly to shoulder troubles, never has a year anywhere near as good after that. For his career, Queen was 20-17 with a 3.14 ERA in 140 games as a pitcher. Hitting, the story is less impressive, a .179 average in 53 games in the outfield.

More celebrated, and somewhat better known, was Wonderful Willie Smith of the Angels. Like Bentley, he earned his reputation in the minors, hitting .380 while posting a 14-2 record on the mound for Syracuse in 1963. That performance earned him a shot at the majors later that same season, originally as a pitcher (1-0, 2 Sv, 4.57 ERA) for the Tigers. The Angels picked him up for 1964, and he appeared in 87 games in the outfield and 15 games as a pitcher. At the plate he was a respectable .301/.317/.465, while his pitching line wasn't that bad either, although he was 1-4, he did have a 2.84 ERA.

However, that was his last significant mound time… he only pitched in three more games (with the Indians and the Cubs) during the 1968 season. For his career, his pitching line was 2-4 in 29 games with a 3.10 ERA and two saves. Hitting, in 339 games in the outfield and 93 games at first, he went .248/.295/.395 and never had another year anything like his 1964 season.

And, to this day, no one else has ever really been a two-way player in the majors during the course of a single season.

So, can Kieschnick do it? First, it might be interesting to note that two-way players were quite common in the 19th Century, when rosters were much smaller and ace pitchers on their day off (that's often all they got… one day off at a time) played the outfield. (An aside – this was somewhat like high school players still do today… would it be correct to speculate that, during the 19th Century, the best professional athletes gravitated to the mound, as they do today in high school?) Some of the most notable of that breed were Dave "Scissors" Foutz, Parisian Bob Caruthers, Guy Hecker (who won a batting title) and the Old Hoss, Charlie Radbourn.

However, after the turn of the century, two-way players became almost extinct. Among the few that come to mind in addition to Bentley are Otis Crandall (the first true relief pitcher and an excellent hitter, he was McGraw's secret weapon before WWI), Clint "Floppy" Hartung (one of the biggest flops of all time), Johnny O'Brien (a rare infielder/ pitcher) and Al Orth (the last of the 19th Century two-way players, and a 200 game winner who regularly filled in the outfield for a few games each year).

The word on Kieschnick as a hitter is that he's got power, but no plate discipline. From 1996 to 2001, his hitting numbers in 173 major league at bats are .220/.297/.405 with 19 walks and 47 Ks for the Cubs, Reds and Rockies. Pitching in Triple A last year, struck out 26 in 31 innings with a 2.59 ERA. And, like John Olerud (who's never pitched an inning in the majors), he was a two-way star in college, going 16-4 for the University of Texas and hitting .364 with 17 homers.

This leads to another question – why wasn't Olerud ever tried as a two-way player? You have to think the answer is that his teams (notably the Blue Jays, who drafted him) didn't need him to do it. However, the Brewers, who are short of BOTH major league pitchers and hitters, just might need him. Sometimes, opportunity is being in the right place at the right time.

And maybe this is the right place and the right time for Brooks Kieschnick. The guess here is that he does break the 37-year-long absence on two-way players by getting into at least five games as a pitcher and 25 games in the field (no fair DHing… that's not real baseball!). The Brewers can hardly do any worse.

CHAPTER 14

March 17, 2003

Item – March 1900: The National League buys out the Cleveland, Washington, Louisville and Baltimore franchises.

Would the Angels have played in the 2002 World Series if Major League Baseball had gone through with certain plans following the 2001 season? As I recall, those plans were called "contraction," and some scenarios included Tinseltown's Number Two Team. Said plans brought down a firestorm of controversy on the head of Bud.com… a fuss surpassed only by one of the other smart moves he's made – cutting short an extra-inning exhibition game so that two outstanding young pitching prospects wouldn't chance damaging their arms. However, if the truth be told, both contracting the majors and the 2002 All-Star Game were good moves – it's just that Commissioner Bud Selig apparently doesn't know PR from a used Yugo and both decisions were handled terribly. That's right, contraction was (at least potentially) a good idea, and could have benefitted baseball. But first, let's look at the last time this happened… 103 years ago.

Following the untimely demise of the American Association in the fall of 1891, the National League ruled baseball with a less-than-admirable monopolistic grip. Syndicate ownership, rowdyism (the Baltimore Orioles and the Cleveland Spiders being the foremost practitioners), violence, competitive imbalance and salary classifications that resulted in a theoretical $2,400 per man salary cap, had taken a lot of the fun out of the game. After all, "monopoly" is an ugly concept, unless you're playing an Atlantic City-based board game. It was into this unseemly situation in 1901 that Ban Johnson, Connie Mack, John McGraw, Charles Somers, Charlie Comiskey, et al, brought the American League – an idea whose time had come.

And why was that? Well, part of the reason was because there were several markets for major league baseball teams available… due to the incident noted previously.

Actually, given present-day major league baseball's problems with ownership, hopelessly outclassed and under funded teams and labor troubles hinging on salary issues, it wouldn't be surprising if some free-thinkers considered harking back to the good old days of 1901 and tried starting a new major league. Although a tempting prospect, the cost and availability of playing sites – a new league can no longer quickly throw up a 15,000-seat wooden ballpark in a few months and expect to make money – unfortunately now makes this a practical impossibility.

It is safe to say the National League was not an especially successful organization during its 12-team monopoly from 1892 to 1899. Despite its monopoly position, most teams lost money, and the competitive balance was terrible. Even before the March 1900 shakeout, the competitive situation in the National League was a strange combination of haves and have nots. Due to syndicate ownership, the Baltimore, Louisville and Cleveland clubs had become virtual farm teams for Brooklyn, Pittsburgh and St. Louis. That's not quite the situation in 2003, but does anyone out there think that shoestring (and badly run) operations like the Pirates, Royals and Marlins can ever really compete over the long haul under the present circumstances with the Yankees, Braves and Red Sox?

Certainly the competitive results of syndicate baseball in the National League in the 1890s were astounding, and predictable. In the years from 1892 to 1899, the first place teams in the National League finished with an average record of 94-43, a .686 winning percentage. The 12th place team's average record was 35-102, a .255 winning percentage. The average difference? The last place team finished 59 games out of first each year.

Apparently, no one ever thought to provide for better competition by breaking the league up into two six-team divisions, so, the key moment in the development of 20th Century baseball came in March 1900 when the National League cut loose Washington, Baltimore, Cleveland and Louisville from its unwieldy 12-team set up. This not only strengthened the remaining eight NL teams (especially in Pittsburgh, a club that made good use of that Honus Wagner they picked up from Louisville), but it also gave Ban Johnson, lying in the weeds with his Western League, the chance to upgrade his operation into the major league cities of Cleveland and Chicago. Baltimore and Washington would follow (along with still-current NL cities, Philadelphia and Boston) in 1901 and, presto, a second major league was formed.

Now, as previously noted, that scenario really can't happen in the 21st Century… but, contraction could provide an opportunity for baseball to rid itself of some bad markets and maybe get some better-funded ownership in place in some other markets (which is what happened in Seattle and, originally, Kansas City.) Yeah, yeah, yeah, I know… this year's humpty-dumpties might be the studs in a couple of years, and vice versa. Like the Royals and Pirates went from penthouse (in the 1970s & 1980s) to outhouse and the Twins came back from the dead in the last two years. But, what happens when the Twins' top players get to free agency? And what happens if someone with brains AND money doesn't take over the Buccos?

The fact is that major league teams without sufficient income – in other words, under funded teams – don't really have a prayer, unless they have Billy Beane as GM… and even then you have to wonder if the Athletics are living on borrowed time until their players get ready to fly the free agency coop. You will note, of course, that the Athletics have announced they won't even try to re-sign the reigning AL MVP.

Notice, the determinant isn't "market size," it's access to capital. The city of Atlanta has one-third the population of the city of Philadelphia. How many times have the Phillies ended a season on top of the Braves since 1992? (Answer, once.) However, Ted Turner had a national cable network and spent money like it was peanuts (and was fortunate enough to hire John Schuerholz), while the Phillies' (relatively impoverished) ownership group collectively would have trouble buying one of Turner's yachts.

Having said that, if there was a major league contraction wand, which teams should be dubbed "Out of Here?" First, the criteria… choose among: under funded teams, teams in poor baseball markets (yes, there are some at the moment), bad teams, teams with owners that MLB would love to get rid of, teams without a hope of a new stadium and the attendant revenue and interest said stadia bring. Of course, this isn't to suggest that ALL of these teams have to be contracted, maybe just two or four, just enough to put some talent on the market and hopefully restore some competitive balance. These are just the best candidates… too bad it can't be done until the 2007 season (according to the new labor agreement.)

The top of the list obviously belongs to the Montreal/San Juan Expos. They don't even have an owner, they play in two cities, when they do play in Montreal it's in a mausoleum in front of less than 10,000 fans a game, and Montreal is too cosmopolitan a city to really support any pro sport well, with the exception of its beloved Les Canadiens.

Number two on the Hit List are the two Florida franchises. Neither the Devil Rays nor the Marlins have much money available, and the entire state, which is largely made up of aging people from somewhere else (who root for their old home town Cubs or Red Sox or Havana Reds), completely forgets about baseball as soon as Spring Training ends.

(By the way… I spent a day in metro Tampa-St. Pete in September 1995, just after the area was awarded a franchise. The reaction? Massive disinterest, at least by observation, the newspapers and the people I talked to.)

Number four is the Royals. Kansas City, although a small market, may or may not be a particularly strong baseball market (despite the writers and players who have come out of that region), at least given what seems to be a fair level of apathy toward the state of the team and the lack of a drive for a new ballpark. Or, it might just be a situation like that of the Minnesota Twins – a bad ownership situation in a potentially good market. Certainly, the team has no dough available and a badly-flawed idea as to what it takes to win (see; Perez, Nefi.)

The aforementioned Twins come next, mainly as a way of getting Carl Pohlad (who has money, but who won't put it into the team) out of baseball. If he stays on as the owner, you can write it in stone that the Twins will flop again, and flop hard.

Bud.com's Brew Crew is next, due to lack of funds and lack of a clue, as well as a terrible team. Obviously, this isn't going to happen, and not just because they're owned by the Commissioner's family and they have a new park, but, you have to think better (and better-funded) ownership would help – the Braves drew tremendously well here in the 50s and 60s, even if it is baseball's smallest market.

You might also want to mention the "secondary" teams in three additional markets – the Angels (LA), Athletics (the Bay Area) and White Sox (Chicago). All three are at least adequately funded (though the A's walk a knife-edge, thanks only to Beane's brilliance), but they play in lousy parks (even though the Sox' is pretty new) and are clearly second rate to their hometown fans, behind the Bums, Bonds and Bruins. Of course, the World Series champions aren't going to be contracted, but they were looked at in 2001, largely because Disney wanted to dump the team. Hey, maybe the A's – who want to move – can come back to Philadelphia – there's a new ballpark going up, and a renewed interest in baseball (in what has always been a good baseball town) as well.

Would any or all of these actions cause massive angst among the fans (such as they are) of these teams? Sure. But, that doesn't preclude baseball moving back in to some of these areas with better-funded, better-run teams in new parks at some point in the future. That's how contraction could benefit baseball, if handled correctly – dispose of a couple of bad markets, and eventually bring new ownership into some under-performing markets.

Finally, a dark horse for contraction. During the fall of 2001, the general feeling was that baseball wanted primarily to ditch teams that had old stadiums with no hope of building newer facilities, and/or teams with owners that the rest of baseball would love to get rid of. Well, what team has the second-oldest stadium in baseball, no hope of a new stadium (not with property values they way they are) and an owner who practically everybody hates?

That's right… Break up the Yankees!

CHAPTER 15

March 24, 2003

Item – March 27, 1902: An anonymous sportswriter for the *Chicago Daily News* **notes that, "Frank Selee will devote his strongest efforts on the teamwork of the new Cubs, this year."**

Well, besides providing a good example of the somewhat stilted style of sportswriting around the turn of the last century (did people also talk like that 100 years ago?), this excerpt from the pages of the *Daily News* is good for a couple of interesting reflections.

First, this is apparently the initial usage of the "Cubs" nickname in conjunction with the Chicago National League franchise.[16]

Second, there was a reason why the Chicago Orphans (that name, along with "Colts" stuck around for about another three years before fading out) were now just a bunch of new (or young) Cubs. One of the certified brilliant minds of baseball – Frank Selee – had taken over the fortunes of the once-proud Chicago NL franchise.

The former Chicago White Stockings had dropped that nickname around the time of the Players League War, becoming known as the Colts, in honor of long-time player/manager Cap Anson. However, by the end of the 1901 season, they were better known as the Orphans, because long-time leader Anson was gone, largely because the team had finished ninth, eighth, fourth, fifth and ninth in his last five (1893 to 1897) seasons. For a team that had finished first six times between 1876 and 1886 (and had been in contention for four of the five years after that), this would not do.

So, club President James Hart brought in the best manager in baseball for the 1902 season. Frank Selee had established his credentials with the Boston Red Stockings in the 1890s, building the best team of that decade (yes, better than the much-publicized "Old Orioles") and finishing first five times from 1891 to 1898. After Selee had the temerity to have off-seasons in 1900 and 1901, he was canned by dictatorial Boston owner Arthur Soden.

Moving to Chicago, it was Selee who built the fabulous team that would dominate baseball from 1904 to 1912, winning more than 90 games every year along with four pennants. Present day Cubs' fans (you know who you are…) may want to make sure to sit down before reading this… but, during that nine-year stretch the Cubs averaged 99.8 wins per year. From 1906 (the record-setting 116-36 team) to 1910, they ran up a staggering mark of 530-235 (that's 106-47 per year).

When Johnny Kling showed that he was a first-rate catcher, it was Selee who moved Frank Chance from catcher to first base, and also installed rookies Johnny Evers and Joe Tinker at second and short. Three-Finger Brown came in a trade with the St. Louis Perfectos, Ed Reulbach was also brought up from the minors and Wildfire Schulte took over left field. Unfortunately, Selee developed tuberculosis during the 1905 season, giving new owner Charley Murphy an excuse for bringing his own man – Chance – in as manager. Selee would die in Colorado in 1909, 90 years before his much-deserved election to the Hall of Fame.

Even after the team Selee started came back to earth just before World War 1, the Cubs were usually in the thick of things in the NL pennant race, at least from 1918 to 1945. Indeed, although they never could quite take the World Series after demolishing the Tigers in 1908, there were pennants in 1918, 1929, 1932, 1935, 1938 and 1945.

And then, the bottom fell out. They haven't been to the World Series since 1945… in fact, they've only come close once in the last 57 years. What happened?

There are no simple answers, but, there is at least one very interesting statistic that might prove revealing. Starting with some mid-1980s research by Chicago-based sabrmetric whiz, Don Zminda (and initially reported in the *1986 Bill James' Baseball Abstract*),[17] we can learn that the Cubs have, over all those years, played pretty lousy baseball in the month of September. Indeed, they've been even worse down the stretch than their records for the season as a whole.

How bad has it been? Let me count the ways…

Over 56 seasons (we're not counting 1994, since there wasn't any baseball in September) the Cubbies have played sub-500 ball 41 times (plus two seasons at .500). In fact, since 1946, the Cubs have NEVER gone more than two consecutive seasons where they've played better than .500 during September. (We're also not counting the handful of October games played over the years… that would be unfair, since the Cubs are almost total strangers to meaningful games in October.)

Want more? In 34 of those 56 seasons, their record during September was worse than their record during the rest of the year. Overall, since 1946, the Cubs are 4163-4799, a .465 winning percentage. For the same period of time, they are 653-844 in September, .436 winning percentage. It's kind of hard to make a rush for the pennant when, on the average, you win less than 44% of your games in the last month of the season.

You would think, given a 57-year sample, that this can't be a statistical illusion. This takes in generations of players, managers and front office types. It accounts for players like Lee Walls, Taylor "T-Bone" Phillips and Brooks Kieschnick, but also players like Ernie Banks, Billy Williams, Ron Santo, Ferguson Jenkins, Bruce Sutter, Lee Smith, Ryne Sandberg, Andre Dawson, Greg Maddux and Sammy Sosa (all of whom will be in the Hall of Fame, if they aren't already.) And all sorts of managers… big name mangers like Charlie Grimm, Frankie Frisch and Leo Durocher… less-than-sterling managers like Jim Frey and Don Zimmer (who nevertheless brought in the 46-02 era's only two first place teams)… and even no manager – the famed College of Coaches from the early 60s.

So, what do all those Cubs teams have in common? There's only one thing – they all played their home games in Beautiful Wrigley Field. And that means two things – they've played in what has essentially been a good hitter's park, and they've played a lot of games in the sunlight – generally, a lot more than the rest of the NL teams.

The good hitter's park/bad results scenario is tempting. After all, the good hitter's parks in long-term usage since the start of the big-hitting era in 1920 (Wrigley Field, Ebbets Field, Fenway Park, the Colorado and the new Texas parks, maybe Fulton County Stadium?) have produced exactly two World Series winners (1955 Dodgers, 1995 Braves) in a combined 254 seasons.

However, that doesn't explain the Cubs' September Swoon. Could it be that playing a lot more games in the summer sun, and having to adjust their schedules from day games to night games, back to day games, back to night games, etc., etc., etc., has made just enough difference that the Cubbies traditionally run out of gas in September?

So, what's the price of day games in the Windy City?

CHAPTER 16

April 1, 2003

Item: April 1, 1876 – The "Father of Baseball," Henry Chadwick, pens (literally, they didn't have typewriters then) the first baseball predictions for the first year of the National League in his column in the *Brooklyn Eagle*. Chadwick picks the Chicago White Stockings for first, on the strength of their signing (actually, thievery would be more like it) of the Boston Red Stockings' "Big Four," Al Spalding, Cal McVey, Ross Barnes and Deacon White, plus the Philadelphia Athletics' Cap Anson.

Well, if it was good enough for Father Chadwick and the *Brooklyn Eagle*, it's good enough for this book. Herewith are the Official *Baseball: 1862 to 2003* Predictions…

National League East
Phillies (for once, the stars are in alignment for Philly)
Braves (ding, dong, the witch is dead)
Mets (as predicted previously)
Expos (Vlad and the Seven Dwarfs)
Marlins (Pudge and the already-fragile Mound Kiddie Corps? Fahgeddaboutit!)

Comments: Too much Thome and Millwood in Philadelphia and too little Glavine and Millwood in Atlanta would seem to spell the end to the Braves' run. However, there's more to it than that. The Braves were, quite simply, lucky last year. The team they are putting on the field is much more indicative of the 88-win team of 2001 than the 101-

win team of 2002. First of all, last year they were five games over their projected (Pythagorean) record. Second, they were 28-17 in one-run games... another indicator of good luck, since success in one-run games has been shown to be largely a product of luck. Third, the Plexiglas Principle (what goes up must come down... or, a team that makes a big jump – up or down – in their record one year is likely to go the opposite direction the next year)[18] is working against them. Fourth, any team with an infield of Robert Fick (2002 OPS–.764), Marcus Giles (.714), Rafael Furcal (.710) and Vinny Castilla (.616) and Javy (.671) Lopez catching isn't likely to scare too many good pitchers, no matter how wonderful their outfield may be. Finally, does anyone really think that a rotation of a 37-year-old Greg Maddux, Mike Hampton (his last three **road** ERAs are 4.83, 5.10 and 6.44... of course, if his calf injury continues to be a factor, well, who knows?), Russ Ortiz, Paul Byrd (if he comes off the DL... don't bet on it with his injury history) and an unknown rookie (one of four on the staff this year) will be better than a rotation with a 36-year-old Greg Maddux, Tom Glavine, Kevin Millwood, Damian Moss and Jason Marquis? If so, there's a bridge in Brooklyn I'll be glad to sell you.

But wait! What about those Mets? Well, Mike Piazza (and some other misguided souls) may think they're the favorites, but Pedro Astacio has already gone down (what a shock) and no one else on the team has gotten any younger since the start of Spring Training. Indeed, they've gotten older, since 40-year-old David Cone has made the starting rotation... and they might be looking at Shane Reynolds as well.

The fact that the San Juan Expos (despite, or maybe because of, the Hernandez Brothers) and the Hooked Trout can actually be mentioned in a prediction just goes to show that the NL East is the weakest division in the league this year.

National League Central
Cardinals (just enough pitching... maybe)
Astros (teams that play in big hitters parks seldom come in first)
Reds (even Junior's re-birth can't save this pitching staff)

Cubs (young pitchers will break your heart… as will Wrigley Field)
Pirates (the Mets of the Central… but with less talent)
Brewers (a candidate for relegation under European Soccer rules)

Comments: The key to this race could well be Matt Morris… the Cards' undeniable ace with an undeniably serious arm operation in his background. If he goes down, I wouldn't want to depend too heavily on Woody Williams (age 36, career ERA 4.06), Garrett Stephenson (his medical bills are higher than Morris'), Brett Tomko and Italian League refugee Jason Simontacchi to carry my rotation. And, with Jason Isringhausen's health questionable as well, I sure wouldn't play my cards on a bullpen featuring Cal Eldred (who practically invented the elbow injury) and the latest victim of Steve Blass Disease (who admittedly was just sent to the minors, in favor of – are you ready for this – Lance Painter and Russ Springer.) Yes, the team the Cards put in the field could well be the best in the NL, however, a full year of Scott Rolen won't be enough to make the difference if the pitching doesn't come through.

The Astros? Teams that play in extreme hitters' park don't often shine (two pennants in 254 seasons). However, speaking of more substantial shortcomings – you have to wonder why they dropped Shane Reynolds to give not one, but two unproven youngsters (along with the immortal Brian "Right Rear" Moehler) rotation spots. Remember these famous words – young pitchers will break your heart. More famous words – never try to convert a 37-year-old former catcher (whose offense is rapidly going downhill) from a second baseman to a centerfielder – you weaken your defense at two key positions.

Cincinnati unfortunately celebrates its new ballpark with the same old pitchers. They're likely to play a lot of 8-7 games. As for the Cubbies, when it's all said and done, and even with the uncertainties of depending on young pitchers, the definitive statement on the chances of an all-Chicago World Series is the fact that Mark Grudzielanek (.301), Alex Gonzalez (.312) and Cory Patterson (.284) all appear to be ready to appear in starting roles. Those are their respective on-base averages last year (and only Grudzielanek's career mark – .324 – is any better). The Cubs just won't get enough men on base to win in Wrigley.

National League West
Diamondbacks (you can't beat Schills and the Big Unit)
Dodgers (this should be a good race)
Giants (overachieved last year with Jeff Kent… and the Marquis and the Neifi won't help)
Rockies (another team of 8-7 losses)
Padres (they're signing the Brewers' pitching discards, since their entire bullpen is trashed)

Comments: This should have been a pretty good three-way race… until Felipe Alou (and Brian Sabean… that's a really bad sign) announced that he was worried about not getting enough at bats for Neifi Perez! Since Neifi is probably the worst offensive player in the National League (with Rey Ordonez now in the American League), that's enough right there (i.e.; wasting 300 at bats on Neifi) to knock the G'ints into third. Well, questions about their rotation after Jason Schmidt and the health of Rob Nen also play a part in that as well, but any team that's counting on Neifi Perez and Marquis Grissom is in trouble.

While it's tough to pick a team as old as the D'Backs for first (see: Mets, New York), it's equally hard to pick against the best one-two pitching punch since Koufax and Drysdale (or maybe Maddux and Glavine). Johnson is clearly a Ryanesque freak of nature and Schilling is simply the one pitcher you want on the mound above all others for a big game. The man is all heart, brains (that's been his biggest improvement over the years… he has a thought out there) and mouth, and he clearly loves baseball. How can you not go with a guy who named his first son Gehrig?

As for the Bums… they're the best bet to get the Wild Card.

American League East
Yankees (Steinbrenner's $$$ will make the difference)
Red Sox (even Bill James can't overcome the Evil Empire)

Blue Jays (a good, middle-of the-road team)
Orioles (give thanks for the D'Rays, O's fans)
Devil Rays (the AL's prime candidate for contraction… what was Pinella thinking of?)

Comments: Why not, it's been this same order for the last five years. If July comes around and the Yankees are in trouble, Steinbrenner will just take advantage of some impoverished team and buy the pennant again. Let's see, what shortstops might be available? (Maybe they can pick up Neifi Perez.) Can you say, "bad for baseball," children?

American League Central
White Sox (by default and deColon)
Twins (coming back to reality)
Indians (though they'll be back in the hunt again soon)
Detroit (with a starting rotation of Mike Maroth, Jeremy Bonderman, Adam Bernero, Nate Cornejo and Gary Knotts)
Kansas City (here I come... back to the basement – their rotation may do worse than Detroit's)

Comments: Although the White Sox and the Twins figure to do battle for first place this year, the really interesting team in this three-team division (what, you mean the Tigers and the Royals are still in the majors?) is the Indians. Just because they were outbid for Thome by the Phillies doesn't mean they aren't in there pitching… particularly with top prospects Jeremy Guthrie, Brian Tallent, Billy Traber, Jake Westbrook and Ricardo Rodriguez along with Cliff Lee, Jody Gerut, Josh Bard, Victor Martinez (where did all these catchers come from?), Brandon Phillips and Travis Hafner. Whew!

Although an awful lot of people seem to be in love with the Twins (is that because they were contraction candidates in 2001?), I'm not one of them. Last year they played a full eight games over their Pythagorean projection (in other words, eight games better than their runs scored and runs allowed would indicate)[19] and also improved 9.5 games in the standings… so, the Plexiglas Principle is working against them as well.

Further, they were ninth in the AL in runs scored, and that fabled staff of starters seems to keep getting hurt. Time for a reality check, folks. This team isn't that good.

So, it's the Sox, by default and by de Bartolo. Actually, that's unfair to the Southsiders. If the Big Hurt can make another comeback, this is a team that can throw some runs at you... Paul Konerko, Maggie Ordonez, etc. And, behind aces, Colon and Mark Buehrle, you've got a good pen led by Flash Gordon and Billy Koch.

American League West
Athletics (Billy Beane... and a tremendous pitching staff)
Mariners (going down, not up)
Angels (never count on a high average/low power and low walks offense to succeed for more than a year)
Rangers (similar problems to the Reds – good hit/no pitch)

Comments: With the Mariners getting older and their pitching not really developing, and the Angels' offense clearly having over-achieved last year (they were 10th in the AL in home runs and 11th in walks, and have added NO one who will help that), the Athletics may just waltz to the title this year. Now, as to what may happen in the playoffs... that's another story, although I will go with the Red Sox for the wild card.

Oh, by the way, in case you haven't figured it out... Henry Chadwick really didn't write a column in the *Brooklyn Eagle* predicting the order of finish for the first National League season. A weak April Fool's joke maybe, but it makes more sense than trying to sell the idea that the Mets have discovered a pitching prospect in a Tibetan Monastery who throws 163 MPH... or whatever it was Sidd Finch supposedly could do.

CHAPTER 17

April 8, 2003

Item: April 8, 1974 – Hammering Henry Aaron hammers a 1-0 pitch from Al Downing into the Braves' bullpen in left center field of the Toilet Bowl (if you ever went to a game in Fulton County Stadium, you know how accurate that appellation was), thus providing Tom House (who caught the ball) with his one moment of glory as a major league pitcher.

Of course, that home run also provided Aaron with some glory as well, since it was career home run number 715, breaking arguably the most important, and certainly the best-known, record in baseball history. In case you lost interest after Aaron hit number 715, he ended his career two years later with 755 home runs. Now, while that number is certainly not as fabled as 714, it has withstood the test of time (and the test of Schmidt, Jackson, Murray, etc.) quite well over the past 28 years. However, it now seems as if Aaron's record will not last the 38 years that Ruth's did. Indeed, speculation has been rampant going into the 2003 season that Aaron's mark is doomed to fall.

But, to whom?

Well, A-Rod just became the youngest player to hit 300 home runs. Slamming Sammy has just joined the 500 Club. Junior Griffey was showing promise of a resurgence in his drive for 755... until he landed the wrong way on his right shoulder. Raffy Palmeiro and The Crime Dog will become the 19th and 20th members of the 500 Club. Don't forget Juan Gone, Jeff Bagwell, the Big Hurt, Piazza, Sheffield, Thome and You the Manny. And, oh yeah, that fellow out in San Francisco is closing in on his godfather's third place mark of 660 dingers. Talk about a crowded field…

Actually, at this point, there are really only three (well, maybe four) viable candidates to hit a 756th home run. With all due respect to the other sluggers mentioned (and a tip of the cap to upcoming young power hitters like Pat Burrell), the Big Four of the Aaron Chase are (in no particular order) Alex Rodriguez, Sammy Sosa, Ken Griffey, Jr. (with a BIG question mark), and Barry Bonds. Palmeiro and McGriff are just too old to qualify, and everyone else is still too far away, given their ages, to get into a serious discussion.

Now, while discussions are the lifeblood of baseball, this issue does not entirely have to live and die at the discussion stage. Thanks to the Boston Red Sox Vice President of Sabrmetric (or whatever his title is), Bill James, we have a way to estimate a player's chance of getting to a specific numerical goal. In this case, 756 home runs.

It's called "The Favorite Toy." (How can you not pay homage to someone who can create these metrics, and also come up with clever names for them? Let's take a moment and bow to Boston…) And here's how it works (from the *1988 Bill James Baseball Abstract*)…

You need four pieces of information for each individual and situation (in this case, the chance of getting to 756 home runs);

The needed number of home runs (call this "A" – I took Algebra at Germantown Friends School, many years ago…);

The years remaining in their career. (call this "B") James' formula for this is 24–.6(age). This gives (among other things) a 35-year-old player three years still to play, and also assumes that anyone still playing regularly has 1.5 seasons left, regardless of how old they are. While the longevity and productivity of certain players may now call this formula into question, we'll go with this version for the moment;

The established home run level. (call this "C") The formula for this number, at least going into the 2003 season – is – three times last year's HR + two times 2001's HR + 2000's HR, and divide by six. In this case, injuries or anomalies in the record have a major effect on this number;

The projected remaining home runs. (call this "D") This is the second number, multiplied by the third number, or BxC=D.

Once you figure (remember when people who were into statistics were called "Figurin' Filberts" by BBWAA types?) the projected remaining home runs (or whatever), the chance of getting to the goal is… D/A–.5 (or, projected remaining home runs, divided by needed home runs, minus .5). If you come up with a number like .362, that would mean the person has a 36.2% chance of reaching the goal.[20]

OK, assuming we haven't lost anybody thus far, here's how following "The Favorite Toy" assesses the chances of reaching 756 home runs for the four players in question before the start of the 2003 season…

Alex Rodriguez – 36.2%
Sammy Sosa – 25.9%
Barry Bonds – 8.2%
Ken Griffey, Jr. – no chance

However, there's more here than meets the eye. Let's take each candidate in turn.

A-Rod clearly has the best chance by the numbers. He won't be 28 until July 27, and he's already to 300 long flies. But, a lot can happen in the next eight to 10 years or so. For instance, if you go back to when Junior Griffey was 29 (following the 1998 season), he had a better than 39% chance of making 756. And, if you look at Jimmie Foxx, who's record for the quickest to 300 A-Rod just broke, when he was 27 (following the 1935 season), he had almost a 26% chance of reaching 756 home runs (he retired with 534). So, A-Rod still has a long way to go, especially if he keeps having disc problems, such as sidelined him during Spring Training.

Slamming Sammy is as close to a miracle as we're likely to see in baseball. It's unlikely that anyone would have given him any chance of reaching 756 home runs after the 1997 season, when he hit 36 home runs, walked 45 times and struck out 174 times. That's Juan Samuel Territory – no one with that kind of strikeout to walk ratio sets any kind of (positive) offensive records. And yet, Sosa learned plate discipline starting at the age of 29. Over the next five seasons his home runs totals have gone: 66, 63, 50, 64, 49. The most amazing five-year run (average 58.4) in history. Correspondingly, his walks/strikeouts have gone: 73/171, 78/171, 91/168, 116/153, 103/144. Given this trend, and the fact that he has averaged more than 157 games per year during that stretch, and the fact that he plays half his games in little Wrigley Field, it would be very unwise to assume that Sosa will not pass Aaron.

Alright, it's time for another math test, class. What number is out of sequence in the following? 40, 37, 34, 49, 73, 46. If you don't know, you get an "F." Those are Bonds' home run totals for the past six years. If you want, you could go back through his entire career, and the pattern will continue all the way back to 1992… Bonds typically gets around 40 home runs per year. What happened in 2001? I won't touch that one with a 10-foot pole. However, it says here that those 73 home runs are a fluke… just like Roger Maris' 61 home runs. If you give Bonds his average HR total for 2001 (41), then The Favorite Toy shows he has NO chance of reaching 756.

On the other hand, Bonds shows no signs of slowing down at age 38 (he turns 39 on July 24). So, maybe giving him 1.5 years still to play is unfair. Let's give him three more seasons (or until he's 41) and 41 home runs in 2001 (however, he gets to keep the extra 32 home runs in his career total.) Now The Favorite Toy pegs his chances at 44%. Can he play at that level for another three entire seasons? Who knows? Aaron hit 20 home runs when he was 40, Willie Mays hit 18, Dave Winfield hit 26, Eddie Murray 22, Reggie Jackson hit 18, Willie McCovey hit 12, Ted Williams hit 29 at 41. To hit 41 at 41 would be, to put it mildly, unprecedented, even in the Rocketball era. Unless they ban intentional walks, or radically change the game in some other fashion, don't invest in Bonds standing atop the heap when he retires.

Finally, there's the sad case of Junior Griffey. At the end of the 2000 season, he still had a 16% chance of reaching 756. Leg, and now shoulder, injuries would appear to have robbed this remarkable talent of his chance… after what happened last weekend, he indeed would seem to have no chance to reach 756 home runs.

In fact, it is injuries, and the lack thereof, along with the ravages of age, that lead to the (tentative) conclusion that, when the four above-mentioned stars are inducted into the Hall of Fame… Sammy Sosa will hold the career home run record.

CHAPTER 18

April 16, 2003

Item: April 12, 1909 – On the first Opening Day of the first all-concrete and steel baseball stadium, Philadelphia Athletics catcher, Michael "Doc" Powers, runs into the concrete wall behind home plate at Shibe Park and suffers abdominal injuries that will take his life two weeks later.

A thorough study of the 150+ years of baseball history would provide the careful researcher with a goodly number of careers that have been either cut short or severely inhibited by on-the-field injuries. Indeed, *Total Baseball* has an entire section on "Tragedies and Shortened Careers," written by eminent historian Joe Overfield.[21] And while many of these on-the-field mishaps have involved pitchers throwing their arms out, there have also been some famous cases involving collisions with walls, bean balls, collisions with other players, line drives through the pitchers' box and even injuries sustained while batting that had nothing to do with a wild (or malicious) pitch.

As often seems to be the case in baseball, irony plays a part in many of these tales of woe… in several cases, the injured party was a star or a coming star, whose career was either ended or badly derailed. Actually, Doc Powers doesn't really fit this category. Although he was an outstanding defensive catcher (he was known as Eddie Plank's personal catcher, much in the same way Tim McCarver would be Steve Carlton's personal catcher 70 years later), he couldn't hit a lick. His career OPS was an incredibly bad .514. However, Jim Creighton, Ray Chapman, Dizzy Dean, Mickey Cochrane, Herb Score, Tony

Conigliaro and Dickie Thon do fit the mold of stars who never reached their fullest due to on-the-field injuries. And then, there's Ken Griffey, Jr., is he fated to join this unfortunate club?

Of the other stars already mentioned, Chapman (the majors' one bean ball fatality), Cochrane (who made the Hall of Fame anyway), Conigliaro and Thon were all victims of bean balls. Pitchers Dean (who also made the Hall) and Score were hit by line drives, off the bats of Earl Averill (in the 1937 All-Star Game) and Gil McDougald, respectively. Creighton, who maybe you've never heard of, was baseball's first superstar, the first pitcher to use a wrist snap in his delivery (which was against the rules at that time) and an outstanding hitter who legend has it once went an entire season without making an out. He died on Aug. 14, 1862, having injured himself at bat while hitting a home run. Oddly enough, Creighton's fate was almost shared by Cleveland Indians pitcher Don Black, who ruptured an aneurysm in his brain while at bat on Sept. 13, 1948. Black lived, although he never played again.

And then, there's the most famous one of all… the non-pareil coming star who, like Doc Powers, couldn't stay away from walls – Pistol Pete Reiser.

Harold Patrick Reiser was personally discovered by Branch Rickey when The Mahatma was running the Cardinals. A native of St. Louis, Reiser was scouted out by Rickey while he was a teenager playing sandlot baseball. Why wasn't a talent like Reiser playing in high school? He was ineligible because he'd already played professional… soccer. (Talk about your natural athletes…) Rickey kept Reiser hidden away, serving as his chauffeur until he was old enough to sign and send to Class D ball. However, Rickey kept him hidden a little too much, and he was one of the hundred or so Cardinal minor leaguers let go when Commissioner Kenesaw Mountain Landis freed the slaves in 1938. Reiser was still only 19 years old.

Never one to take another's authority lying down, Rickey broke every rule in the book by conspiring with another of his protégés, Brooklyn Dodgers President Larry MacPhail, to have Reiser sign with the Bums for $100, and then have Brooklyn hide him for a couple of years before sending him back to the banks of the Mighty Mississippi. Indeed, a trade was already worked out, wherein Reiser and three other minor leaguers (to make it look good) were to go the Cardinals for none other than Joe Medwick, who had only won the National League Triple Crown in 1937.[22] That's how good a prospect Pete Reiser was.

Unfortunately for MacPhail and Rickey, and maybe Reiser, Dodgers Manager Leo Durocher gummed up the plan when he saw how good Reiser was in Spring Training 1940. Maybe Reiser's going seven-for-seven with four walks in his first three exhibition games had something to do with it. Even though MacPhail ordered Durocher not to play Reiser anymore, the cat was out of the bag, and MacPhail would have been lynched even if he traded Reiser for Medwick, even up. Durocher had talked the kid up too much, and the victory-starved Brooklynites had heard every word.[23]

So, what happened? Reiser hit .378 for the Dodgers' Elmira farm club in 1940, earning a July call-up to Brooklyn. He was incredibly fast, could play anywhere on the field exceptionally well, ambidextrous (he had two super arms), and hit line drives all over the place. Think a left-handed hitting Willie Mays without quite as much home run power, and you've got the idea. He hit .293 in the last 58 games of 1940, and scored 34 runs.

The next year, he went wild, leading the Dodgers to their first pennant in 21 years and leading the NL in batting (.343), slugging (.558), OPS (.964), runs (117), total bases (299), doubles (39), triples (17), extra base hits (70) and superlatives. The Knights of the Keyboards (as Ted Williams used to call them) couldn't make up enough adjectives to describe him. He was 22 years old.

And that was the last full season he would spend at his peak. In July 1942, he was leading the NL in batting, hitting .383, when he set off in pursuit of a long fly hit by (ironically enough) the Cards' Enos Slaughter, and ran head-on into the center field wall, fracturing his skull and separating a shoulder.[24] For, along with his other sterling qualities, Pete Reiser was fearless, and, like Mike "The Ghost" Rama of Phillip Roth's *The Great American Novel*, he apparently did not understand the reality of walls. The basic is – Reiser played baseball with a football mentality, and that's a good way to get hurt. Indeed, in 1947, he was given the Last Rites of the Catholic Church after another encounter with a center field wall.[25]

(An interesting *aside* here… the date, location and result of the 1942 incident vary depending on who is telling the story. The only points of agreement in the many versions of the story are that it was in July, against the Cardinals, and that the RedBirds' team physician, the famous Dr. Robert Hyland, told MacPhail, Durocher and Reiser that he thought Pistol Pete was out for the season… something none of the three wanted to hear.[26] If those facts are true, it had to have happened in St. Louis – since Hyland wouldn't be in Brooklyn – during back-to-back doubleheaders on July 18 and July 19.)

A shadow of his former self, Reiser's playing career was over after just 10 seasons at age 33, with a .295 average, an .830 OPS and one major league record (in addition to: Most Walls Run Into)… he still was fast enough to steal home seven times in 1946.

Now, Junior Griffey has already run up career numbers far better than Reiser's. However, it's interesting to note that a broken wrist, incurred while reaching OVER the fence for a home run cost him most of the 1995 season, and that a shoulder separation, incurred diving for a ball, will cost him most of the current season. Are these signs that Junior also has the football mentality – the going all-out, no matter what the consequences, mindset – that cost Reiser most of his career? (And also cost Lenny Dykstra a good bit of his career.) Will these injuries (along with the leg injuries of 2001 and 2002) keep him from the Hall of Fame, to say nothing of his ultimate potential?

The jury is still out, but, at this point, it doesn't look good. And that's a shame… to see such a marvelous talent unfulfilled. Remember when Junior came up? They called him "The Natural." Pete Reiser finished his career the same year that Malamud's book was published (1952), but he, too, was The Natural. If only he could have stayed away from the wall.

CHAPTER 19

April 21, 2003

Item: April 18, 1942 – Steve Blass is born in Canaan, Ct.

It is the most dreaded malady among pitchers. Worse than a torn rotator cuff. Much worse than tendinitis. Worse than a hangnail for a knuckleballer. Worse than a torn elbow ligament – Tommy John Surgery can fix that. But, nothing can fix Steve Blass Disease. Or, is there a cure? And, is there any hope for the most recent sufferer, Rick Ankiel?

If you were to pull out your Medical Dictionary of the Major Leagues and turn to the "S" section, here's what you would see… **Steve Blass Disease:** (1) A complete and almost total inability to throw a strike to major league (and sometimes minor league) batters. Named after Pittsburgh Pirates pitcher Steve Blass (1964-1974), the first known victim. (2) Sudden, extreme and protracted wildness on the mound in a game setting. (3) Also known as the Wild Man Syndrome.

This isn't Tommy Byrne wild or Rex Barney wild, or even Steve Dalkowski wild. Their control was lousy from the start. This is a loss of control, where it previously existed… to at least a certain extent. Ever since the 1973 season, when Blass suddenly and totally lost the ability to throw the ball over the plate when there was someone in the batters' box; baseball clinicians, theoreticians, sabrmetricians and every other kind of ician have been wishin' they could figure out, A) what causes Steve Blass Disease, and B) what to do about it.

While there have only been six (or maybe eight) clinically diagnosed pitching sufferers to date, it is possible to make some tentative generalizations about the type of pitcher that may be more prone to develop the disease.

-A tendency to have some control problems beforehand
-Closers
-Pitchers with psychological issues

To briefly re-cap the progression of Steve Blass Disease… after derailing the career of its namesake in 1973 and 1974, all was quiet until 1982, when the Tigers' 1981 closer, Kevin "Hot Sauce" Saucier suddenly developed an extreme fear of hitting a batter, lost his control, and retired in mid-season. The next sighting came five years later, after the Phillies picked up Joe Cowley in a trade with the White Sox. Cowley was coming off a 1986 season when he went 11-11 with a no-hitter. For the Phillies in 1987, he started four games, lost all four, walked 17 men in 12 innings, and was peremptorily sent to the minors, never to be seen again. The very next year, another Phillies pitcher, Bruce Ruffin, normally a ground ball/control-type pitcher, started walking men at a rate of five per nine innings (maybe he caught the disease from Cowley), sidetracking a promising career (Ruffin had previously taken Steve Carlton's place in the Phillies' rotation.) Just two years later, reliever Mark Davis came off a Cy Young Award-winning 1989 season with the Padres, signed a big contract with the Royals, and proceeded to more than double his walk rate and almost triple his ERA. All was quiet until Braves' closer (note that this has happened to three closers – Saucier, Davis and…) Mark Wohlers completely lost the plate in 1998. In 21 major league innings in 1998 and 1999, he walked 39 men.

Two other possible cases that could be included in this uncontrolled litany are Pete Harnisch, who took a walk on the wild side for one year (1997… he had more walks than strikeouts, but he only pitched 40 innings) as a side effect of tobacco withdrawal, and a Yankees prospect named Sam Militello. According to Joe Ptak, Militello had some pretty phenomenal minor league numbers and a decent 1992 debut with the Yanks (3-3, 3.45 ERA). However, he pitched briefly and ineffectively in 1993 (7 walks in 9 innings and a 6.75 ERA) after problems surfaced in the spring. Ptak says he subsequently gave it a couple of tries in the minors over the next couple of years and then disappeared forever.

After the dreaded malady struck down Wohlers, discussion of Steve Blass Disease went into remission until the 2000 playoffs, when it flared again in the most dramatic case yet diagnosed – 21-year-old Rick Ankiel, the hottest young pitching prospect in the majors. Like the previous six victims, he has yet to completely recover. After posting an 11-7 record with a 3.50 ERA with 194 strikeouts in 175 innings in 2000 regular season, Ankiel developed an incredible record-setting wildness in the playoffs. He was so highly thought of that he started the post-season opener against the Braves, and, out of nowhere, he became the first major league pitcher since 1890 to throw five wild pitches in one inning. He ended up tossing nine wild pitches in four innings during the postseason. Things did not get better in 2001, he walked 25 in 24 innings in the majors and was sent to Triple-A Memphis, where he ran up a 20.77 ERA in three starts. Finally, he fell all the way to the rookie leagues before he could get anyone out. And then, he promptly hurt his elbow and missed the entire 2002 season. This is generally not the way an organization would like to treat its outstanding (better than Matt Morris, better than Bud Smith, a whole lot better than Jason from the Italian League) young pitching prospect. But, what are you going to do?

Well, disregarding the fact that half of the previous Steve Blass sufferers were closers, the Cards tried to make Ankiel a relief pitcher this spring. When he was last heard from (on April 6), he had thrown six straight balls and made a wild throw to third that led to two runs in a one-inning stint for Double-A Tennessee. This was after Ankiel made nine appearances of an inning or less in spring training, allowing eight runs and nine hits while walking nine and striking out nine. Clearly, whatever the Cards have tried so far is not working.

And yet, as serious as Steve Blass Disease may be, there is some small hope. Yes, it did end the careers of Blass, Saucier and Cowley. But, it did not end the careers of Ruffin, Davis and Wohlers. They may not have come all the way back to where they were before they lost the plate, but they did keep pitching.

It has been suggested that Steve Blass Disease is all in the mind.

While arm injuries suffered by Ruffin, Wohlers and Ankiel would seem to dispute that (although all three were injured *after* coming down with Wild Man Syndrome), it is true that psychological factors do seem to have played a role in most of the cases. It's also worth noting that, except for Blass and Ruffin, none of the victims were what you would call control pitchers before the onset of the disease. Or maybe, it's just a case of the pressures of the major leagues getting to a pitcher. However, after losing their control, Blass, Cowley and Ankiel were just as wild in the minors as they were in the majors.

Saucier was generally considered flaky (why do you think he was called "Hot Sauce"?) even before he developed the overwhelming fear of hitting a batter. Cowley was said to have had a unique enough personality that his teammates were rooting *against* him in his no-hitter. Davis was burdened by the expectations of the largest contract (at that time) ever given a relief pitcher. Wohlers was suffering through a painful divorce. And Ruffin and Ankiel are both lefties… and you know what they say about left-handed pitchers. Actually, to be fair – Ruffin was supposed to take the place of one of the greatest pitchers of all time, and Ankiel was asked to start the opening playoff game against the best team in the league – not that those types of difficult assignments have never been given before or since to other pitchers.

Perhaps the most careful study of Wild Man Syndrome came in relation to its namesake. In his classic essay, *Gone for Good*, Roger Angell looked at several possible causes of Blass' total loss of control… and many of them had psychological underpinnings. Among the possible causes that Angell looked at was the possibility that Blass was afraid of hitting a batter – since he was able to through strikes as long as there wasn't anyone in the batter's box.[27] Or maybe he was afraid of getting hit himself – by a batted ball. Or maybe the Dec. 31, 1972 death of Roberto Clemente in a plane crash so upset Blass that he couldn't pitch. Perhaps Blass suffered a loss of confidence in himself, which led to a loss of control (or maybe vice versa.)[28]

Interestingly, Blass' own diagnosis of the cause of his problems (which he bore with remarkable good will, it should be noted) was that maybe control was just something you could lose… that it could come and go.[29] And, in some of the milder cases, maybe that's true. Here are the major league walks per nine innings rates for the seven established patients, from just before they contracted Steve Blass Disease, until they retired…

Blass – 2.55, 3.02, 8.49, 12.60
Saucier – 3.60, 3.86, 6.53
Cowley – 4.78, 4.61, 12.75
Ruffin – 2.69, 3.20, 5.00, 4.43, 3.74, 2.87, 6.36, 4.44, 4.82, 5.03, 3.72, 7.36
Davis – 3.86, 3.00, 6.78, 5.57, 6.96, 5.66, 7.18, 2.76
Wohlers – 2.45, 4.96, 14.85, 81.00, 5.46, 3.31, 3.30
Ankiel – 3.82, 4.63, 9.37

As noted, wildness ended the careers of the first three sufferers. However, Ruffin, Davis and Wohlers all persevered (and were all allowed to do so) and kept pitching in the majors. In Ruffin's case, he actually became a fairly successful closer for the Rockies – he pitched another nine years after his awful 1988 season, although his control generally wasn't very good. On the other hand, it appears as if he had the mildest case of the disease, or, at least, he went into remission for a couple of seasons. Davis, who "peaked" around seven walks per game three times, and who averaged 6.43 walks per game over five years, never was real effective after he lost control of his big curve in 1990. Nevertheless, either patience or optimism led teams to keep giving him the ball for five more seasons, even though his control was awful except for his brief 1997 comeback with the Brewers. Although arm problems continue to trouble Wohlers (he's back on the DL again), and he's nowhere near the 100 MPH fireballer and closer he was before 1998, his control does seem to have rebounded the best after his 33 walks in 20 innings adventure in 1998.

On the weight of the evidence, and given that a sample size of six is pretty small, it would seem that Wohlers' or Ruffin's scenarios are the best that the Cards can hope for. Certainly, it appears as if the Cardinals are willing to be very patient with Ankiel (which is probably the main reason why Ruffin, Davis and Wohlers were able to stick around), plus he does have one additional factor in his favor – he's by far the youngest sufferer of Steve Blass Disease. Blass was 31 when he lost it, Saucier 25, Cowley 28, Ruffin 24, Davis 29, and Wohlers 28. There's still a lot of pitching (potentially) ahead for the still only 23-year-old Ankiel. Just don't expect him to become the star that the Cards thought they had prior to October 2000. He's got Steve Blass Disease. And there is still no known cure.

CHAPTER 20

April 28, 2003

Item: April 28, 1961 – Forty-year-old Warren Spahn no-hits the Giants.

Warren Spahn was a great pitcher at 40. Just the year before (1960), he had set a record as the oldest pitcher to throw a no-hitter in the major leagues. Then, he came back and broke that record on his way to a 21-13 season. Incredibly, Spahn came back TWO years after that (1963), at the age of 42, and went 23-7, matching his personal record for wins in a season. And then… he crashed, going 6-13 and 7-16 over his final two seasons.

It's hard to say how many current fans or sportswriters remember what happened to Spahnie, however, even without that reminder, we have seen near panic in the stadiums in Atlanta, Phoenix (especially Phoenix), Boston and New York early in the 2003 season. Why? Because all four cities have seen their Hall of Fame-caliber pitchers torched in at least one outing in the early going. Now, a key point to remember is that it is still very early in the season. Indeed, the current campaign isn't yet a month old. Nonetheless, no fewer than five excellent starters have had some rocky starts, leading to much speculation as to whether they've "lost it." The early struggles of Greg Maddux, Randy Johnson, Curt Schilling, Pedro Martinez and Tom Glavine have occasioned much comment – too much, in fact, since there is still plenty of time for all five aces to righten the ship and resume their accustomed places in the pitching universe. However, it is still instructive to take a look back at no less than eight outstanding pitchers – seven of whom are in the Hall of Fame (no, the eighth is NOT

Nuke LaLoosh), who "lost it" very suddenly.

While it is certainly premature to suggest that any of the five 2003 aces have "lost it," it does happen. Looking back over the list of lifetime 250+ game winners, it is possible to identify Grover Cleveland Alexander, Burleigh Grimes, Red Ruffing, Robin Roberts (he's a special case, it happened twice to him), Warren Spahn (the most extreme case), Jim Palmer, Steve Carlton and Jack Morris as certifiable aces who were still near the top of their games one year, and ready for the scrap heap the next year. Let's look at some of their key statistics, with the retirees' last good year listed first.

Alexander	**W-L**	**H/9**	**K/W**	**ERA**
1929	9-8	10.16	1.4/1	3.89
1930	0-3	16.6	1/1	9.14

Grimes				
1931	17-9	10.17	1.1/1	3.65
1932	6-11	11.08	.7/1	4.78

Ruffing				
1946	5-1	5.46	.8/1	1.77
1947	3-5	10.7	.7/1	6.11

Roberts				
1960	12-16	9.71	3.6/1	4.02
1961	1-10	11.85	2.3/1	5.85
1965	10-9	8.07	3.2/1	2.78
1966	5-8	11.33	2.6/1	4.82

Spahn				
1963	23-7	8.35	2.1/1	2.60
1964	6-13	10.57	1.5/1	5.29

Palmer

1982	15-5	7.73	1.6/1	3.13
1983	5-4	10.09	1.8/1	4.23
1984	0-3	11.2	2 .2/1	9.17

Carlton

1984	13-7	8.41	2.1/1	3.58
1985	1-8	8.2	2.9/1	3.33
1986	9-14	9.98	1.4/1	5.89

Morris

1992	21-6	8.30	1.7/1	4.04
1993	7-12	11.14	1.6/1	6.19

Not a pretty sight, is it? Although Carlton and Palmer took two years to completely drop off the face of the earth, it's clear to see their slides begin just one year after winning 15 and 13 games respectively. (Check out Carlton's strikeout/walk ratio in 1985 and recall that this man struck out more batters than anyone but Nolan Ryan.) In every other case, from one year to the next, ERAs soared while either their hits per nine innings went up or their strikeout to walk ratio dropped. (And, sometimes, all three happened at once.)

As noted, Robbie was a special case. After serving as the bellwether of the Phillies' staff since 1949, he was awful in 1961, having seemingly lost a foot off his fastball and not having developed another pitch to take its place. A July leg injury suffered while sliding into second didn't help, either.[30] So, the Phillies let him go to the Hated Yankees. He spent about a week with New York, and they similarly ditched him. Then he was picked up by the Orioles, and, voila!... (that's French, not the former Twins pitcher) he learned guile and cunning, and pitched excellent ball for four more years before old age finally caught up with him for good.

In fact, old age is largely what caught up with all eight of our aces in question. Here are their ages in the seasons when they "lost it..."

Alexander (43), Grimes (38), Ruffing (43), Roberts (34 and 39), Spahn (43), Palmer (38), Carlton (40) and Morris (the one of this group not in the Hall–38). Maybe the most amazing stat is that Alexander, Ruffing and Spahn were all still pitching effectively when they were 42. It was worth noting that none of the five contemporary hurlers in question is anywhere near 43 yet. Johnson is 39, Maddux and Glavine 37, Schilling 36, and Martinez just 31.

And, in reality, all five of our current aces are still pitching pretty effectively, although you would not normally expect them to be a collective 9-10 with a 4.52 ERA after 159 innings of pitching. Maddux's numbers aren't especially pretty (2-3, 11.4, 2.9/1, 5.94) after getting shelled in four of his first five starts, however, that 5.94 ERA is a lot better than the 11.05 he had at one point. Similarly, Schilling (1-2, 6.25, 3.6/1, 4.28) and Johnson (1-2, 11.6, 6.2/1, 6.94) have each posted good starts the last time out. (On the other hand, who would have thought that two guys with nine Cy Young Awards between them would have ERAs of 5.94 and 6.94?) Glavine (3-2, 9.26, 1.5/1, 3.60) has had two poor outings in his six starts, and, despite the frightful pounding he received at the hands of a bad Orioles team (4 1/3 IP, 9H, 10R/ER, 4BB, 5SO), it's clear that Pedro (2-1, 6.03, 2.5/1, 2.90) is still Pedro.

Of course, it was the shelling of Martinez on the same day (Apr. 12) that an equally bad Brewers team hung the following pitching line of the Big Unit (4 2/3 IP, 10H, 10R, 2 BB) that started all this talk in the first place. Adding fuel to the fire was the beating Maddux took (5 2/3 IP, 12H, 10R 7ER, 3BB 7SO) from the Phillies three days earlier on Apr. 9. Nevertheless, their ages and the small sample size thus far this season indicate that Johnson, Maddux, Schilling, Glavine and Martinez are likely to bounce back… this year. However, if any of them do not, it won't be the first time that a great pitcher lost it all of a sudden.

CHAPTER 21

May 5, 2003

Item: May 5, 1984 – The Detroit Tigers edge the Cleveland Indians, 6-5, to go 21-4 on the year.

Yes, children, there once was a major league baseball team in the state of Michigan, just north of the province of Ontario. And, in 1984, they were the hottest thing around, roaring off to a remarkable 35-5 start on their way to a five-game World Series triumph over the San Diego Padres. They had stars like Alan Trammell, Kirk Gibson and Lance Parrish, and one of the game's great managers, George "Sparky" Anderson.

In 2003, the big question in the American League is whether or not Detroit is still fielding a major league team. Yes, Trammell, Gibson and Parrish are still there, but, hey, they're all over 50 years old, and they don't get around on the fastball as well as they used to.

Actually, the sad state of the Tigers wasn't the only hot topic in the first month of the season. Also in the news was the team that was expected to share the tenements of the American League Central with the Tigers, the Kansas City Royals. Only, in this case, the question, "Can the Royals keep it up?" was being asked in a positive light.

As of the morning of May 5, 2003, the Royals were in first place with a record of 19-9, while the Tigers were an exceptionally dead last, at 4-25. Clearly, these two teams have, thus far, gone in opposite directions. Now, the reasons for this dichotomy can be debated ad infinitum and ad nauseum. However, no matter how you slice it, what you have to date is the potential for two historic accomplishments – a true "Cinderella" team and a truly awful bunch of losers.

Given that the season isn't quite one-fifth over, what are the chances that the Royals will indeed find the glass slipper before they turn into a pumpkin? And, what are the chances of the Tigers really posting an historically bad record? Maybe not an 1899 Cleveland Spiders bad (20-134), but at least a 1962 Mets bad (40-120)?

Interestingly, true Cinderella teams are about as rare as historically bad teams. Although exact definitions of such rare birds (yes, the 1988 Orioles are in there) can also be argued, here are two lists for the 20th Century – eight really bad teams, and seven true Cinderella teams.

Cinderellas	**Cinders**
1914 Braves 94-59	1904 Senators 38-113
1950 Phillies 91-63	1915 Athletics 43-109
1961 Reds 93-61	1916 Athletics 36-117
1969 Mets 100-62	1935 Braves 38-115
1991 Braves 94-68	1942 Phillies 42-109
1991 Twins 95-67	1952 Pirates 42-112
1993 Phillies 97-65	1962 Mets 40-120
1988 Orioles 54-107	

Actually, you can say there are seven of each, if you wish to consider the 1915 and 1916 A's the same team. (Although Connie Mack ran high schoolers and sandlotters through the rotunda of Shibe Park so fast they had to install a revolving door.) Looking at the time frame from late April to late May, how did these 15 teams start their seasons? First, the Cinderellas.

The Miracle Braves of 1914 truly deserved that title. They were 2-9 on May 2, and 3-16 on May 16, and manager George Stallings – one of the most foul-mouthed managers of all-time – was undoubtedly cussing up a storm. Coming off four straight last place finishes, each of which saw more than 100 losses, the Braves had "jumped" all the way to fifth in 1913. Still, in May 1914, no one expected them to catch fire in the late Summer and storm to the World Series title. The 1950 Phillies – the Whiz Kids – had been similarly down and out for years.

Although they had made it to third in 1949, prior to that they had been over .500 once in 32 years. Only 8-8 on May 5, they won nine of their next 10 and, by May 28, stood 23-12. The 1961 Reds? Well, no one predicted they were going anywhere but the second division. Porkopolis (as the city was known in the 1860s) hadn't seen a pennant winner since 1940. Only 5-10 on Apr. 30, they then won nine straight and stood 26-16 by Memorial Day. Shortly thereafter, the Mets became the laughing stock of baseball (everywhere but in New York), until they got hot in the Summer of 1969. However, they were only 9-14 on May 3 and 18-23 on May 27 of that year.

The last three teams, all from the Nineties, are the three Worst-to-First teams. The Braves and the Twins did it in the same year, 1991. The Braves, who had been worse than awful since winning their first 13 games of 1982, were only 8-10 on Apr. 30, 1991, and drawing crowds that sometimes actually broke into five figures. However, they went 17-9 over the next month on their way to a pennant race with the Dodgers. The Twins, after winning the World Series in 1987, went back to mediocrity, and started 1991 the same way, with a 2-9 mark on Apr. 20. However, by May 14 they were back to 17-15, and by June 16 they were 38-25. The 1993 Phillies had to overcome a recent legacy of injuries and ill-luck, and sometimes both (the car crash that disabled Lenny Dykstra and Darren Daulton). However, they started off the first month 17-5 and never looked back. They were 27-10 by May 18 and led the division for all but one day of the season.

Note, if you will, that six of the seven Cinderella teams started off the season at .500 or worse for the first month or so. Only the 1993 Phillies got hot from the start and stayed that way. Might it be postulated that teams that come out of nowhere are unlikely to sustain a hot start and go all the way to first place at the end of the season? That's what happened in both 2001 and 2002, when the Phillies (a 35-18 start in 2001) and the Indians (11-1 to start 2002) both couldn't keep up the pace. Perhaps the better road to Cinderella success is ask the Fairy Godmother to wait as couple of months before swinging her magic wand. (Rumor has it she's left-handed all the way.) Sorry, Royals fans.

Now, as to the truly awful teams… oddly enough, they weren't all truly awful to start the season. The 1915 (8-13) and 1916 Athletics (13-17) were at least respectable starters, and the 1935 Braves of Babe Ruth were 5-7 on Apr. 29. However, the other five teams… well, the less said about them, the better. Check out these starts…

    1904 Senators – 0-13, 1-16, 6-29
    1942 Phillies – 3-12, 8-23
    1952 Pirates – 2-12, 3-18, 5-28
    1962 Mets – 0-9, 3-16, 12-36
    1988 Orioles – 0-21, 6-34

What's really scary, if you're a Tigers fan, is that only the 1988 O's of sainted memory (where do you think the "O's" nickname came from?) got off to a worse start than that assayed by Alan's Awfuls. On the other hand, there was some good news at Comerica Park last week… Tigers outfielder Gene Kingsale made a one-day trip to his native Aruba, where Gov. Olindo Koolman knighted him (along with Baltimore's Sidney Ponson and Dodgers minor league pitcher Calvin Maduro.) The bad news is that Sir Gene is currently carrying a .632 OPS. The worse news is that Sir Gene is third on the Tigers in OPS, behind just Craig Monroe and Bobby Higginson. It's going to be a very loooong year in Detroit.

CHAPTER 22

Item: May 15, 2002 – San Diego Padres pitcher Bobby J. Jones goes on the Disabled List.

Bobby J. Jones is a pioneer. While he is not to be confused with Bobby M. Jones, Bob G. Miller (1953-62), Bob L. Miller (1957-74) or Bob J. Miller (1949-58) (fortunately, the last three were not all in the majors at the same time), Bobby J. nevertheless made his mark on history last year when, as a member of the San Diego Padres, he went on the DL.

You see, in 2002, Bobby J. was the victim of what has this year become the "in" reason to visit the DL – the strained oblique muscle. (The left one, in Bobby J's case.) Although oblique muscles have been strained before, clearly an epidemic has broken out during Spring Training and in the first month of the 2003 season. In less then seven weeks (Mar. 19 to May 5), no fewer than 10 major league players (plus three French Hens, two Turtle Doves and a Partridge Family in a Pear Tree) have visited the DL due to problems with that old oblique muscle. And, it appears to be spreading faster than SARS at a Blue Jays' game.

First of all, just what the heck is an oblique muscle anyway? Anatomically, it refers to any muscle that is obliquely placed (meaning slanted or inclined) or attached. And while we all have oblique muscles around the eye sockets, it seems unlikely that those muscles are getting strained at a record pace… unless, of course, this is part of a larger problem involving the worst thing you can do in baseball – not keeping your eye on the ball. Since that seems unlikely, we'll assume the rash of oblique injuries come from the muscles in the abdominal area which are supposed to prevent too much rotation in the back. So, there's been a whole lot of rotating going on this year, either from over-swinging, or over-throwing, or over-something, since Seattle Mariners' catcher Dan Wilson went down on Mar. 19. In fact, no less than five players suffered oblique injuries during Spring Training, leading one to speculate that either there was a LOT of swinging going on in Florida and Arizona, or maybe there wasn't enough stretching done prior to doing early workouts. It's also possible that the wet fields you get in the early spring may be a slip and fall factor in oblique injuries. Here's the current list of 2003's oblique casualties…

Mar. 19 – Dan Wilson, C, Mariners
Mar. 21 – Kevin Mench, OF, Rangers
Mar. 21 – Carlos Beltran, OF, Royals
Mar. 26 – Ben Broussard, 1B, Indians
Apr. 1 – Jason Michaels, OF, Phillies

After the season started, there was a two-week hiatus before the oblique bug bit again (it's worth noting that only nine players were disabled with oblique injuries all last year)…

Apr. 17 – Jeff Cirillo, 3B, Mariners
Apr. 20 – Josh Fogg, P, Pirates
Apr. 29 – Chad Fox, P, Red Sox
May 2 – Rodrigo Lopez, P, Orioles
May 5 – Stephen Randolph, P, Diamondbacks

Now the pitchers are getting into the act. After being strictly confined to position players in the preseason, four of the five most recent victims have been pitchers. Did they take it easy in Spring Training, and then do too much after the season started? Not exactly. Starters Fogg (88) and Lopez (91) both averaged fairly moderate pitch counts in their three (Fogg) and five (Lopez) starts before getting hurt in their fourth and sixth starts. And neither one threw as many as 100 pitches in any one start. However, short reliever Fox threw 35 pitches in a game against the Rangers the week before he was hurt, and middle reliever Randolph threw 299 pitches in just 15.1 innings (that's the equivalent of 176 pitches per nine innings), including two 50+ pitch outings, providing some more intriguing, though inconclusive, evidence on the importance of pitch counts, especially early in the season.

Actually, as indicated by Mr. Jones, major leaguers didn't just start pulling their obliques this year. It just seems that way… sort of like the epidemic of hamate injuries that first struck in the 1990s. However, it turns out that fractures to the hamate (it's one of the eight bones in the wrist, in case you flunked anatomy in Med School) are fairly common in athletics. The hook of the hamate (not to be confused with a hook slide – although that's one way to break it) is fractured most often in one of two ways… falling on an outstretched hand or, more frequently, while the individual is engaged in a sport involving a racquet, bat, or club, most often through a misjudged swing. If the centrifugal force of the bat exceeds the grip of a baseball batter, you get a hook of the hamate fracture. Similarly, in golf, it will happen if you hit the ground instead of the ball.

And while the Phillies' Dave Hollins was probably not the first baseball player to fracture the hamate, when he did it in July 1994 (while sliding), everyone (or at least everyone in Philadelphia) was trying to figure out just what he'd done to what. (Hollins is the same player who missed most of last year after a reaction to a spider bite… so he's no stranger to unusual medical problems.) Since then, the list of players hooked by the hamate has included; Benny Agbayani (1994, when he was in the minors), Todd Hollandsworth (1995), Rey Sanchez (1996), Cleatus Davidson (1999), Kevin Nicholson (2000), Wendell Magee (2001), Erubiel Durazo (2001   he gets a special award for a hamate injury in March and an oblique injury in July) and Darin Erstad (2002).

So, don't be surprised if a player on your favorite team goes out with a hamate or oblique injury. It's the thing to do.

CHAPTER 23

Item: May 1912 – 21-year-old Clarence Arthur Vance makes his professional debut as a pitcher for the Superior Brickmakers (!) of the Class D Nebraska State League.

He was known as "Dazzy," or "the Dazzler," and dazzle the hitters he did... but not on the major league level until 1922, when he was 31 years old. One of the most unique stories among major league pitchers, Vance is the only Hall of Fame hurler who didn't establish himself as a star until after his 30th birthday. And, you have to wonder why, since he possessed a fastball which supposedly gave him the ability to throw a creampuff through a battleship, and a drop curve that fell off the table. If you're thinking about Dazzy Vance, who led the National League in strikeouts seven straight times and won 197 games after his 30th birthday, think Mike Scott. Or think Curt Schilling.

While neither Scott, nor Schilling, is an exact match for the old Dazzler, all three strikeout pitchers could boast essentially the same "stuff," good fastballs, along with a pitch that dropped out of sight... in Vance's case, a curve, in Scott's and Schilling's, a splitter. And, all three had their greatest success after turning 30. Vance was held back partly by an arm injury suffered after he had brief trials in 1915 with the Yankees and Pirates. Scott just didn't have quite enough stuff until Roger Craig taught him the split-fingered fastball (or was it the scuffball?) after the 1984 season. In Schilling's case, shoulder troubles and a certain lack of focus held him back until 1997, when, at age 30, he blazed to 319 strikeouts (still the modern-day NL record for a right-hander) and 17 wins for a bad Phillies team.

The book is closed on Vance's and Scott's stories. The Dazzler finally ran out of steam in 1935 at the ripe old age of 44. Scott, who absolutely terrorized National League hitters from 1985 to 1989 – remember the famous 16 inning game that concluded the 1986 NLCS… the Mets were aghast at the possibility they would have to face Scott again in a seventh game… so they were fighting for their lives to avoid the same – had his arm fall off in 1990.

But, whither Curtis Montague Schilling? Certainly the best pitcher ever born in Anchorage, Ak., Schilling has terrorized NL hitters as much as Vance and Scott, at least in those seasons when he's been healthy. There have only been six such occasions, that is, when he's spent an entire season as a starter without being on the DL. But, they have been worth recalling.

Year	W-L	ERA	K	K/W
1992	14-11	2.35	147	2.5/1
1993	16-7	4.02	186	3.3/1
1997	17-11	2.97	319	5.5/1
1998	15-14	3.25	300	4.9/1
2001	22-6	2.98	293	7.5/1
2002	23-7	3.23	316	9.6/1 (That's Incredible)

As Lee Sinins has noted, Schilling is also second in strikeout/walk ratio among all pitchers with more than 2000 Ks. Better than the Rocket, way better than Sir Walter, better than Matty, better than Lefty, better than the Big Unit, better than anybody but Pedro.

	K/W	K	W
Pedro Martinez	4.35	2282	524
Curt Schilling	4.12	2408	584
Mike Mussina	3.53	2002	567
Greg Maddux	3.26	2675	821
Dennis Eckersley	3.25	2401	738
Juan Marichal	3.25	2303	709
Ferguson Jenkins	3.20	3192	997

Randy Johnson	3.06	3777	1236
Christy Mathewson	2.96	2502	844
Roger Clemens	2.96	3969	1340

In the past two seasons, Schilling has won 45 games, struck out 609 batters and walked only 72. And, while some may have wondered about his health or effectiveness after he got off to a slow start this year, his past two outings (after coming back minus his appendix, no less) would seem to indicate he's still got it… a 10 strikeout, no-walk, four-hit shutout and a remarkable 14 strikeout, one-walk, two-hit shutout (Game Score 96 – the highest in the majors this year, in case you're not scoring at home).

In answer to the question, "Whither Mr. Schilling?" there are currently two issues at hand… Is he going to the Hall of Fame? And, is he going back to Philadelphia?

First, the Hall of Fame. At age 36, Schilling is currently 158-110 with 2408 strikeouts and a 3.35 ERA over a 16-year career. Good numbers, but not Hall of Fame numbers, although he does score 33 on the Black Ink Test and the average for a HOF pitcher is just 40.

It's also interesting that the pitchers with career numbers most comparable to Schilling are an outstanding crew (Bret Saberhagen, Mike Garcia, Dennis Leonard, John Candelaria, Doug Drabek and Ron Guidry among them), but none of them are in the Hall of Fame, nor are they likely to be added at some point in the future.

However, John Smoltz, Mike Mussina and Kevin Brown are on Schilling's comp list, and, like Schilling, they are far from done. So… let's see… would a pitcher with 200 wins (and a .589 W/L percentage) and 3000 strikeouts make the Hall of Fame? Could be. Others have made it with worse records. (As to whether they should have, or whether Schilling should be judged against them, that's not the point… The fact is, he will be judged against them.) Without counting this year's efforts to date, and using The Favorite Toy as a calculator, we find that Schilling has a 60.2% chance of reaching 200 wins and a 54.4% chance of reaching 3000 Ks.

Given the continued health of his shoulder (admittedly, that's a significant "if"), it's not hard to visualize Schilling reaching those goals. He still should get another 25 or so starts this year, which should be good for another 200Ks and a dozen or so more Ws. So, let's say he ends 2003 with 170 wins and 2600 strikeouts. That will give him three consecutive years that look like this…

22-6 293K (age 34)
23-7 316K (age 35)
15-9 260K (age 36)

Is it so far-fetched to project the rest of his career (starting at age 37) along these lines…

18-10 300K (age 37)
15-12 250K (age 38)
12-6 200K (age 39)
5-5 100K (age 40)

For comparison sake, Vance's years from 37 to 40, in an era with far fewer strikeouts, looked like this…

22-10 200K (age 37 – the last year he led the league in Ks)
14-13 126K (age 38)
17-15 173K (age 39)
11-13 150K (age 40)

Such a record would leave Schilling with career totals of 210-150 (.583) and 3450 strikeouts (a total that would put him 10th in career strikeouts, just behind Walter Johnson.) It might also be instructive to look at the career totals of two other Hall of Fame pitchers, each with something in common with Schilling…

Don Drysdale – 209-166 (.557) and 2486K
Lefty Gomez – 189-102 (.649) and 1468K

Drysdale was another power pitcher, a strikeout pitcher, whose career W-L record could well end up similar (though very possibly slightly inferior) to Schilling's. Gomez, on the other hand, is in the Hall of Fame partly because he had some monster seasons (as has Schilling), partly because he was a character (as is Schilling) and partly because he was the dominant post-season pitcher of his era.

And that may be Schilling's trump card for the Hall of Fame. Even if he never pitches in October again, he has established himself as a dominator when it counts. He is 5-1 with a 1.66 ERA, four complete games, and strikeout/walk numbers of 91/17 in the postseason.

Now, as to what team he might be doing all this for… well, unlike Schilling's splitter, that's up in the air. Certainly, the Phillies recent visit to Arizona (when Schilling's current teammates hung a Phillies jersey in his locker), and the D'Backs visit to Philadelphia last week (when he threw the two-hitter and continued to make noises about how good a team the Phillies have put together and how much he liked playing in Philadelphia) re-sparked the fuss that was kicked up during the past off-season, when the Phillies indeed approached the D'Backs about their former ace's availability (and were told to get lost) and Schilling (who still has a house in Philadelphia) himself publicly brought up the subject of waiving his no-trade clause (at his Philadelphia golf tournament to raise money for ALS) to Phillies manager Larry Bowa and pitching coach Joe Kerrigan (who almost swooned on the spot).

Does Schilling really want to go back to Philadelphia? Could be. His public pronouncements, as opposed to those attributed to him by second-hand sources, indicate so. In either case, there's no question the man wears his heart on his sleeve, and there seems to be little doubt that he has changed his feelings (the ones that led to the disastrous – for the Phillies – 2000 trade) about the Phillies while he still maintains his passion for baseball and winning therein. And, Schilling's deeds (both on and off the field) since leaving Philadelphia clearly indicate a new level of maturity and accomplishment.

Do the Phillies want him? What, are you crazy? Picture a Schilling/Wolf/Millwood/Padilla rotation and watch out, Braves. Besides, how can you not want a pitcher who named his first son "Gehrig?"

Will Arizona trade him? Maybe yes, maybe no. GM JoeGJr says no way… for now. Of course, Arizona isn't going to pack in the 2003 season before Memorial Day. On the other hand, one can imagine a scenario wherein the D'Backs realize in July they're not going to win with an old (Randy Johnson is 39, Schilling 36, Mark Grace 38, Steve Finley 38, Matt Williams 37, Luis Gonzalez 35, Carlos Baerga 34, Tony Womack 33… can you say, "New York Mets, class?") highly-paid team. What's worse, Grace, Finley, Williams, Baerga and Womack shouldn't bring more than a case of Patio Diet Cola apiece in a trade. Hence, their tradable assets for re-building are exactly… Schilling and Gonzalez. (They'd never get comparable value for the elderly Unit.) And, no matter how good the team, every team has to re-build at some point… and, for an old team with money troubles, it's that much harder. (The 1983-84 Phillies were a good example of this.)

Can the Phillies afford him? Maybe yes, maybe no. Although it does seem likely that they could take on the balance of his 2003 $10 million salary in, say, late July… about the time the most heavily debt-laded team in the league might disappear in the Giants' rear-view mirror.

Now, as to whether the Phillies can afford to pay Schilling and Millwood both $12 million or so in 2004… that's another issue, and, for the Phillies, it should be an issue for another time. To quote that noted baseball philosopher Joaquin Andujar, in baseball, you just never know. The Phillies, if they get the opportunity, should follow the Bill Veeck theory of team building… when you get a chance for a pennant; you go for it with whatever it takes, because you never know when you'll get another chance.[31]

CHAPTER 24

May 27, 2003

Item: May 27, 1916 – The New York Giants sweep a doubleheader from the Boston Braves, 4-3 and 2-1, running their winning streak to 16 games.

In 1916, the Giants were as hot as they come. Their May 27 doubleheader win over the Braves was part of a 17-game winning streak within a 19-1 tear. Then, in August and September, they got even hotter – running off a still-record 26 game winning streak as part of a 32-5 burst. But, what did that get the McGrawmen at season's end? Fourth place.

The 1916 Giants are only the most dramatic, and probably best-known, example of a team that was red hot during an extended stretch… and didn't win the pennant. However, in this case, there were some extenuating circumstances for this seemingly inexplicable development. First, the '16 Giants were almost two different teams. They started the season with an old team that was basically the remnants of the great 1911-13 team. However, John McGraw saw that his old stars were over the hill, and conducted a mid-season purge that, among other things, saw Christy Mathewson go to the Reds in a trade. The 26 game streak was pulled off by the "new" 1916 Giants, after a couple of months of stumbling. And, in 1916, all the power in the National League was in the East – the Giants, Dodgers, Phillies and Braves tromped all over the Cards, Reds, Cubs and Pirates that year. So, while the G'ints were running wild from Aug. 24 to Sept. 30, they stayed in fourth place the whole time, because the other three contenders were also beating up on the Western teams.

However, the 1906 New York Highlanders, the 1907 Giants (they liked this sort of futility so much they did it in two different seasons… and you wonder why John McGraw died young), the 1924 Brooklyn Dodgers and the 1936 Cubs also had tremendous hot streaks that got them nothing but a "close, but not cigar." And, in some cases, they weren't even very close.

Team	Hot Streak	Dates	Overall	Finish
1906 Highlanders	18-2 (.900)	8/23 to 9/11	.593	2nd
1907 Giants	24-2 (.924)	4/15 to 5/18	.536	4th
1916 Giants	19-1 (.950)	5/9 to 5/31	.566	4th
	32-5 (.865)	8/24 to 9/30		
1924 Dodgers	32-7 (.821)	8/6 to 9/11	.597	2nd
1936 Cubs	24-5 (.828)	5/31 to 7/4	.565	3rd

Of course, hot streaks do lead to pennants. Here are seven of the best-known instances where a team got really hot during the season, and swept to a pennant…

Team	Hot Streak	Dates	Overall
1906 Cubs	42-4 (.913)	8/6 to 9/26	.763
1914 Braves	30-5 (.857)	8/29 to 10/1	.614
1935 Cubs	24-2 (.923)	8/28 to 9/27	.649
1942 Cardinals	30-5 (.857)	8/23 to 9/27	.688
1954 Indians	28-6 (.824)	7/30 to 8/31	.721
1955 Dodgers	22-2 (.917)	4/13 to 5/10	.641
1984 Tigers	35-5 (.875)	4/3 to 5/24	.642

Now, while these lists are not meant to be comprehensive (yes, the A's won 20 straight last year… but we're talking HISTORY here), and they do represent a small sample from the past 103 seasons. They are interesting, and, perhaps, some inferences can be drawn from them that are relevant to at least one team in 2003   the 1914 Braves' descendants.

First, no matter how good the team, sustaining a really hot streak for more than about six weeks just doesn't happen. Nobody's that good. No team plays .800+ ball for an entire year… or even half a year. The 20th/21st Century record for overall winning percentage is still held by the 1906 Cubs… and their overall record was .150 under their incredible 42-4 streak. In fact, of the 13 teams listed herein, only the 1954 Indians were able to play within roughly 100 percentage points of their hot streak over the course of an entire season. Furthermore, the teams that did win a pennant didn't get any hotter than the teams that didn't. ("Did. Didn't. Did." Sounds like my kids…) The six teams that finished 2nd, 3rd or 4th played .871 ball (149-22) while the seven teams that finished first played .879 ball (211-29).

Second, while it should be obvious that a really hot streak does not guarantee a pennant, it should also be noted that hot streaks late in the year seem to bring better results at the finish line than hot streaks early in the year. Half of the "hot" teams that didn't win were on fire before the halfway point in the season. Only the 1955 Bums and the 1984 Tigers among the seven pennant winners got hot early and coasted to a pennant.

Even as we speak, on May 27, 2003, the Braves are hot. So hot that even a pundit the caliber of Bill James has now picked them to win the NL East. But, in effect, is James picking them more on mystique than players? More on an early season sample than historical precedence?

We won't know the answer to that for several months. However, in addition to the rather iffy historical precedents, there are some current facts that suggest that the race isn't over yet. These facts are otherwise known, not as the Four Horsemen of the Apocalypse, but the five equus hemionus that make up the Braves' non-outfielders… and that old time sabrmetrician, Pythagoras.

On a more-or-less regular basis, the Braves' infield and catcher are NOT Moe, Larry, Curly, Shemp and Joe; but Vinny Castilla, Rafael Furcal, Marcus Giles, Robert Fick and Javier Lopez. Check out their OPS numbers for the three seasons prior to 2003, and see if you think ESPN.com poet Jim Baker will be writing a Furcal-to-Giles-to-Fick ode anytime soon…

	2000	**2001**	**2002**
Castilla	.562	.775	.616
Furcal	.776	.691	.710
Fick	.714	.815	.764
Giles	DNP	.768	.714
Lopez	.821	.747	.671

To summarize briefly... Castilla's hitting fame is based on his performance in Coors Field. Fick is Travis Lee with a slightly better bat and a worse glove. Lopez is an aging (32) catcher who has already suffered a devastating knee injury. Furcal and Giles, based on their actual performances, would seem to be failed (or at least disappointing) phenoms. Now, look at their OPS numbers for 2003 through the games of May 26...

Castilla –.806
Furcal –.931
Fick –.798
Giles –.956
Lopez –.946

Only Fick is producing at anything near his recent norms. Which leads one to ask... Does anyone think that the 35-year-old Castilla, during his 2000-2001 sojourn in Tampa Bay, took a quick trip over to St. Augustine to find the Fountain of Youth? Does anyone think Lopez, with 12 home runs, has suddenly become the second coming of Mike Piazza (who only has seven homers)? Does anyone think Furcal is a better hitter than Nomar Garciparra (.909 OPS in 2003)? And, does anyone think Marcus Giles (.956) will have a higher OPS than his brother Brian (.868) at year's end?

Clearly, 62.5% of the Braves' regular starters are hitting over their heads. And, while they may all have better years than last year (which would in itself be one strange alignment of the planets), you have to think they can't keep this up, any more than the Braves can keep up playing .844 ball for long. Because, that's what the Braves did between

Apr. 13 and May 18. Helped by a 10-1 record in 11 games against the Wretched of the Earth, otherwise known as the Marlins, Brewers, Rockies and Padres, they went 27-5. (Of course, since May 18 they're 3-4.)

So, five Braves regulars have been, for want of a better word, lucky, in their offensive production. (And, let's face it, luck does play a role in baseball.) What about the team as a whole? Thanks to the Pythagorean Theory (actually promulgated by the aforementioned Mr. James, not the ancient mathematician, who couldn't hit a curveball to save his life) we learn that the team has been lucky as well.

Basically, and based on number crunching from the entire history of baseball, the Pythagorean Theory states that the ratio of a team's wins to losses is the same as the ratio of the square of it runs scored to the square of its runs scored plus the square of its runs allowed.[32] The Braves have scored 290 runs (they are first in the NL in runs scored) and given up 242 (11th in runs allowed and 10th in ERA – have times changed, or what?), which should produce a record of 30-21. They are 34-17.

Interestingly, the third place Phillies' (27-23, 6.5 games out at the moment) runs scored (236) and runs against (196) produce a Pythagorean record of 30-20. And the second place Happy Wanderers' (32-19, 2 games out) runs scored (235) and runs against (189) produce a Pythagorean record of 31-20.

So, here's how the NL East SHOULD stack up at the moment…

Expos 31-20
Phillies 30-20
Braves 30-21

Two game and a six-and-half-game leads at Memorial Day are not overwhelming, especially under the circumstances. The NL East race isn't over, yet.

CHAPTER 25

June 3, 2003

Item: June 9, 1996 – The Pride of the University of Pennsylvania – Doug Glanville – makes his major league debut with the Chicago Cubs.

Multiple choice, class. Rocco Baldelli is…

A)The third cousin of Phil "The Chicken Man" Testa.
B)The new Joe DiMaggio.
C)The great-grandson of Emil "Hill Billy" Bildilli.
D)A younger Doug Glanville.
E)One of the best stories in Baseball 2003.
F)The holder of just about the lowest ID in the major leagues.

The lowest what? Does Baldelli, in addition to his other accomplishments, also have a degree in Psychology? Is he seeing a psychiatrist? What about his Super Id? Or his Ego? And what position did Sigmund Freud play, anyway?

OK. One question at a time. First, the answers to D, E, and F are "yes." Second, the answers to B and C are "no." Third, since The Chicken Man was blown up on his front porch some 20 years ago, we'll take an incomplete on A.

Now, since Baldelli isn't old enough to have graduated from college, and since he seems remarkably well-adjusted, just what is his ID? If you follow baseball statistics, you know what's meant by Isolated Power (IP). It's a somewhat more accurate measure of a hitter's pure power, obtained by subtracting their batting average from their slugging average. The higher the Isolated Power number, the more power a hitter has. Generally, if your Isolated Power is over .200, you have some power.

Well, ID, or Isolated Discipline, is the on-base version of Isolated Power. Isolated Discipline (as in Plate Discipline) is derived by subtracting a player's batting average from his on-base percentage. And, it's helpful in defining players like Glanville and Baldelli.

Going back over the past 42 seasons, or to the start of the Expansion Era (1961), we find that the yearly league average ID is fairly consistent – averaging about .069 in the American League (on a yearly range from .062 to .077) and .067 in the National League (on a yearly range of .059 to .074). On a career basis, an ID of more than .100 is pretty darn good. Here are some of the ID monsters from the past…

Max "Camera Eye" Bishop –.152
Gene Tenace –.150
Eddie Stanky –.142
Eddie "The Walking Man" Yost –.141
Teddy Ballgame –.139
Ferris "Burrhead" Fain –.135
The Babe –.132
Roy Cullenbine –.132
Mickey Tettleton –.128
The Mick –.125
Bernie Carbo –.125

No, this doesn't mean that Roy Cullenbine was as effective at getting on base as Babe Ruth. And, it doesn't mean that Bernie Carbo should be mentioned in the same sentence with Mickey Mantle (oops, I just did!) But, it does give some perspective of the hidden value of players with excellent plate discipline… those players who were willing and able to take a walk.

Where does that leave Rocco Baldelli? He of the .027 ID? (For comparison sake, Alfonso Soriano's career ID is .037) Surprisingly enough, it may well leave Baldelli with a long career… despite his offensive shortcomings and inability to accept charity at the plate. Because, Baldelli is just the most recent example of a type of player that major league GMs and managers seem unreasonably infatuated with… a modestly high average, fast, middle infielder or outfielder with some power and a terrible strikeout/walk ratio. Despite the fact these dudes almost never get on base unless they get a hit, they often bat leadoff or second (like Baldelli). And, what's more amazing, they hang around forever.

Not counting the aforementioned holder of a B.S. from Penn in Science and Systems Engineering (who is still active), here are the career numbers of seven Baldelli clones from the past 25 or 30 years. Note the length of those careers… they average 16 years!

Name	Years	BA	OBP	SLG	IP	ID	SB	K/W
Willie Wilson	19	.285	.326	.376	.091	.041	668	2.7/1
Shawon Dunston	18	.269	.296	.416	.147	.027	212	4.9/1
Gary Templeton	16	.271	.304	.369	.098	.033	242	2.9/1
Garry Maddox	16	.282	.320	.413	.131	.038	218	2.4/1
Juan Samuel	16	.259	.315	.420	.161	.056	396	3.3/1
Enos Cabell	15	.277	.308	.370	.093	.031	238	2.7/1
Mookie Wilson	12	.274	.314	.386	.112	.040	324	3.1/1

Except that Willie Wilson stole a LOT of bases, Dunston's plate discipline was truly awful, and Samuel was a little better hitter than the other six (his IP, ID and OPS – on base plus slugging–are all higher than the rest), these guys could be peas in a pod. One other current player, in addition to Glanville, seems to fit this mold pretty well…

Name	Years	BA	OBP	SLG	IP	ID	SB	K/W
Doug Glanville	8	.280	.318	.386	.106	.038	158	2.4/1
Jimmy Rollins	3	.264	.317	.397	.133	.053	87	2.1/1

Finally, if Shawon Dunston didn't make a deal with Mr. Applegate after last year's World Series to come back as Rocco Baldelli… well…

	IP	ID	K/W
Dunston	.147	.027	4.9/1
Baldelli	.132	.027	5/1

However, if Baldelli can keep up his current pace, he will, at least superficially, have an impressive year that would pretty much equal the best seasons of any of the nine other members of the "Baldelli Family." With the season about one-third gone, here are his projected totals for the entire year…

G	AB	R	H	2B	3B	HR	RBI	W	SO	SB	BA	OBP	SLG	OPS
159	648	80	218	35	12	9	94	27	133	21	.336	.363	.468	.831

Although some of those numbers look pretty good, 80 runs scored for a number two hitter with 218 hits isn't very good – even playing for Tampa Bay. Of course, that's likely to happen if you won't take a walk. Still, if it wasn't for the latest Japanese Import, Baldelli would be a lock for the Rookie of the Year with those numbers… and, in either case, he may well have a long (if somewhat misleading) career ahead of him.

CHAPTER 26

June 9, 2003

Item: August 1923 – Babe Ruth is caught using a bat that is actually four different pieces of wood glued together.

No, not the Babe, too? You got it.

And not only that, but when Dave Henderson had a chance to examine another Ruthian bat in 1983, he noticed that the round end of the bat didn't match the wood of the barrel of the bat. "That's a plug," said Hendu. "This bat is corked."[33]

Maybe Slamming Sammy Sosa getting caught with a corked bat won't be the biggest story of the year… but it'll be close. And, while it's certainly an interesting story… it's just not that big a deal (even if his other 76 bats – the man has 76 bats? – weren't clean), for two reasons.

First, altering bats is an old and (dis?)honored baseball tradition. Here's a very brief list of some of the other players who have been identified with souped-up bats… Albert Belle, Billy Hatcher (super balls), Ken Williams (maybe the first to cork a bat),[34] George Sisler (he drove nails in his bat, and filed off the ends),[35] Norm Cash ("I owe my 1961 batting title to my corked bats," he is supposed to have said), Graig Nettles (he also used super balls), Amos Otis and Wilton Guerrero. Only Hatcher and Guerrero are/were lousy hitters… the rest of these guys could hit, and most of them were power hitters. And yet, according to ESPN.com's Rob Neyer, there has never been any scientific proof that corking a bat makes any difference at all. So, what's all the fuss about?

Second, cork, or anything else in his bat, didn't help Sammy Sosa one lick in becoming a great hitter. He learned that himself, on the major league level, at the age of 29 – an almost incomprehensible accomplishment, since basically no one learns to hit on the major league level. And certainly not at the age of 29. Here are his walk totals, and strikeout/walk ratios for the past six seasons….

Year	Age	Walks	K/W
1997	28	45	3.9/1
1998	29	73	2.3/1
1999	30	78	2.2/1
2000	31	91	1.8/1
2001	32	116	1.3/1
2002	33	103	1.4/1

That is historic, and no amount of cork taught Sammy how to walk.

Item: June 4, 1902 – Napoleon Lajoie plays his first game for the Cleveland Indians.

It's that time again. Interleague play. The worst thing to happen to baseball since the advent of the DH. (Even worse than the Wild Card.) Why? Let me count the ways…

It detracts from the special nature of the World Series. As far back as 1884, the two teams that met for the ultimate in post season play were a unique match up, something that would never happen otherwise in an official contest. Not anymore.

It's helping kill the All Star Game, and the basic division/rivalry between the leagues. Used to be, the two leagues had separate identities, and a sense of competition… and not always friendly competition. Remember when Pete Rose wiped out Roy Fosse at the plate? Remember when Leo Durocher told Dizzy Dean, "They wouldn't let us in the other league. They would that say we are a lot of gas house ballplayers."[36] Remember when Jim Bouton, upon being traded from the Seattle Pilots to the Houston Astros agonized, that, if his knuckleball wasn't working, "They'll kill me in THAT league."[37]

Not anymore. Interleague play is one of the things that makes the All Star Game just another exhibition, and further blurs the line between what used to be two great rivals.

It's undermining the purity of the stats (horrors!) Can you lead the National League in home runs, if you hit 40 in NL games and five in interleague games, when someone else hits 41 in NL games and one in interleague games? Hmmmm??? For that matter, if Roger Clemens wins his 300th game this Friday against the Cardinals, will that make him the fifth 300 game winner in American League history? Or not?

And, possibly worst of all, it's just simply unfair. It's bad for competition. An unbalanced schedule is one thing, but, to be fair, teams in each league should play the same teams, for goodness sakes. What we've got now reeks of, you'll pardon the expression, pro football scheduling.

What's the only good thing about interleague play? Bill Chuck's comment on the recent Yankees/Reds series, to the effect that the Yankees left Cincy with a loss due to Juan Castro's single with two outs in the 9th. What's so great about that? If you have to ask, you don't know Chuck, who added, that, following the game Yankee pitcher and Cuban expatriate Jose Contreras, responding to a "Reds Win Led by Castro" headline, was seen building a raft.

Now, what does this have to do with "King Larry?" Well, once upon a time, he was the centerpiece of real competition amongst the National League and American League. Think lawsuits are a late 20th century addition to the baseball scene? Think again. In 1901 and 1902, there was little brotherly love in the City of Brotherly Love as the Phillies and the Athletics battled over Napoleon Lajoie… pursuant to Connie Mack having pilfered the great second baseman from the Phillies. Court orders, suits, counter suits, hearings enough to warm the cockles of any Philadelphia Lawyer's heart, until finally Phillies co-owner John I. Rogers won the big one in the Pennsylvania Supreme Court on Apr. 21, 1902.

The case was *Philadelphia Ball Club, Limited v. Napoleon Lajoie et al.* (You can probably guess who the et al was.) Reversing a lower court decision, the ruling was that Lajoie was "unique, and impossible to replace easily" and that "the court cannot compel the defendant to play for the plaintiff, but it can restrain him from playing for another club in violation of his agreement."[38] In other words, his original contract with the Phillies.

At the time, it was speculated that the court's ruling might scuttle the upstart AL. However, never underestimate Ban Johnson and Connie Mack. There was a loophole… the Pennsylvania Supreme Court's ruling was only valid in the state of Pennsylvania. As long as King Larry didn't play in Pa., the court had no jurisdiction. So… after a little more legal maneuvering, and a brief tour of other American League towns, somewhat similar to the last year's A-Rod caravan, Lajoie ended up in Cleveland on June 4. And, until the two leagues kissed and made up (at least enough to work under the same agreement), King Larry spent the days when the Indians played at Columbia Park on the beach in Atlantic City.

Now that's a rivalry. And it set up a 50+ year-long struggle between the Phillies and the Athletics for the hearts (and dollars) of the Philadelphia public. The struggle was recalled this past weekend, when the Athletics returned to Philadelphia for the first time since 1954. However, it wasn't any big deal, and though the Phillies promoted the match a little (and drew 36,000+ to Sunday's doubleheader), they certainly didn't go all out. Interestingly enough, the reason for the Phillies' reluctance to really market the Athletics' visit may well reside in the very history of the two teams. You see, Philadelphia WAS an American League town, from 1901 until, at the very least, the late 1940s. And, word has it that the team's primary owner, long time baseball man Bill Giles, knows that all too well, and was hesitant to remind the fans of it. While it has been almost 50 years since the Philadelphia Athletics left, there is an active, 900-member Philadelphia Athletics Historical Society, (Philadelphians have a strong sense of history… why do you think we still revere that cracked bell?) and a lot of older fans still remember that Eddie Joost, Bitsy Bobby Shantz, Indian Bob, Double XX, Lefty Grove, Black Mike, Home Run Baker, Cocky Collins, Stuffy McInnis, The Chief, The Rube and Gettysburg Eddie played in Philadelphia. For that matter, they even remember Jittery Joe Berry and Lynn "Line Drive" Nelson. Why?

"When I was growing up, everybody was an A's fan, nobody rooted for the Phillies." That's the one, the only, the original John A. Shiffert, Sr., speaking… an Athletics fan from the mid-30s until they left town in 1954. (He couldn't care less about those guys in green and gold.)

That attitude lasted a long time, and didn't change until around 1949, when the Phillies finally came out of the doldrums that had stretched back to 1917. And, if you think about it, that makes some sense… even though the A's were awful from the mid-30s on (as were the Phils), they had had so much more success than the Phillies (as well as an on-going icon in Connie Mack) up until then, that people just related more to the city's AL team. In fact, they related to the A's from the start.

"Rain Falls Upon the Just and the Unjust" headlined the Apr. 25, 1901 *Philadelphia Inquirer* as to the fate of rained out National and American League openers, leaving discerning readers to figure out exactly who the just and the unjust were.[39] Of course, regular Inky readers already knew who the paper was backing in the budding war between the leagues. Inky Sports Editor Frank Hough was hardly a neutral reporter on the state of the National Pastime in the city. Hough was an investor in the Athletics franchise and Mack's best PR man.

Whether the newspapers had anything to do with it or not, there was tremendous public enthusiasm for the Athletics from before the beginning of the 1901 season, partly because the shrewd Mack had given his white with navy trim clad team the most distinguished name in Philadelphia baseball history with a very clear purpose, and partly because the National League in general was in ill-repute, due to syndicate baseball, rough play and lack of competition. Certainly, on Opening Day 1901, it seemed as if Mack's naming brainstorm was a success. The Athletics' Apr. 26 paid crowd of 10,000+ was more than a dozen times the size of the intimate gathering of 779 that came to the Phillies' home opener. For the season, the fourth-place A's would end up outdrawing the second-place Phillies by 206,329 to 112,066.

CHAPTER 27

June 16, 2003

Item: June 7, 1983 – Steve Carlton strikes out the Cardinals' Lonnie Smith, his 3522nd K, and takes over the career strikeout lead from Nolan Ryan, who had just taken over the career strikeout lead from Walter Johnson.

There should be no doubt that the last 20 years or so have been the heyday of the K. Starting with the 1983 battle for the career strikeout lead between Carlton and Ryan (Johnson's total of 3509 – which now places him ninth – was once thought to be one of those "unbreakable" records), the last two decades have been a time of Special K.

The freak of nature – as physically unique in his own way as Babe Ruth was in his – who struck out 5714 batters. The all-time lefty K King who worked out in a vat of uncooked rice and threw an unhittable slider. The Dutch curveballer. Greaseball and sandpaper experts. Tom Terrific. They all passed Sir Walter's mark. As have two current pitchers of similarly unsurpassed credentials… Randy Johnson and Roger Clemens.

In honor of his unique double of winning 300 games AND striking out 4000 batters (a place where only two men have gone before), let us then take a moment to honor one of the foremost practitioners of that craft, and admire the Rocket's Red Glare. (We won't say where Roger Clemens is red… you can figure that out for yourself.)

Certainly, the feat of reaching 300 wins and 4000 strikeouts in the same game is mind-boggling. Even in the age of strikeouts, only Ryan and Carlton (4136) had previously passed 4000 Ks. And, what's more, after Johnson also reaches that plateau, it's highly unlikely that anyone else is going to reach 4000Ks in the foreseeable future. To put Clemens' feat of Friday the 13th (clearly an unlucky day for the Cards… sort of like getting stuck with the Queen of Spades in a Hearts game) in another perspective, imagine a hitter reaching 3000 hits and 600 home runs in the same game. The rarity of both of those feats compares quite well with Clemens' Daily Double. There are now 21 members of the 300 Win Club, and 25 members of the 3000 Hit Club. Similarly, the 4000K Club's three members are nicely balanced by the 600 Homer Club's four members. Of course, not only has Clemens made a name for himself as a strikeout pitcher, but, more importantly, his 300 wins also look like an almost insurmountable goal to the younger generation of pitchers. Let's bring Bill James' Favorite Toy back out to assess the 300/4000 possibilities for the rest of the field.

First, the 300 win barrier. Three current trends in pitching would seem to be leading the 300 game winner to, if not extinction, at least Endangered Species status (along with the Kiwi Bird, the Snail Darter and the complete game shutout, among others). The universal acceptance of the five man rotation (no one has started more than 37 games in a season since Charlie Hough – a knuckleballer – in 1987, and no one has thrown more than 300 innings in a season since the aforementioned Mr. Carlton in 1980), along with the proliferation of situational relievers, and an increasing focus on pitch counts have all cut down on the number of decisions a starting pitcher will have in the course of a year. The last two factors have taken away a starter's ability to control his own fate, and the former has taken away his chances to win before he ever gets to the mound.

Now, while it can be argued WHY 300 game winners are becoming scarce, it cannot be argued that they are. After Clemens, only Greg Maddux (62.2%) has a good chance of reaching 300 wins (at least, according to The Favorite Toy). Indeed, among the top 30 in career wins among active pitchers coming in to the 2003 season, the two youngest are Pedro Martinez (152) and Andy Pettite (128) and they're both 30 years old. And while such young guns as Kevin Millwood, Kerry Wood, Mark Prior, Barry Zito, Mark Mulder, Tim Hudson, Matt Morris, Gil Meche, et al., MIGHT get close some day, it's very risky to project pitchers' success 10 years into the future. For further reference, see; Ankiel, Rick.

Among the rest of the current career win leaders, only Martinez (12%), Tom Glavine (5.3%), Pettite (1.2%) and Mike Mussina (.3%) have ANY chance of reaching 300 wins. And, given the current struggles of Maddux, Martinez and Glavine, you have to wonder what The Favorite Toy will say about their chances after the 2003 season.

What about the chances of someone else reaching 4000Ks? Again, Kerry Wood or Mark Prior might get there some day… but, with a pitcher with a history of arm trouble, and a second-year starter, it's safer not to count your batters before they're K'ed.

As for everyone else on the strikeout leader board… The Favorite Toy gives Johnson the maximum chance (97%) of reaching 4000 (he currently has 3777). Of course, that's assuming his knee comes around enough to enable him to get those last 223. See, even predicting the end results for Hall of Famers can be tough. Martinez has a 24.6% chance, and no one else has ANY chance of reaching 4000Ks.

You will note that only Pedro Martinez had a chance of both reaching 300 wins and 4000 strikeouts… and a combined probability of approximately 3% of doing both. And, given his physique and injury history, even that seems optimistic. Anybody think he can do it in the same game?

Oddly enough, as remarkable as Clemens' career has been, and as much fame as he has for his strikeouts, including his five strikeout titles and his two, 20-strikeout games, he's never struck out 300 men in a season. His career high is 292 (with the Blue Jays in 1997). Of course, he has struck out more than 200 a total of 11 times.

There is also some evidence that Clemens' contemporary, the rather large Unit, is actually the greater strikeout pitcher. In addition to Johnson's six-300 strikeout seasons (in addition to six-200 strikeout seasons), Lee Sinins has pointed out that Johnson actually ranks one spot ahead of Clemens in strikeouts above league average for his career…

STRIKEOUTS	DIFF	PLAYER	LEAGUE
Nolan Ryan	2536	5714	3178
Randy Johnson	1677	3777	2100
Roger Clemens	1269	4006	2737
Walter Johnson	1191	3509	2318
Rube Waddell	1116	2316	1200
Dazzy Vance	1086	2045	959
Steve Carlton	981	4136	3155
Bob Feller	963	2581	1618
Sandy Koufax	958	2396	1438
Pedro Martinez	886	2285	1399

Actually, there's another way to slice and dice these stats. Based on their pure strikeout totals compared to their own eras, Ryan, Johnson and Clemens, the three top pitchers of the Special K Era, are the top strikeout pitchers of all time. However, if you take a ratio of their strikeouts to their league's strikeouts (in other words, the player total divided by league total) the top two are a couple of eccentric aces from waaaay back. Now, the top five look like this:

Dazzy Vance	2045/959 – 2.13/1
Rube Waddell	2316/1200 – 1.93/1
Randy Johnson	3777/2100 – 1.79857/1
Nolan Ryan	5714/3178 – 1.79799/1
Sandy Koufax	2396/1438 – 1.67/1

Clemens' ratio is 1.46/1, just behind Sir Walter. However, anyway you look at it, the man can pitch, and his kind is not likely to come along again (at least, not very soon.)

Finally, speaking of great pitching feats, is baseball a great game, or what? Sixty-five years to the day after Johnny Vander Meer threw the first of his two consecutive no-hitters (June 11, 1938), no less than six Houston Astros combined to no-hit the Yankees. If Jimy Williams has his act together, he'll throw the same six pitchers out there the next time that spot in the rotation comes up, to see if they can repeat the no-hitter.

CHAPTER 28

June 23, 2003

Item: May 30, 1989 – Michael Jack Schmidt retires from baseball at the age of 39.

Apparently, late spring is a hard time for power-hitting, slick-fielding third basemen. Just about 14 years after Mike Schmidt called it quits, Matt Williams was ignobly released by the Arizona Diamondbacks (on May 31), and subsequently retired (on June 12) as well.

Back in 1994, when Williams was making a run at Roger Maris' home run record (extrapolations, computer and even table top game projections of Williams' home run pace that year support the theory that he would have hit 62 home runs for the season without a strike), there was talk about Williams' place in the cosmos of great third basemen. Although he's ranked a fairly modest 23rd all-time in the *New Bill James Historical Baseball Abstract*,[40] Williams was a fine player… a good fielder and an imposing power hitter.

So, it seems only logical that Williams' retirement might be a good jumping off point to look for the Greatest Third Baseman Ever… starting with Williams, Schmidt and seven other hot sackers who have either been mentioned as candidates for that title, or who should have been so considered. Let's first compare their career numbers…

	G	AB	R	H	2B	3B	HR	RBI	W	BA	OBP	SLG	OPS
Williams	1866	7000	997	1878	338	35	378	1218	469	.268	.317	.489	.806
Boggs	2439	9180	1513	3010	578	61	118	1014	1412	.328	.415	.443	.858
Brett	2707	10349	1509	3154	665	137	317	1595	1096	.305	.369	.487	.856
Schmidt	2404	8352	1506	2234	408	59	548	1595	1507	.267	.380	.527	.907
Robinson	2896	10654	1232	2848	482	68	268	1357	860	.267	.322	.401	.723

Matthews	2391	8537	1509	2315	354	72	512	1453	1444	.271	.376	.509	.885
Traynor	1941	7559	1183	2416	371	164	58	1273	472	.320	.362	.435	.797
Baker	1575	5984	887	1838	31	103	96	987	473	.307	.363	.442	.805
Collins	1725	6795	1055	1999	352	116	65	983	426	.294	.343	.409	.752

(If you wanted to, you could include Ned Williamson… sometimes mentioned as the greatest third baseman of the 19th Century, Harlond Clift and Ron Santo on this list. All three were fine fielders and good hitters. But, for now, we'll pass on them.)

The most immediately striking thing about the list we do have is that these guys are all so well-known that no formal introductions are needed, with the possible exception of the first man in line, Jimmy Collins, who played from 1895 to 1908, largely with Boston in first the National League and then the American League. Before the advent of Pie Traynor, he was generally considered the holder of the "Greatest Third Baseman of All Time" crown.

Then, when you take a closer look at the numbers, encompassing 108 years of baseball history, you see some remarkable similarities. Just to mention a few… Boggs', Brett's, Schmidt's and Matthews' (who is tied with Brett) runs scored. Matthews' and Collins' doubles. Brett's and Schmidt's RBIs (a dead heat!) Baker's and Collins' RBIs. Williams', Traynor's and Baker's walks. Williams', Schmidt's, Robinson's and Matthews' batting averages. Traynor's and Baker's on-base percentages. Williams' and Baker's on-base plus slugging (OPS). Boggs' and Brett's OPS. There's a less than 1.5 percent difference in all of the figures mentioned. Still, this is really comparing apples to oranges, given the variations in career length. Home Run Baker only played 1575 games, and Brooks Robinson played a whopping 2896 – 84 percent more. So, let's look at their figures based on 162 games played…

	AB	R	H	2B	3B	HR	RBI	W	BA	OBP	SLG	OPS
Williams	608	87	163	29	3	33	106	41	.268	.317	.489	.806
Boggs	610	100	200	38	4	8	67	94	.328	.415	.443	.858
Brett	619	95	189	40	8	19	95	66	.305	.369	.487	.856
Schmidt	563	101	151	27	4	37	107	102	.267	.380	.527	.907
Robinson	596	69	159	27	4	15	76	48	.267	.322	.401	.723

Matthews	578	102	157	24	5	35	98	98	.271	.376	.509	.885
Traynor	631	99	202	31	14	5	106	39	.320	.362	.435	.797
Baker	615	91	189	32	11	10	102	49	.307	.363	.442	.805
Collins	638	99	188	33	11	6	92	40	.294	.343	.409	.752

That levels the playing field a little, and makes clearer some points that eliminate several candidates right off the bat (literally). Williams' lack of plate discipline (his career strikeout to walk ratio was 2.9/1) takes him out of the race for the greatest ever... even his four Gold Gloves can't save him, especially when you consider the case of Brooks Robinson. As great a fielder as The Human Vacuum Cleaner might have been, he doesn't fit in with this bunch offensively. Similarly, it's hard to make a case for the two Dead Ball stars, Baker and Collins. Baker is the better hitter, though a somewhat awkward fielder (he kept getting spiked at third base), and Collins, though a fine fielder, actually played part of his career in a high-scoring era when a .400 average was not uncommon. And, sorry Pirates fans, despite the "common" knowledge of many years, and despite several fielding records, Traynor's lack of power and refusal to take a walk leave him out as well.

That leaves Boggs, Brett, Schmidt and Matthews, who, by what is definitely NOT a coincidence, also happen to have the four highest OPS numbers of the group. Now, what other measures can we use to judge these four stars... two great power hitters and two line drive machines with more than 3,000 hits apiece? How about their standings in the MVP voting? Here's the list of their respective top 10 finishes...

Schmidt   1, 1, 1, 3, 3, 6, 6, 7, 10
Brett   1, 2, 2, 3, 7
Matthews   2, 2, 8, 10
Boggs   4, 6, 7, 9

Hmmm... not much doubt who was considered the best player by the MVP voters of their time – the people who actually saw them play every day.

What about defense? The Gold Glove. They were first awarded in 1957, Matthews' sixth year in the National League. That may be a unfair to him, but, on the other hand, he never won the award from 1957 until his retirement in 1968. Robinson, of course, has the record with 16, but Schmidt picked up 10 as fast as he used to scoop up swinging bunts barehanded. Boggs received two Gold Gloves from the AL, Brett, just one. With Robinson out of the running due to a weak bat, there's not much doubt here, either.

Finally, one last offensive measure. The Black Ink Test. Although a blunt tool, it gives us a chance to make comparisons in different eras. Leading the league in home runs in Frank Baker's Dead Ball Era gets you the same number of Black Ink points as doing so in 1980, or even the present Rocketball Era. Just for comparison sake, here are the Black Ink totals for all nine of the third basemen in question. We'll even throw in Santo, Clift and Williamson for good measure, and to keep all those old Cubs (Williamson played mostly for Chicago in the 1880s) and Brownie fans happy...

Schmidt	74
Brett	39
Boggs	37
Baker	26
Matthews	16
Santo	11
Robinson	10
Williamson	10
Williams	8
Collins	6
Clift	2
Traynor	2

Any questions? Schmidt is also the career leader in home runs, RBIs, slugging percentage and OPS (he's second in walks behind

Eddie Yost) by a third baseman, and still, after 22 years, the single season record holder for home runs by a third baseman (sorry Matt, the strike cost you that record). Looks like he's Number One in the *Baseball: 1862 to 2003* rankings, as he is in the *Bill James New Historical Abstract* rankings.[41]

CHAPTER 29

June 30, 2003

Item: June 29, 1905 – Archibald "Moonlight" Graham appears in his one and only major league game for the New York Giants.

Is *Shoeless Joe* the best baseball book of all time?

That's the subject for another chapter, however, there's no doubt that author W.P. Kinsella hit a home run with his tale of an Iowa farmer who brings the 1919 White Sox, a five-minute major leaguer (Graham), J.D. Salinger (and he isn't even dead yet) and his own father back to life. One way to measure the success of Kinsella's masterwork is to note how two aspects of the book have morphed into popular usage. The first is probably his most famous line, "If you build it, he will come."[42] How many times have you heard that repeated in some version in the past 20 years? The second is Moonlight Graham. Completely unknown when Kinsella wrote *Shoeless Joe* (just a line in the baseball encyclopedias… which makes you wonder how Kinsella found out about him), Archibald Wright Graham, has become a baseball term… describing a player with a career even shorter than the proverbial "cup of coffee." If you want to say someone had a REALLY short major league career, you say he had a "Moonlight Graham" career.

To briefly recap Doc (he was indeed a doctor in northern Minnesota for many years) Graham's career, he was a pretty decent minor league outfielder who made it to the big time in right field for one-half of one inning… the ninth inning of the Giants/Superbas game at Washington Park in Brooklyn of June 29, 1905. The G'ints were killing the hapless Brooklyns (the Dodgers name came back into use more commonly in

1906) 11-1 in front of 2000 probably bored Brooklynites when John McGraw sent Graham out to right field to take the place of George Browne. Christy Mathewson, who started what would become the Giants' eighth straight win (raising their record to 47-18), had long since been excused for the day, as had catcher Frank Bowerman and first baseman Dan McGann.The left-handed hitting, right-handed throwing, 5-10, 170 pound, 28-year-old Graham didn't make a play, and obviously didn't have much effect on either the game, the pennant race (which the Giants would win by nine games) or the Giants. Nonetheless, Graham was a pretty good minor league player, starring for the Charlotte Hornets before coming to the Giants in June 1905, and then leading the New York State League in hitting in 1906, with a .336 mark at Scranton. Some sources indicate he retired on June 30, 1905, but, most likely, he just left the Giants to return to medical school… since he was doubling in the two professions, somewhat in the fashion of latter-day doctor/players, Bobby Brown and Doc Medich. Despite his minor league accomplishments, and his catchy nickname (the origin of which is unknown), that was Moonlight Graham's sole appearance in a major league box score, leaving him forgotten by baseball fans (at least, outside of Chisholm, Mn.) until 1982, 17 years after his death.

However, it is certainly true that he was not alone in having a "Moonlight Graham" career in the majors. There have been many others who have played in just one game… which may not seem like much, but it's a lot more than you or I can say.(An aside… I had a Moonlight Graham career… in high school baseball. I knew at a young age that I was destined to be a sportswriter/statistician, so that's what I did for Germantown Friends School in Philadelphia. The last regular season game of my senior year, we were leading Friends Central 7-1 on their field in the last inning when an altercation broke out at second base, resulting in one of our players getting tossed. Our coach, Harry Gratwick, had already cleared the bench, and since the league rules stipulated that you couldn't play with less than nine men on the field, I was elected to play right field for one-half of the last inning of the game. I put on Ted West's uniform – number 23 in your scorecard – and played right for the last three outs. And, just like Moonlight Graham, I never touched the ball.)

Possibly the most famous Moonlight Graham career (outside of its namesake) belonged to Walter Alston. The long-time Dodgers manager had one at bat (he struck out) on Sept. 27, 1936 for the Cardinals. At first base, he had one putout and one error in two chances. And, that was it for "Smokey." However, there have been Moonlight Graham careers hidden throughout baseball history. For instance, if your last name is Harrington, chances are pretty good you played just one game in the majors. Well, that may be an exaggeration, but no fewer than three Harringtons have had Moonlight Graham careers; Andrew Francis (1913 Reds), Andrew Matthew (1925 Tigers) and Mickey (1963 Phillies). The latter had a really brief major league career – the 28-year-old Mickey pinch ran on July 10, 1963, didn't score, and never played again in The Show. By comparison, A. Francis was practically a vet – pitching four innings for the Reds (and giving up four runs) and going 1 for 1 at the plate. On the other hand A. Matthew pinch hit on Apr. 18, 1925, didn't get on, and was never heard from again. Maybe he gave manager Ty Cobb some lip.

The briefest major league career belonged to Larry Yount (Robin's older brother). His elbow acted up while he was on the mound, warming up for a late-season 1971 game for the Astros, and he never threw a pitch in the majors. However, since he was announced as the pitcher, he is considered as having played in the majors.

More recently, 24-year-old Beiker Graterol (is that a great name, or what?) was the starting pitcher in the fourth game of the 1999 season for the same Tigers that once employed Andrew M. Harrington. The date was Apr. 9, 1999 in Yankee Stadium, and ole Beiker hasn't been seen in a major league game since. Mainly because he lasted just four innings of a 12-3 rout by the Yankees (the game only went seven innings – maybe they invoked the "mercy killing" rule used by high schools), and gave up three home runs on the way to a 15.75 ERA. If Graterol indeed ends up with a Moonlight Graham career, it's going to be an awkward one to explain to the grandkids.

Maybe Moonlight Graham careers follow the Tigers around

because of what happened on May 18, 1912. That's the day of the first player strike in history, when the Bengals refused to take the field against the Philadelphia Athletics in protest of the suspension of the aforementioned Mr. Cobb. (Ban Johnson sat him down for going into the stands in New York to silence an abusive fan… but, that's another story as well.) Now, Manager Hughie Jennings knew beforehand that his players were going to walk, and, with the help of Connie Mack, he had lined up some replacements from the Philadelphia sandlots. Although the final score of the game was 24-2 (guess who won?), the efforts of Bill Leinhauser, Jim McGarr, Ed Irvin, Dan McGarvey, Vincent Meaney, Hap Ward, Jack Smith and Aloysius "Allan" Travers are certainly worth a tip of the hat (undoubtedly the classic "pillbox" cap worn by the A's at that time). The Rev. Travers' (he was a seminary student at the time, and went on to a long career as a Catholic priest and teacher… in fact, he taught my friend Dave Glielmi at St. Joe's Prep in Philadelphia) efforts were particularly notable, as the 20-year-old right hander went the whole way, giving up 26 hits and 14 earned runs (also leaving him with a 15.75 ERA) to the defending World Champions.

If he heard about the game up in Chisholm, Moonlight Graham would have been proud.

Item: July 6, 1882 – Tom Brown makes his major league debut with the Baltimore Orioles of the American Association.

Tom who? Well, he had a longer career than Moonlight Graham. In fact, Brown would go on to play the outfield until 1898 and would steal 657 bases in 1786 games in the process (although stolen bases were computed differently at that time.) And, I'll bet you've never heard of him. Well, neither had I until I came across his name on Baseball-Reference.com. And therein lies a point to be made.

There was some serious moaning, most of it coming from the Left Coast and ESPN, last week when one of the now San Francisco Giants' (the team moved west from New York in 1958, in case you missed it) players passed what was considered (at least by the Giants' front office) a significant milestone. Can't think of his name right now, but, the fuss that was made was enough to make you think that the Fed's lowered interest rates had made U.S. Savings Bonds worthless. Wait, that's it. Bonds. Barry Bonds. Plays left field (like his feet hurt) for the Giants. Anyway, there was some comment that Bonds was shortchanged by the media in terms of the notoriety for his becoming the first player to have 500 career home runs and 500 steals. That is, in comparison to the hoopla over Roger Clemens reaching 300 wins and 4,000 strikeouts.

Well, one of the reasons for that is the same reason you've never heard of Tom Brown... 500 steals isn't that big a deal, and stolen bases in general just aren't that big a deal, certainly not in comparison to wins or strikeouts. Here's one way to look at it. Brown is 13th on the career stolen base list, but Bonds, with his 500SBs, is all the way down at 36th, just ahead of the fabled Omar "The Outmaker" Moreno. That's right, 35 other players have stolen 500 bases. That's in comparison to just 21 300 game winners, and only three men with 4,000 Ks.

In addition, it's been two years since Bonds hit his 500th home run (there are 19 total members of that more exclusive club), so his reaching the less significant milestone of 500 stolen bases didn't really have another aspect to it... unless you follow the concept of the power/ speed number. That's the Bill James-created metric used to measure an individual's home run power in combination with his steals.[43] Bonds does indeed have the highest career power/speed number in history, but few outside of the membership of the Society for American Baseball Research have ever heard of a power/speed number... hence, the relatively massive disinterest in Bonds' feat which, despite its nice symmetry, is something of an artificial landmark in any case. As James has noted, you can make up exclusive groups for just about any set of statistics.[44] For instance, Stan Musial is the only player in history to amass more than 450 home runs and more than 175 triples... which may be a more valuable offensive accomplishment in his era that 500 home runs and 500 steals is in Bonds'.

Of course, the other reasons for the heightened hype over Clemens' feat(s) arc the facts that he did them in the same game (an incredibly unique double) and the fact that he pitches for a team with "New York" on its uniforms (at least, on the road.) And, it may just be possible that

Bonds' rather objectionable personality may have something to do with the lack of fanfare as well.

Add it all up, and the public notice over Bonds' accomplishment deservedly pales in comparison to Clemens' same-day double. Sorry, Barry. You'll just have to pat your own back on this one.

CHAPTER 30

July 7, 2003

Item: June 12, 1898 – Michael "Doc" Powers makes his major league debut for the Louisville Colonels.

Item: June 13, 1878 – Bill Bergen is born in North Brookfield, Massachusetts.

Item: June 14, 1982 – Hitting .118, Mario Mendoza is released by the Texas Rangers, ending his major league career.

A veritable tripleheader of offensive ineptitude.

One of the worst hitters to have a substantial major league career, Doc Powers appeared in 647 games over 11 seasons, mostly with the Philadelphia Athletics. In fact, he caught their very first game on Apr. 26, 1901, and was their regular catcher in their inaugural season, also getting in about 60 games per year from 1902 until 1908. All this despite the fact that he just could not hit. For instance, in 185 at bats during the 1906 season, he managed exactly one extra base hit (a double) and one walk. And that wasn't totally out of character for him. In 1904, he had three doubles and six walks in 184 at bats. When he died on Apr. 26, 1909 – eight years to the day after he caught Chick Fraser's first pitch, he had a career batting average of .216, an on base percentage of .248 and a slugging percentage of .268. That's a career OPS of .516. His ID of .032 and his IP – Isolated Power – of .052 weren't exactly anything to write home about, either.

And yet, as bad a hitter as Powers was, Bill Bergen was worse. Even taking into account the dead ball era in which he (and Powers) played, Bergen may well have BEEN the worst hitter ever. He actually played in 947 games from 1901 to 1911, mostly with Brooklyn (no, they didn't change their name from Superbas to Dodgers during that time because of him), "hitting" a stunning .170 with a .194 on base percentage and a .201 slugging percentage. Add 'em up, that's an OPS of .395, with an ID of .024 and an IP of .031. Although he didn't have any seasons with just one extra base hit and one walk (although his 1907 season featured three doubles and one walk), he never had more than 11 extra base hits or 14 walks in any one season, and he played a lot more than Powers. However, as bad as Powers and Bergen were, at least they didn't suffer the fate of Mario Mendoza. Offensive ineptitude, thy name has been The Mendoza Line. In a deathless quote generally attributed to George Brett, The Mendoza Line was fixed at a .200 batting average. Sink below .200, and you're below The Mendoza Line. Supposedly, Brett said that he checked the batting stats every day to see who's below The Mendoza Line. This momentous occasion may have happened in 1979, when old Mario hit .198 as the regular shortstop for the Seattle Mariners.

However, there is another version of the story. Pittsburgher Kevin Warren says that, originally, The Mendoza Line was NOT a specific batting average, nor did it even originate with George Brett. According to Warren, it is the batting average below which even a great fielder shouldn't/won't play, and it was in common use in Pittsburgh by June of 1977, when Mendoza was the Buccos' shortstop.

Either way, for his 686 game career, Mendoza actually hit above The Mendoza Line, finishing with a .215 average (although he did hit under The Mendoza Line for five of his nine seasons) to go along with a .248 on base percentage and a .262 slugging percentage, as well as a .507 OPS (worse than Powers) and ID and IP numbers of .033 and .047. In other words, he had less power than Powers.

Nonetheless, the time has come for Mario and The Mendoza Line to step aside. As the understanding of baseball statistics becomes more sophisticated, people are beginning to realize that batting average really doesn't tell that much about as player's offensive contributions. A truer measure of offense is OPS a metric where .800 is usually considered pretty good, and 1.000 will put you up among the league leaders. But, what about the other end of the scale? What's a really bad

OPS? Upon careful consideration, it can be stated that an OPS below .600 should be just cause to never stick your head out of a major league dugout again. However, that hasn't stopped players or managers from dragging sub-.600 OPS' up to the plate. And, nowadays, when you think of a really bad hitter, you think of the immortal Rey Ordonez, the Mets' once and futile shortstop, who is now on the disabled list of the Tampa Bay Devil Rays. By a strange and wonderful coincidence, coming into the 2003 season, Ordonez's career on-base percentage was .290. His career slugging percentage was .304. (In case you're interested, his career batting average was .245) Put those two numbers together, and you have a career OPS of .594. Close enough. From here on in, when we wish to express the measure of a really bad hitter, one with a sub-.600 OPS, we can say they are below The Ordonez Line.

Now, that naturally leads to another question. At mid-season 2003, who's below The Ordonez Line?

Well, it turns out that four regulars, four guys who have batted enough to qualify for the various batting championships (fat chance of that!), are below The Ordonez Line at mid-season. They are (and the names have NOT been changed to protect the guilty)…

David Bell, Phillies, 272 AB, .593 OPS
Cesar Izturis, Dodgers, 277 AB, .577 OPS
Alex Cora, Dodgers, 247 AB, .570 OPS
Brandon Phillips, Indians, 268 AB, .555 OPS

Even realizing that Dodger Stadium is a tough place to hit, doesn't this at least partly explain why the Dodgers, who have the best pitching in baseball, aren't running away with the NL West? At least the Phillies and the Indians have excuses. Bell just signed a big free agent contract and Phillips is a highly-thought of prospect playing for a team that's going nowhere this year. But, what in the world are Izturis AND Cora doing making outs in the lineup of a contender?

Bell, Izturis, Cora and Phillips aren't the only ones below The Ordonez Line. Four other players with more than 200 at bats reside there, although two of them are now back in the minors – the Indians'

Josh Bard (.596 OPS… I guess the Indians don't have unlimited patience with all of their non-hitting prospects) and the Tigers' Omar Infante (.517 OPS… that's Mike Powers territory.) Shockingly, one of the other two is the White Sox' Paul Konerko at .546. Not so shockingly, the other is a latter-day Bergenesque/Poweresque catcher, the Astros' Brad Ausmus (also .546).

The Mariners' Dan Wilson (.597), the Expos' currently disabled (with a bruised bat?) Fernando Tatis (.543) and the Tigers' Brandon Inge (.500, he's back in the minors, too) all have between 150 and 200 at bats, and all reside below The Ordonez Line. In addition, another eight players with at least 100 at bats on the year are below .600 in OPS. Although there's no need to embarrass them all, it should be mentioned that the lowest OPS among all players with 100+ at bats belongs to the Athletics' Jermaine Dye, who came into the 2003 season with a career OPS of .818, and now sits at – stand back – .458! Gag! That's getting near Bill Bergen territory, and makes you wonder why he REALLY went on the DL the other day. Others in this group include the Pirates' sterling second base pair of Pokey Reese (.533) and Abraham Nunez (.512), and Sir Gene Kingsale (.540), whose Arubian Knighthood didn't stop the Tigers from sending him back to the minors… and bringing up somebody almost as bad.

And what of Rey Ordonez? Well, as mentioned, he's currently on the DL, probably with symptoms of severe shock. Having never topped .636 in OPS for a complete season previously, he was, thanks to an unprecedented power surge (his IP is .171, though his ID is still down at .012) in 117 at bats, at .815 when he was hurt.

Which just goes to prove that either the American League really is inferior, or that every dog has its day. Or something like that.

CHAPTER 31

July 14, 2003

Item: July 9, 1957 – The American League beats the National League 6-5 in the All-Star Game.

Traditionally, not much is supposed to happen during the All-Star break. That's especially true now that the game is meaningless, except in three cities – the host town and the two places that will eventually split this year's World Serious. However, this year, the week leading up to the All-Star break provided plenty of food for thought… with no fewer than three good stories running around the bases, though, hopefully, not being chased by Randall Simon waving a bat.

Starting with the 50s… a time when the AL pretty much dominated the All-Star Game. So, the Junior Circuit's win in St. Louis in '57 wasn't a great shock. What would have been a shock was if the National League had won the game, because manager Walter Alston was playing with a stacked deck… stacked against him, that is. The stacking was done by the good burghers of Cincinnati, who, along with a little help from one of the bastions of impartial journalism in town, had managed to vote seven (some sources say eight) members of the eventually fourth place Redlegs (you didn't dare call them "Reds" in the McCarthy Era) onto the NL's starting team. Even though Commissioner Ford Frick (in one of his few decisive actions as commissioner) managed to get a couple of ringers named Mays and Aaron onto the starting team in place of their crimson-hued hose counterparts (Gus Bell and Wally Post), the NL team still looked like a Cincy intrasquad game.

While that little bit of skullduggery may be the worst example of ballot box stuffing visited upon the Mid-Summer Classic by fan voting, it is far from the only such bit of madness that has come about since Arch Ward had his brainstorm back in 19 and 33. Unrestricted fan voting, once described by Bill James as leaving an open ballot box on the street on the second Tuesday in November,[45] was an unrestricted disaster, especially in conjunction with the requirement that every team must have a representative in the game. Even now, with Internet voting (even limited to 25 votes per e-mail address), special ballots, players voting and the ever-popular one rep per team rule, giving the basic vote to the fans is a sure recipe for either unfair representation or really dumb choices. Like Mike Williams, he of the 0-3 record and 6.62 ERA. Like Marcus Giles (does three good months erase the fact that he's been mediocre in his other two years?) Like Hideki Chop Suey (or is that Hee Seop Choi?) getting on the starting AL team through the Internet vote from the Lefty O'Doul League. Like Brian Giles (a far better choice than either teammate Williams or brother Marcus) staying home. Like the really popular (in the U.S., at least) rookie in the AL, Rocco Baldelli, staying home. Like a genuine star, who happens to play half his games in the city where the All-Star Game is being held, buying a ticket to get in. You get the picture.

Look, you can't entirely blame the fans for this mess... even though a large percentage of them may well have been accurately characterized by Lee Elia in his famous diatribe when he was the Cubs manager, or by James' statement about the "idiot vote."[46] First of all, no one has ever defined just what the heck an All-Star is supposed to be. Is it someone who's had three hot months (M. Giles)? Is it a faded star that the fans want to see one last time (numerous examples)? Is it a retired star (Mike Schmidt was voted to the 1989 starting team AFTER he retired)? Is it a genuine star who's having a poor start to the current year (Slamming Sammy)? Who knows?

One suggestion might be that the voters be given some guidelines for weighted voting. As to who should do the voting… well, baseball writers come first to mind… why do you think they vote for the Hall of Fame? However, I wouldn't give the vote to just the BBWAA types. Include the really knowledgeable (and usually more impartial) scribes from the national and electronic scene… Rob Neyer, Jim Baker, Jayson Stark, Lee Sinins, the guys from Baseball Prospectus, some of the Elias troops, etc. Have them take into account, in this order…

-The player's entire career to date
-His performance in the current year
-His performance in the second half of last season
-His number of previous All-Star appearances

Such a weighted system would, hopefully, make it more likely that true stars actually play in the game. I mean, isn't an All-Star Game supposed to be for the "Stars?" However, until such time that the Lords of Baseball (take a bow, Bud.com) define All-Star as something rational, it's time to move on to bigger and better things. The REAL All-Star teams. Here are three of them…

The All-Fish Team
1B – Sid Bream (Captain)
2B – Johnny Ray
3B – Chico Salmon
SS – Irv Ray
OF – Lip Pike
OF – Tim Salmon
OF – Kevin Bass
C – John Bass
RHP – Dizzy Trout
LHP – Steve "Rainbow" Trout
RP – Jim "Sting" Ray
Mgr – Lip Pike

The Bench
Dick Bass
Norm Bass
Carl Ray
Farmer Ray

Ken Ray
Roger Salmon
Roy Crabb
Doc Bass
Jay Pike
Jess Pike
Larry Ray
Randy Bass

Honorary Nickname Members
George "Catfish" Metkovich
Jim "Catfish" Hunter
Johnny "The Crab" Evers
Jesse "The Crab" Burkett
Camille "The Eel" Henry (OK, so he was a hockey player, it's still a great nickname)

Note: This is only for complete last names – no Oscar Grimes, Ray Semprochs or Estell Crabtrees on this squad. Bream's the captain because his name spawned the idea for this team.

The All Fowl Ball Team
1B – Dave Winfield
2B – Billy Herman
3B – Garry Templeton
SS – Phil Rizzuto
OF – Indian Bob Johnson
OF – Rickey Henderson
OF – Eric Davis
 C – Birdie Tebbets
PH – Dion James
RHP – Kirby Higbe
LHP – Randy Johnson
RP – Ellis Kinder (Captain)
MGR – Casey Stengel

Notes: These are all players who have been associated with our feathered friends in some fashion.

Winfield: Probably the fowlest ball of all – killed a seagull in Toronto with a warm-up throw between innings. Was arrested for it. Got off cheep, though just escaped being tarred and feathered.

Herman: Used to shoot skeet (live pigeons, in this case) with Ernest Hemingway during Spring Training in Havana.

Templeton: Gave the fans the "bird" in St. Louis after being booed.

Rizzuto: He was terrified of birds. Teammates once tied one in the team valuables drawer and almost gave him a heart attack.

I.B. Johnson: Once stuck a bird in his brother's (Roy) glove in the outfield between innings.

Henderson: Killed a bird with a fly ball.

Davis: Also killed a bird with a fly ball (in the minors).

Tebbets: George Tebbets was so-named because he used to chirp like a bird behind the plate.

James: Still another to kill a bird with a fly ball. Got a double out of it. (About the only way he could get a double.)

Higbe: Used to shoot skeet (live pigeons, in this case) with Ernest Hemingway during Spring Training in Havana.

R. Johnson: Nailed a bird with a pitch during Spring Training. A for-certain "Owie!"

Kinder: Smacked on the head on the pitcher's mound at Fenway Park by a mackerel dropped by a seagull. Probably the greatest "bird" incident in major league history. That's why he's captain.

Stengel: Tipped his cap to the fans when he was being booed (aka, being given the bird) as a manager... and a bird flew out.

The All Eye Chart Team
1B – Kent Hrbek
2B – Winston Llenas
3B – Jerry Dybzinski
SS – Ken Szotkiewicz

OF – Mike Krsnich
OF – Lenny Dykstra
OF – Joe Zdeb
C – Doug "Eye Chart" Gwosdz (Captain)
RHP – Eli Grba
LHP – Kevin Mmahat
RP – Al Hrabosky
Mgr – Hugo Bezdek

The Bench
John Tsitouris
Emil Yde
Mike Blyzka
Bob Chlupsa
Mike Cvengros
Radhames Dykhoff
Mike Fyhrie
Joe Grzenda
Ricky Trlicek
Sal Yvars
Sig Gryska
Walt Hriniak
Joe Kmak
Rocky Krsnich
Monte Pfyl
Scott Lydy

Note: These players are chosen more so for their unusual names than for their ability.

Item: June 19, 1903 – Ludwig Henrich Gehrig is born in New York City.

Lou Gehrig is probably the most famous case of a star player "losing it" very suddenly. Although his 1938 season wasn't up to his normal standards (.295 BA/.410 OPB/.523 SLG – that was an off-year for him), no one dreamed he would start off 1939 so terribly that he would take himself out of the lineup, ending his 2130 game streak. Of course, there was a reason. An extreme reason. Gehrig was dying of a form of Muscular Dystrophy – ALS – that would eventually be named after him.

As we hit the All-Star break 100 years following the Iron Horse's birth, it seems likely that at least three players will welcome the break. While one would certainly hope that there is nothing seriously wrong with Pat Burrell, Jermaine Dye or Paul Konerko, and while it is far too early to assume that any or all of these three relatively young sluggers has had it, you have to wonder just what's wrong with all three of them. A slump is a slump, but, at the half-way point of the season, they're all hitting like, well, Rey Ordonez. Indeed, Dye and Konerko are way below The Ordonez Line, and none of them are old enough to be dismissed as being over-the-hill… in fact, none of them are even close to Gehrig's age when he retired. Let's run the numbers…

Burrell – age 26

	G	AB	R	H	1B	2B	3B	HR	RBI	W	K	BA	OBP	SLG	OPS
2002 Phi	157	586	96	165	87	39	2	37	116	89	153	.282	.376	.544	.920
2003 Phi	80	294	35	57	24	21	1	11	31	45	92	.194	.304	.384	.688
Career	503	1827	258	467	352	116	6	93	315	267	546	.25	.352	.478	.830

Burrell's numbers come from last week, when he had almost exactly half as many at bats as he had in the entire 2002 season – making the comparison a little easier. At this point, he's actually hitting more doubles and walking more (hence his ID is actually up from last year), while his singles and home runs are way down (which is why his slugging average is down.) And, his strikeouts are way up.

One must be tempted to assume that pitchers are throwing him almost ALL bad pitches... a lot of which (but not all, since he still will end up with almost 100 walks at this rate) he's swinging at and missing, and some of which he's strong enough to still muscle into the outfield for doubles. His strikeout to walk ratio this year is much worse than in

2002 and 2001, but, interestingly, it's about the same as it was in his rookie year, 2000.

As bad as Burrell has been, Konerko and the now-disabled (maybe for the rest of the year) Dye, have been worse.

Konerko – age 27

	G	AB	R	H	1B	2B	3B	HR	RBI	W	K	BA	OBP	SLG	OPS
2002 CWS	151	570	81	173	116	30	0	27	104	44	72	.304	.359	.498	.857
2003 CWS	71	216	18	40	28	8	0	4	18	21	23	.185	.261	.278	.539
Career	744	2629	367	732	473	139	5	115	428	228	366	.278	.341	.466	.807

This poor soul's struggles caused the White Sox to go out and get Carl Everett. Konerko's problems are even harder to figure out – since his Strikeout/Walk ratio (and his ID) has actually improved significantly from last year. However, his power has gone way down, and, he isn't even getting many singles. Is it possible to hit in bad luck for more than 200 at bats? Yes, it is, just like Norm Cash seems to have hit in good luck (or with corked bats) for the entire 1961 season. Still, luck this bad over an entire season would be historic.

Dye – age 29

	G	AB	R	H	1B	2B	3B	HR	RBI	W	K	BA	OPB	SLG	OPS
2002 Oak	131	488	74	123	71	27	1	24	86	52	108	.252	.333	.459	.792
2003 Oak	42	150	16	24	18	4	0	2	12	15	30	.160	.235	.227	.462
Career	879	3215	466	882	55	182	13	136	523	287	632	.274	.335	.466	.801

Dye, slightly older than the other two, and not quite as good a hitter, is still having an historically bad year. A .462 OPS for anybody is awful… that's terrible, even for Rey Ordonez. Dye's Strikeout/Walk ratio hasn't changed much from last year, but, like Konerko, he has no power and doesn't even have the bloops falling in for singles. You have to wonder if maybe he hasn't been hurting physically all year.

Item: July 11, 1961 – Stutterball Stu Miller is blown off the mound at Candlestick Park during the All-Star Game.

A lot of strange things have happened during the course of baseball games since Alexander Cartwright drew up the first set of rules back in 1845. Similarly, a lot of strange things have happened to baseball players, both on and off the field, in the past 160 years or so.

Certainly, Stu Miller's moment of embarrassment is one of the All-Star Game highlights of this genre, but, there have been plenty of other odd occurrences in baseball. Without a doubt, the leader in this year's "Oddball Derby" is Randall Simon of the Pirates, who, on July 9 in Miller Park in Milwaukee, became, to the best of anyone's knowledge, the first major leaguer to attack a seven-foot Italian Sausage with a baseball bat between innings. (Actually, it was during a smoked meat footrace.) And, to get suspended for three games for same.

There has been much speculation as to the possible reason for the Simon Sausage Slashing… some of which you may not have heard previously…

He thought the offending link was mocking the Pittsburgh team's former nickname. In 1887, when they first jumped from the American Association to the National League, the Pittsburgh team wore gaudy blue and black striped uniforms, leading some sportswriters to call them the "Smoked Italians." (No, I'm not making this up.)

Simon thought that John Rocker had taken up a new career, dressing as a sausage and running through ballparks (he might as well, he certainly can't pitch anymore). In case you've forgotten, Rocker was thought to have been referring to Simon in his "fat monkey" comment in his infamous Off-the-Rocker *Sports Illustrated* interview.

Since he was dressed all in bright yellow (the Pirates' hideous late 70s retro unis), Simon was just trying to put some mustard on the hot dog in the race, and missed.

He knew the person in the Sausage outfit was a young woman, and, caveman-style, he was trying to get a date.

Since Simon is 6-0 and about 250 pounds, and the game was running long, he wanted to spear a snack with his bat.

Finally, since Simons' career Strikeout/Walk ratio is 2:1, he'll clearly swing at anything.

Whatever the reason, Simon has passed the Padres' Jay Witasick (who hurt himself taking out the garbage) for the Oddball Story of 2003.

Now, that's not to say there haven't been plenty of other strange happenings in baseball in the past, both on and off the field of play. For instance, also in the mascot category, there was the time in 1978 when the San Diego Chicken almost caused a riot in Veterans Stadium by virtually molesting the Phillies' pin-up ball girl, Mary Sue Styles, on the field before a game.

Also in the assault category, the most famous event took place on May 15, 1912, when Ty Cobb went unto the stands in Hilltop Park in New York and attacked Claude Lueker, a crippled Tammany Hall flunky with a vile tongue. What's not commonly known about this event is that the two protagonists to the one-sided fight knew each other, and there was already bad blood between them from earlier contretemps down South. That's right sports fans. Ron Cobb (according to a family story, they're related, but Ron doesn't know how, although his dad was a spitting image of the Georgia Peach… however, Ron has published two books on Tyrus, and is on the Advisory Board of the Cobb Museum in Royston, Ga.) reports that, thanks to a choice bit of information uncovered by baseball researcher Bill Burgess, "Lueker and Cobb had a long running feud from down south, and Cobb selected Lueker to pounce on because he recognized him when he jumped into the stands." Cobb (Ron again, by way of Burgess) even provides a quote from an article by *Cincinnati Times-Star* Sports Editor Bill Phelon in the Feb. 27, 1913 *Sporting News…*

"Tyrus Cobb may have a rocky session or two when he visits New York this summer. The man he walloped that fateful day on the bleachers has not forgotten or forgiven–I know, because I know him and have talked with him. By the way, but little attention, at the time, was paid to the fact that his famous fracas was only part of an old Southern feud, entirely disconnected with base ball. Long ago Cobb and Claude Lueker, who received the wallops, were Georgia boys, and never harmonized, having many fights and contracting a strong personal enmity."[47]

Actually, no direct quote of what Lueker said has survived, so we'll speculate that maybe he was singing (to the tune of "Dixie")…

"Oh, I wish I was in the land of cotton.
I smell you, and you smell rotten.
Get away, get away, get away…
you stink!"

Maybe… hey, this is a family publication!

Off the field, one of the great all-time stories came from Cardinals' pitcher Flint Rhem who, on Sept. 15, 1930, in the midst of a hot pennant race with the Dodgers, failed to show up for his start against the Bums. The admittedly alcoholic Rhem finally re-appeared two days later, somewhat the worse for wear, claiming he had been kidnapped by persons unknown, and forced to drink large quantities of bootleg liquor. Right, Flint.

Finally, June 30, 1959 is a day that will go down in history for unintentional low comedy on the diamond. The Cardinals are playing the Cubs at Wrigley. Bob Anderson is on the mound, pitching to Stan Musial in the top of the fourth. A 3-1 pitch gets by catcher Sammy Taylor, who, instead of pursuing the ball (while Musial is heading to first, and subsequently second) stops to argue with umpire Vic Delmore, claiming the ball hit Musial's bat. Meanwhile, despite the fact that no one has called "time," the Cubs' batboy gives the ball to famed PA announcer Pat Pieper (who sat right next to the field) just before Cubs' third baseman Alvin Dark arrives on the scene to retrieve same in an attempt to prevent Musial from getting three bases on a walk (was Stan the Man great… going for a triple on a walk). He guns the ball down to Ernie Banks in the neighborhood of second base. With "time" still not having been called or granted, the harried Delmore, still at home plate, does the unthinkable… he pulls out ANOTHER ball, and plops it in Anderson's glove, at just about the same time Dark makes his throw from way behind the plate. Anderson, seeing The Man on the base paths, guns the new ball toward second base, only to have it go into center field. Stanley Frank, seeing this ball sail by him, lights out for third, only to run into future fellow Hall of Famer, Banks, who is holding the original ball. After a 10-minute argument featuring extended legal briefs from all parties involved (can you imagine what would have happened if this was 10 years later, and Leo Durocher was the Cubs' manager), Musial is called out. Well, Banks DID tag him with the original ball. Cards' manager Solly Hemus (a notorious crybaby, anyway) protests the game, which turns out to be meaningless when the Cards win 4-1. And you wonder why one of the Cards' broadcasters of that game, Joe Garagiola, wrote a book called, *Baseball is a Funny Game*...

CHAPTER 32

July 21, 2003

Item: July 18, 1961 – Cincinnati Reds relief pitchers Jim Brosnan and Bill Henry both get shelled in a 12-8 loss to the Milwaukee Braves.

What major league team has, so far in 2003, gotten the most grief from the media, fans, and other assorted observers of the National Pastime? Not the Tigers or the Brewers or the Padres or the Mets or the Pirates, who have received justifiable flak for ineptitude. Not even the Expos, who would seem to be doomed to fail at the expense of their 29 fellow owners in MLB.

No, as the 2003 season passed the halfway point, the team with the biggest "Kick Me" sign on its back was the Old Towne Team in Boston. And why? Because the Red Sox had the nerve to go against what is perceived as tradition, and not anoint a single closer in their bullpen. Indeed, no single development so far this year has received as much negative attention as the Sox' ill-fated "Closer by Committee." While no one, including the Sox' hierarchy, would state that the Boston bullpen set-up has been a success – why do you think they fleeced the D'Backs for Byung-Hyun Kim – it is equally flawed logic to assume that what the Red Sox tried was stupid or doomed to failure. Since when has it been a baseball law that a team MUST have a single closer? Well, since you asked, from about 1990 on or so.

However, let's not go back to 1990 to study the makeup of major league bullpens. Let's go back a lot further, to 1871, when Bob Ferguson, the first switch hitter, was playing in the National Association. Ferguson's action of batting both left and right-handed implies an understanding that there is such a thing as what is now called a platoon advantage… in other words, left-handed batters are generally better hitters against right-handed pitchers, and vice versa. So, it's long been recognized that lefty-righty match-ups make a difference. Hence, is it so radical a thought to have two closers, a lefthander to deal with the Jim Thomes of the world, and a right hander to get out Mike Sweeney? Maybe not a bullpen by committee, but, at least a bullpen structured to take better advantage of the platoon advantage.

That's where Messrs. Brosnan and Henry come in. Actually, the game of July 18, 1961 was an aberration in that pennant-winning season.[48] Both Brosnan (the right hander) and Henry (the lefty) were outstanding throughout the year as manager Fred Hutchinson (a former pitcher, it might be noted) used his two closers like Bobby Fischer used to use the pieces on a chessboard. Brosnan finished 10-4 in 53 games with 16 saves (and a 3.04 ERA) and Henry was 2-1 in 47 games with another 16 saves and a 2.20 ERA. Together, Brosnan and Henry helped lift the Reds to the pennant and marked the first extensive use of a lefty-righty closing duo. Call them, Platoon Closers.

For the sake of argument, let's define a team with Platoon Closers as one where one (or more) lefty and one (or more) righty have 10+ saves in a season, and appear in 40+ games, and where both pitchers are relieving in save situations at basically the same time. Sound like a radical concept in 2003? Well, that hasn't always been the case. Starting with, of all teams, the 1958 Boston Red Sox (and the immortal Leo Kiely and Murray Wall), 107 teams in the 45 seasons between 1958 and 2002 have had a matched set of firemen who fit the description of Platoon Closers.

It is especially instructive to see how the teams with Platoon Closers break down by decade…

1950s – 2
1960s – 17
1970s – 30
1980s – 41
1990s – 15
00/02 – 2

Starting with Brosnan and Henry on the 1960 to 1963 Reds (Al Worthington took over for Broz in 63), about two teams per year had Platoon Closers in the 60s, and three teams per year, on the average, had them in the 70s. The average jumps to four per year in the 80s, before the practice dies a sudden death with the advent of the one-inning specialty closer (largely beginning with Dennis Eckersley, Bobby Thigpen and Lee Smith) in the period 1989 to 1991. Actually, the heyday of the Platoon Closer was in the seven seasons from 1982 to 1988, when 34 sets of Platoon Closers flourished (the single season record is six in 83 and 84.)

How successful were Platoon Closers? Well, 25 of the 107 Platoon Closer teams finished first. Do you think that any other pitching strategies work out to a 20+ percent success rate?

Who used Platoon Closers the most? The pioneering Reds have had 11 teams with Platoon Closers, the Mets nine, the Giants eight and the Red Sox, Orioles and Pirates six each. The Mets' group including a consecutive run of six years (a record) from 1983 to 1988, which happens to include the period of the team's greatest sustained success... they finished 6, 2, 2, 1, 2, 1 in that span with Jesse Orosco, Doug Sisk, Roger McDowell and Randy Myers doing the honors at various times (although this run was mostly Orosco and McDowell).

And while the Platoon Closer concept seems to have all but died out (it's only been done six times since 1995), have you forgotten last year's Chicago White Sox? Righties Keith Foulke (who admittedly lost his job fairly early in the year) and Antonio Osuna both had 11 saves and lefty Damaso Marte had 10. And, as recently as the 2000 season, the Braves used lefties John Rocker (24 saves) and Mike Remlinger (12 saves) and righty Kerry Ligtenberg (also 12 saves) to get to the National League Division Series where they lost to the Cards. (Some trends are harder to overcome, even by Platoon Closers.)

So, let's lighten up on the Sox, and remember that there might actually be something to having both a left-handed closer and a right-handed closer.

Item: August 28, 1993 – The New York Mets sign draftee Kirk Presley to a $960,000 contract.

It's time once again for the REAL All-Star teams. And, the first one in the building is…

The All The-King-Has-Left-The-Building Team
1B – Mark Grace(land)
2B – Jeff King
3B – Jim Presley
SS – Elvis Pena
OF – Jim King
OF – Tim "Rock" Raines
OF – King Kelly
C – Earl Grace(land)
RHP – Runelvys Hernandez
LHP – Vida Blue (Suede Shoes)
MGR – King Kelly
Minors – Kirk Presley (Elvis' cousin never made the majors)

The All Music Team
1B – Jack Norworth (wrote the words to "Take Me Out to the Ballgame")
2B – Jim Steinman (and his collaborator…)
SS – Meatloaf ("Paradise by the Dashboard Light," Scooter)
3B – George Thorogood (the rest of his semi-pro team, the Delaware Destroyers, don't make the squad)
LF – Terry Cashman ("Talkin' Baseball," etc.)
CF – John Fogerty (who else?)
RF – Paul Simon (and Joe DiMaggio)
C – George M. Cohan (friend of John McGraw, he also wrote some baseball-themed music, along with his regular "stuff")
RHP – Bruce Springsteen ("Glory Days")
LHP – Albert Von Tilzer (wrote the music to "Take Me Out to the Ballgame")

RP – David Frishberg ("Van Lingle Mungo")
MGR – Bruce Springsteen (Why? Because he's The Boss!)

The All Hogan's Heroes Team
1B – Howie Schultz
2B – Sam Crane (there were two of them, this one became a New York sportswriter in the early 20th Century)
SS – Sam Crane (this one got locked up on a murder charge after his playing days)
3B – Joe Schultz, Sr. (father of future Seattle Pilots manager)
OF – Willie Hogan
OF – Shanty Hogan (normally a catcher, but also played some OF)
OF – Joe Carter
C – Gary Carter
RHP – Joel Newkirk
LHP – Joe Klink (nicknamed "Colonel" by his teammates)
RP – Bob "Ach" Duliba (one of the great baseball nicknames of all time)
MGR – Joe Schultz, Jr. (and just as funny as John Banner)

The All Accessories Team
1B – Socks Seybold (also played the outfield, with a first baseman's glove)
2B – Cap Peterson
3B – Cap Anson (started out at 3rd)
SS – Socks Seibold (note the different spelling from the first baseman)
OF – Ty Cobb
OF – Shoeless Joe Jackson
OF – Harry "The Hat" Walker (pretty good outfield… Carlos Beltran didn't make the cut)
C – Cap Clark
RHP – Cletus Elwood "Boots" Poffenberger
LHP – Rigo Beltran
MGR – Cap Anson

CHAPTER 33

July 28, 2003

Item: July 18, 1961 – Commissioner Ford Frick rules that, if either Mickey Mantle or Roger Maris breaks Babe Ruth's single season home run record, they will have to do so within 154 games, or the accomplishment will go in the record books with a "special mark."

During his entire career of service to major league baseball, Ford Frick made one definitive stand, one definitive ruling. And, in the tradition of most of baseball's commissioners, he blew it.

In *Veeck as in Wreck*, Hall of Famer Bill Veeck noted that, when Frick was president of the National League, he would pass the buck up the ladder on difficult decisions by saying an issue wasn't under his jurisdiction. Then, said Veeck, when Frick was commissioner, he would invariably say that such controversies were "a league matter."[49] Well, this was one controversy that wasn't a league matter, because Frick had been the Babe's ghostwriter in years past, and he was determined to keep the Bambino's most revered record intact. (Note that he didn't say "asterisk," the sportswriters came up with that term.)

Usually, Frick wasn't much when it came his asterisk, unlike some of his predecessors and successors. Most of them were all too willing to make decisions… usually the wrong ones. Let's recall some of the worst…

Judge Landis… he banned Buck Weaver when it was clear that the White Sox third baseman had taken no bribe money and had played his best in the 1919 World Series. Landis also swept the Cobb/Speaker bribery scandal under the rug to stick it to Ban Johnson. However, his greatest sin was keeping major league baseball lily white, something Veeck intimated,[50] as did Peter Golenbock in *Bums*.[51]

Senator Chandler… actually, he was a pretty good commish… opening the doors to Jackie Robinson, Larry Doby, et al. Even his year-long ban of Leo Durocher, though done on rather tenuous grounds, could hardly be said to have hurt baseball. Ultimately, Chandler was let out to pasture on his Kentucky horse farm because of his health. In other words… the owners were sick of him.

Spike Eckert… the unknown soldier. Did he do anything?

Bowie Kuhn… too many faux pas to mention all of them. Certainly trying to squash *Ball Four* wasn't a highlight of the free speech movement. Banning the Mick and Willie for working for casinos was pretty silly, too.

Olympic Peter… should have stuck with the Olympics, where the athletes were more professional.

A Bartlett Pair (Giamatti and Vincent)… believing The Dowd Report regarding the activities of Mr. Rose.

That brings us to… Bud.com, who says he's outta here when his current contract runs out. Probably the best move he's made. So, there's going to be a job opening soon. Here is my platform if I were running for Bud.com's job: Now if I were commissioner…

Let me make one thing perfectly clear (as a former chief executive once said… I think he was related to nonpareil baseball fan, David Eisenhower), I am not a crook (a good job requirement for this position) and baseball isn't broken, and it doesn't need fixing. Tweaking maybe. Fixing no. And, I'll base my campaign for the job on this platform… a platform designed to improve play and competition, because, as Veeck used to say, a good team is the best promotion.[52]

Other than getting rid of Bud.com and getting a true baseball fan in the Commissioner's Chair, the Number One Priority for the new Commissioner is the immediate (if not sooner) abolishment of the designated hitter (it's so repulsive, I won't even capitalize it, and won't even allow the term to creep into the rest of this essay).

All right, in reality the American League teams (and the player's union) might pitch a fit if it's outlawed mid-season. So, we'll wait until the off-season. But then, it's bye-bye. Nothing more than a hype for the offense from the very beginning, this abomination to the basic concept that baseball is a two-way game (hitting and fielding) is no longer necessary in the Rocketball Era. Maybe, in 1968 or 1973, it might have livened things up a bit for the AL, which was undergoing a hitting drought and was getting beat regularly in the All-Star Game, but now it just detracts from the strategy of the game and allows latter-day Smead Jolleys to extend their careers. What's more, with this insidious plague having filtered down to the high school level, we have raised a generation of one-way players. About the only aspect of this rule that has any value is that it helps maintain the vanishing separation between the leagues. Which leads to ruling number two…

The next thing to go is interleague play. As mentioned previously, it's the worst thing to happen to baseball since the advent of the you-know-what. Why? Let's quickly recall the ways…

It detracts from the special nature of the World Series. As far back as 1884, the two teams that met for the ultimate in post season play were a unique match up, something that would never happen otherwise in an official contest. Not anymore. It's helping kill the All Star Game, and the basic division/rivalry between the leagues. It's undermining the purity of the stats. And, possibly worst of all, it's just simply unfair. It's bad for competition. An unbalanced schedule is one thing, but, to be fair, teams in each division should play the same teams, for goodness sakes.

Third move… let's really level the competitive playing field. There once was a rule passed that no team could trade with the team that had won the previous year's World Series (honest). Guess what team that rule was enacted against? That's right, the Hated Yankees, during one of their previous periods of domination. It's time for real competition. It's time for a rule that says the playoff teams can't sign free agents during the year after their appearance in the playoffs. And, while we're at it, let's institute a serious salary cap and a serious salary floor.

Fourth… it's contraction time, guys. There are too many mediocre teams, players and markets. Exit the Expos. Toodle-oo Tampa Bay.

Farewell Florida. Pittsburgh, you're the pitts. Turn PNC into a playground. Bye-bye Brewers. Detroit? You're dead. Turn Comerica into Coney Island. That gets us back to 24 teams, 12 in each league.

Fifth… while were at it – cutting back on the number of teams – let's ditch the Wild Card and go back to a couple of two team divisions in each league. New York, Boston, Toronto, Baltimore, Chicago and Cleveland in the AL East. Minnesota, Kansas City, Seattle, Oakland, Anaheim and Texas in the AL West. Atlanta, Philadelphia, New York, Chicago, Cincinnati and St. Louis in the NL East. San Francisco, L.A., Colorado, Arizona, Houston and San Diego in the NL West. And, let's relegate (ala soccer) each division's last place team to AAA for the next year, and bring up the four best minor league teams – that gives you pennant races at both ends of each division… and, some real competition.

OK, so pure relegation won't work, since the triple A teams are all part of major league organizations. Still, you'd think something could be worked out wherein cities like Buffalo, Charlotte, Indianapolis, Louisville, Memphis, New Orleans or Salt Lake (all of which are, or have been, "major league" cities in other sports… for that matter, Buffalo, Indy and Louisville were once major league baseball cities) could at least have a one-year shot at the majors, and a chance to prove they're better for baseball than Tampa, Pittsburgh or Montreal. Maybe we can have the Padre, D-Ray, Tiger and Brewer organizations mix their erstwhile major league and minor league personnel and send the best combined teams to Portland (the Padres AAA site), Durham (D'Rays), Indianapolis (Brewers) and Toledo (Tigers) for the 2004 season. Hey, they can't be any worse than the current Tigers, or draw worse than the Expos or Marlins.

Sixth, and this one really can't be enforced since it's an amateur baseball issue… ban metal bats. Send them back to softball where they belong. The pitcher's life you save may be your son's. In fact, along with disposing of the abominable rule previously mentioned, this might actually bring some good young talent to the mound… so that every major league team won't be short of pitching any more. How can this be done? Well, major league baseball probably has $50 million or so in excess TV money lying around… spread that among the colleges and high schools to pay for the extra cost of broken wooden bats.

That's what I would do, if I were commissioner.

CHAPTER 34

August 5, 2003

Item: August 13, 1993 – The Phillies beat the Mets, and the immortal Anthony Young, 9-5, on a ninth inning grand slam by the equally immortal Kim Batiste.

Do you have a favorite team? No, not a team like the Kansas City Royals or the Chicago White Sox or the Chicago Cubs. A single team, like the 1985 Kansas City Royals, the 1983 Chicago White Sox or the… well, there must be some Cubbies teams that still-living fans remember fondly. (I don't think there are too many 1908 Cubs fans left around.) A team and a season, that brings to mind all that's good for you about baseball. A single team that you can say, "Weren't they something?" about.

My favorite team is the 1993 Phillies, and even while getting old and decrepit, I can still remember some great moments from that highly unusual season. Like watching a game (with my dad, of course) on a motel TV screen in Stone Harbor, New Jersey, and marveling as Kim Batiste, not exactly the first coming of Alex Rodriguez, added another chapter to their growing legend with a grand slam to pin another loss on the luckless (1-14 at that point, on his way to 29 straight losses) Anthony Young. (Of course, another memorable highlight was Curt Schilling coming back after that 15-14 abomination and just throttling the Blue Jays in game five of the World Series.) And, you better believe it, that team was already a legend in its own time by mid-August. Although they became the third worst-to-first team of the 20th Century, the '93 Phillies were actually better known by August as the most scrofulous bunch to play the national game since the Gas House Gang.

So, it only figures that, when Bob Gordon and Tom Burgoyne wrote an "insider's" book on the 1993 Phillies, *More than Beards, Bellies and Biceps*, a review was necessary. How insider is *More than B3*? About as inside as you can get, because Burgoyne is inside the Phillie Phanatic costume for every game at the Vet, or, at least he has been since 1994. (Prior to that he was the pinch-hit Phanatic for the equally immortal Dave Raymond.)

Now, what you see is what you get with an insider's book like this. You know right up front that this is likely to be advocacy journalism, and not a hard and fast sabrmetric view of the subject in question. Having said that, there's no getting away from the fact that this book has a lot of insider information, and is fun to read… on several levels. It's a clubhouse-level look at a pennant winner that almost no one expected to win (ala Jim Brosnan's *Pennant Race*). It provides behind the scenes insight to some highly unusual characters (ala Jim Bouton's *Ball Four*). And, you get an interesting layout with multiple sidebars about the ace mascot of the major league, the Phanatic (the sidebars are, at least in style, a method well-used by both Bill James and Rob Neyer)… but more on that later. In addition, this kind of insider book provides insights you can't get anywhere else. Like Brosnan admitting he couldn't stand Solly Hemus in *The Long Season*. And Bouton's highly controversial statements about the Mick. You want to know what Dave Hollins really thought about Greg Maddux and the Braves? Or what Jim Fregosi felt his one mistake in the World Series was? It's in here.

The reader also gets a bonus beyond the baseball. *More than B3* also provides some of the best insight this native Philadelphian has even seen into the nature of Philly natives and Philly baseball fans. And, interestingly, the most insightful comments come from a non-Philadelphian. See if you can guess whom this is talking…

"You don't shortchange fans in Philly, and you don't fool them... In Philly, and a few other eastern cities, like Boston, New York, and Baltimore, fans really are different. They have the pride and tradition that newer franchises haven't built yet... In Philly, kids are raised to be

Phillies fans by their fathers, whose fathers raised them to be Phillies fans [Editor's Note: Or Athletics fans, if you go back far enough], as did their fathers before them. You are born a Phillie fan – born into a Phillie-fan family, but, more importantly, you stay a Phillie fan for life, even if you move away from the Delaware Valley. You don't feel that kind of intensity in many other cities."[53]

Very true, Mr. Schilling.

Using that quote, and many others, very effectively, Gordon builds both the story of the 1993 Phillies and their fans – a group as interesting as the team itself. While Philadelphia may be a very patrician city in some areas (e.g.; Society Hill, the Main Line, Chestnut Hill, etc.) this city of neighborhoods is also a very blue-collar town (e.g.; Roxborough, the Greater Northeast) that indeed wears its heart on its sleeve. And, when Philadelphia falls for a team (the Flyers of the mid 70s are another example of this), it falls hard. Clearly, that's what happened in 1993, when the Phillies set the all-time Philadelphia attendance record (3.1 million) with as scruffy a bunch of players as you'll ever see. Any team with John Kruk, Lenny Dykstra, Mitch Williams and Pete Incaviglia isn't likely to go on the cover of GQ. And, any team with Kruk, Dykstra, Williams, Dave Hollins, Danny Jackson ("the craziest guy on the team," according to Incaviglia) and Larry Andersen can probably be said to have more than its share of characters. And that's all part of the story in *More than B3*. However, the main thrust of the book, and the reason for the title, is what Gordon and Burgoyne would say is the team's character (as opposed to characters). Maybe that angle is overdone a little bit, and it certainly isn't a sabrmetric treatment of the team, but there's no doubt that the authors, as well as the members of the team (most of whom were interviewed for the book) truly believe it. And there also can be no doubt that one of the things that did set the 1993 Phillies apart from the average pennant winner was the "Macho Row" attitude embodied by Kruk, Dykstra, Hollins and the team leader, catcher Darren Daulton. And now, that's part of the historical record, just like the Gas House Gang's attitude.

On the other hand, Gordon also includes an intelligent look at the argument most used to explain the success of the 1993 Phillies – they all had career years together. Gordon refers to this theory as, "a credible argument; however, the data supporting the argument is far from compelling."[54] Gordon quite rightly assigns only Batiste (who was basically a utility infielder), rookie shortstop Kevin Stocker and lefty set-up man David West to the "Career Year" category, and points out, also quite rightly, that Dykstra (who did have the best single season totals of his career), Incaviglia, Hollins (his '92 and '93 season were almost identical), Tommy Greene, Daulton and platoon outfielder Wes Chamberlin had years that were, at the very least, congruent with at least one previous season. And, as Gordon also notes, Kruk, platoon outfielder Jim Eisenreich (whose teammates called him "Dahmer," apparently because he looks like the famous cannibal), platoon second baseman Mariano Duncan, starter Terry Mulholland and the Wild Thing all had years that were very much in keeping with the rest of their careers.

Had I been writing this book, I would have added one further codicil. A lot of players did have good years, but this team won mainly because this was the one year that the entire cast of characters was healthy. Dykstra had previously missed a lot of time because of his habit of running into walls (on the field) and trees (in his car). Daulton's knees were a disaster area. Hollins began to have serious hand problems right after '93. Kruk had cancer in 1994. And right there, that's the heart of an offense that always seemed to have two men on base. (On base averages for '93 – Daulton .392, Kruk .430, Hollins .372, Dykstra .420.) As for the pitching staff, although Mulholland and Schilling have both lasted a long time, they have also spent time on the DL, along with Jackson and the ill-fated Greene.

More than B3 is not a strictly linear history of the '93 Phillies. It skips around, somewhat like Hollins' throws from third base. Profiles of team members, Philadelphia tidbits, and *The Phanatic Phile* (Burgoyne's priceless sidebars on life as the Phanatic, and not the story of infielder Bobby Pfeil, who played for the Phillies in 1971) pop up at unexpected intervals, sort of like the way the Phanatic will pop up at various times during a game at the Vet.

(An aside… Dave Raymond, the original Phanatic whose story also appears in quotes throughout the book… almost got popped on his green snout during a game in one of his early years. He tried to "kiss" my Aunt Katherine Shiffert in a box seat down the third base line. Big mistake. Aunt Katherine, who was a pretty fair fastball pitcher for the Mermaid AA back in WWI when my grandfather – her brother – was their catcher, was not someone that fuzzy green mascots were wise to mess with, and she was tempted to lay him out. Fortunately, granddad and I restrained her.)

As a result, reviewing *More than B3* lends itself to picking and choosing some favorite highlights… jumping around, just like the Phanatic.

Ever get tired of the Atlanta Braves' "we're better than you" act? The Phillies were already tired of the Braves' arrogance by 1993. Especially Dave Hollins (known as "Head" or "Headley," because, well, he was a head case.)

"I hated the Braves. Never liked them from day one. They acted like they were better than us, like we didn't belong on the same field with them," says Hollins. It should also be noted that Atlanta's notorious headhunter, Greg Maddux, plunked Hollins four times in 1992, and Headley did not approve of that. After that season, Kruk took Hollins to a charity affair in Vegas (where Maddux lives in the off-season). They ran into Maddux at a casino, and Hollins told him, "if you ever hit me or one of my teammates again, I'm gonna kill you." Maddux, according to Kruk, never hit Hollins again.[55]

That little contretemps (and others) makes *More than B3 's* blow-by-blow account of the 1993 NLCS especially memorable – recalling Schilling's two outstanding outings, Dykstra's pivotal 10th inning home run in game five, and Jackson doing his "Jason" routine, tearing off his shirt and pumping up like The Incredible Hulk on the pitcher's mound, after the final game.

The 1993 World Series has been rehashed at great length, largely due to Joe Carter's dramatic, walk-off home run to win it all. However, Gordon brings a bit of extraordinary insight into the Series' key circumstance… the state of the Phillies' bullpen. In an interview for the book, 1993 Phillies manager Jim Fregosi defends the indefensible… his continued use of Mitch Williams to try and close out games in the post-season. Even before the regular season ended, it became clear, to both the Philly media and perceptive fans, that the Wild Thing, who lived and died with his fastball, has lost a few feet off his heater. A wild fastball pitcher with an 85 mph fastball is not going to close many games successfully. Nevertheless, Fregosi kept calling on the exhausted (and very possibly hurting) Williams, who would only pitch 38 innings in the majors after 1993, walking 52 and giving up 45 hits. Why?

"Just because a guy struggled recently, you still use the guys who got you there… Probably the only change I'd have made going into the '93 Series is that I'd have gone with an extra pitcher. I would have included Mike Williams on the Series roster," says Fregosi in the interview.[56] When "the guy who got you there" has clearly thrown his arm out, that's as sure a recipe for disaster as you can come up with.

And, it's insights like that that make *More than B3* an entertaining read and, in its own way, a seasonal diary as compelling as *Pennant Race* or *Ball Four*. If you're a Phillies' fan, or just someone who wants an inside look at the 1993 National League East race and the subsequent playoffs, it's a must-read.

Of course, there are people out there who have other favorite teams, like the Fly Creek Philosopher, Bill Deane. A world-class baseball historian and former Senior Research Associate at the National Baseball Library at the Baseball Hall of Fame (Fly Creek is three miles from Cooperstown), Deane recently wrote this column for the Oneonta Daily Star.

—By Bill Deane

John asked me and several other baseball gurus and nuts – he didn't say which category I fall into – to submit essays about our favorite team. And not just a team, but a specific year's edition of it. My choice is the 1976 Cincinnati Reds, the only team since divisional play began to go through the post-season without a loss.

Now, I've never seen much point in rooting for a particular team. As Jerry Seinfeld says, "The players change, the manager changes, the ballpark changes. About the only thing that stays the same is the uniform. When you get down to it, what you're really rooting for is the shirt."

Since age ten, my favorite team was simply the team with my favorite player. On one of the first games I ever watched on TV, there was this guy slashing line drives all over the field, sliding head-first into bases, making diving catches in the outfield, and I thought he must be about the best, most exciting player in the game. I wasn't far off. So Pete Rose became my favorite player, and the Reds my favorite team.

After several years of mediocrity, the Reds seemed to be arriving in 1970. They won 70 of their first 100 games and were dubbed "The Big Red Machine." But the engine sputtered as their best pitchers went down with injuries, and they were stopped cold by the Orioles in the World Series. After an off-year, Cincinnati lost another World Series in 1972, this time to the A's. Then, the unkindest cut of all, in the 1973 NLCS, when the Reds, winners of 99 games, lost to the Mets, winners of just 82. And more frustration in 1974, when the Reds won 98, second-highest total in the majors, but finished behind the team with the first-highest total, the Dodgers.

The Big Red Machine finally put it together in 1975. Manager Sparky Anderson made a key move in May, shifting Rose from left field to third base to replace the light-hitting John Vukovich, and opening a regular spot for slugging reserve outfielder George Foster. They joined Hall of Fame catcher Johnny Bench, Hall of Fame first baseman Tony Perez, Hall of Fame second baseman Joe Morgan, Gold Glove shortstop Dave Concepcion, Gold Glove center fielder Cesar Geronimo, and All-Star right fielder Ken Griffey, Sr. in the Reds' potent lineup. The Reds won 108 games, 20 more than the second-place Dodgers, swept the Pirates in the NLCS, and then edged the Red Sox in a memorable World Series.

They were just warming up. Though the '76 Reds won "only" 102 games, they are commonly and properly ranked among the best teams of all time. Due to injuries and rest, their starting eight played together in only 46 of 162 games, but the team still won the NL West by ten games, and the octet was ready to go for the post-season. Griffey, Rose, Morgan, Geronimo, and Foster all topped .300; Rose led the league in runs, hits, and doubles, Foster in RBI; Morgan won the MVP, pitcher Pat Zachry was Rookie of the Year, reliever Rawly Eastwick was Fireman of the Year, and Bench, Morgan, Concepcion, and Geronimo were Gold Glove winners. The Reds led the National League in runs, hits, doubles, triples, home runs, RBI, stolen bases, walks, and batting, on-base, and slugging averages. Their underrated pitching staff led in wins and saves, and their defense led in fielding percentage. What else is there?

The Reds swept the Phillies in the NLCS, 6-3, 6-2, and 7-6, then squared off against the Yankees in the World Series. The Yanks were a team on the rise led by the best manager of all time, but were not in the same class as the Machine. Living in New York, I was surrounded by fans who believed otherwise. Though I was working my way through college and tight with a buck, I bet more than half-a-week's salary on the outcome of the Fall Classic. The Reds didn't disappoint me, demolishing the Bronx Bombers, 5-1, 4-3, 6-2, and 7-2.

My best-liked player, historical greatness, and money in my pockets – what more could I ask of a favorite team?

Another pretty fair wordsmith and historian is Jim Baker of ESPN.com. A former research assistant to the estimable Red Sox executive known as Bill James, Baker is the current Poet Laureate of Baseball, and his favorite team is, interestingly enough (since he's a Mets fan), the 1975 Red Sox, who lost to Deane's Reds in the World Series.

—By Jim Baker

My favorite team is probably the 1975 Red Sox because they seemed to have the situation covered everywhere on the diamond. They had a Hall of Fame catcher – when he was healthy – in the person of Carlton Fisk. At first base was Yaz and I was still convinced that it was only a matter of time before he would find himself in 1967 mode again. I was too young to know that seasons like that only happen once every 50 careers or so.

The outfield had so much promise it made one shake. The rookie Fred Lynn played the game like he'd been a professional for an entire decade. Some scoffed at the notion that Ichiro Suzuki deserved to be Rookie of the Year because he had playing at an advanced level for so long. That is just how Lynn looked at the time as well – although he, unlike Ichiro – hadn't been stashed in the Japanese leagues but in college and the minors. Jim Rice got injured but before that a lot of people were saying he was the more talented of the two rookies. They were wrong, of course, but I believed them at the time. Dwight Evans in right had that rocket arm and seemed a lot older than 23 to me.

There were talented players like Cecil Cooper and Bernie Carbo spending a lot of time on the bench – a sure indication that this was a juggernaut of a team.

Of course, in the cold light of analysis years later, some of the shine rubs off. I had this problem then (that many general managers still have) that I thought that if a guy once had a good season or was once good, I assumed that was he would be forever.

For instance, I didn't notice that Rico Petrocelli had lost it completely and I never understood just what a bad season Doug Griffin was having. But I was young and still believed everything I read in the sports pages or was told by the announcers on Game of the Week. But none of that matters. They almost made it. They came within three innings shy of winning it all and that's saying something.

One of the charms of *More than B3* is its characterizations of Philadelphia baseball fans. Here's another classic on Philadelphia baseball fans, this time from a quintessential fan, my father, who also happens to be John Shiffert. Holding a B.A. and M.A. in English from the University of Pennsylvania, and the former sports editor of the U of P's *Daily Pennsylvanian*, he's the first sportswriter in the family.

—By John A. Shiffert, Sr.

When Mr. 19 to 21…Baseball Then and Now *asked me what my favorite team was, I immediately answered, "The 1947 University of*

Pennsylvania Football Team!"

"No, Dad," he said, "this is all about baseball." That's OK, baseball is my favorite sport by a wide margin. My choice of those Penn gridders wasn't based on the sport they played, rather other factors.

I am a somewhat elderly Philadelphian and a baseball fan. That translates into...an ardent devotee of the A's...and not those green and gold aberrations!

My team died on that day of perfidy, November 5, 1954. As a gesture of revenge, I cut the American League out of my will. Today, I am interested only in the National "Real Baseball" League, and pay little attention to the post-1954 AL, with its abominable DH!

Well, back to the favorite team. As noted above, in 1950 I was still an A's man, positing that the skills of Eddie Joost made him a better lead-off man than Richie Ashburn, So, while I was certainly pleased with the Whiz Kids' success... my favorite team? No.

My father was probably responsible for my bias, with his stories of the 1910 and 1911 White Elephants, and particularly the '29, '30 and '31 Mackmen. (Forget the '27 Yankees. That '29-'31 team was the best ever.) While I was around in those years, I was pretty young, and never had the pleasure of seeing them.

So, ergo: My favorite team: the 1993 Phillies! Ooops, son John already opted for them.

Well, reluctantly, I have to say those 1964 Phillies!!!

"Why?" With every right, you may say, "Why?"

No, I'm not a masochist; it's just because they were the archetypical Philadelphia sports team!

We were at the Jersey shore that summer. Didn't see too many games at Shibe Park (oops, Connie Mack Stadium), but never missed one on TV or radio. What an idyllic summer it was. Weather was great; I commuted every day (except for long weekends) to Ocean City in my new TR – 4; the kids, at seven and twelve, were lots of fun; and the Phillies, after a year of promise in '63, were winning, winning, winning.

Every day a new hero. Memories of that year: Young Johnny Briggs rattling the right field tin to pull out one game (over my portable radio between innings of a wiffle ball game), the same portable sending me running home from the beach to catch the last two innings of Jim Bunning's perfect game; on the Black Horse Pike, from the top down TR-4 radio when, after kicking a ground ball at third, the out-of-position Richie Allen redeemed himself with a mammoth home run. And, we were lucky enough to be at the ball park to see that titanic shot over the Coke sign, atop the left field bleachers...the longest batted ball I have ever seen...and, I'd stack it up against anyone else, from the Babe to McGwire to Bonds.

And, there was Mr. Steady. Little Johnny Callison, all 5'10, 170 pounds of him. He carried his winning magic to the All-Star Game. When he came up in the ninth with two outs and two on, I just knew he'd take Dick Radatz deep. And don't forget the other "John Wesley" on the team: Wes Covington. He seemed to save his hits for big occasions.

And, lest we forget the pitching, it did the job. While Bunning and Short will forever be linked with those last 12 games, the staff was an effective one. Dennis Bennett and Art Mahaffey won twelve games each, and Jack Baldschun and Eddie Roebuck were outstanding relievers. And in five key instances, eighteen-year-old Rick Wise supplied a "W." And, mirabile dictu, my all time favorite A's pitcher, Bobby Shantz, showed up from the Cubbies. (I remember my son's birthday, August 6, because he was born the day after Shantzy won his 20th in 1952.)

Ah, well, the summer must end. Back home in September (the 21st, to be exact), the Phils have a six and a half-game lead; there are twelve games left. They are playing the Reds on my trusty portable radio, while son John and I are stacking firewood in the garage, getting ready for winter. Mahaffey is pitching a gem. Then in the sixth inning, with Chico Ruiz on third and two outs, and, for heaven's sake, Frank Robinson at bat, Ruiz tries to steal home. Mahaffey, startled, pitches high. Ruiz is safe. The Phils lose 1 to 0.

I shall not, indeed I need not, dwell on the rest of the season. Every baseball fan knows what happened. One vignette I remember. It is Saturday, September 26. We are back at the shore. Disgusted that the

Phils have lost five in a row, the kids and their friends are out playing basketball. I'm alone at home watching the Phils and the Braves. Bobby Shantz is pitching late in the game, tied at four. Two men on, Rico Carty at bat. Shantzy pitches. Carty swings. The camera follows the ball to the outfield, it is windy; hotdog wrappers are blowing around; the ball carries to the wall as Callison chases. I leave to join the basketball game.

Oh, well. To a sports-loving kid growing up in Philadelphia, then a more philosophical 36, there was a kind of fitness to that scene. At least it was better than checking the paper every morning to see how many games we were behind seventh place.

Despite what the media thinks, I believe that Philadelphia sports fans are the best in the world. They care, but they have been annealed by decades of disappointment. The ups are few, the downs frequent. "What can go wrong now?" is too often quickly followed by the answer. Star-crossed? I don't know. But I do know that those wonderful, tragic 1964 Phillies are archetypical of the Philadelphia sports experience.

CHAPTER 35

August 11, 2003

Item: August 29, 1990 – The St. Louis Cardinals trade Willie McGee to the Oakland Athletics for Felix Jose and two minor leaguers.

Willie McGee was a sneak. He snuck around the outfield, robbing other people of extra base hits. He snuck around the bases, stealing them (352 in all), for goodness sakes. He snuck into Oakland after nine years as a Cardinal regular, and took part in a World Series wearing those awful green and gold uniforms. And, he snuck around baseball for 18 years, pretending he was an outstanding offensive player. And thereby lies a tale. (Though not the one where he was busted flat in Baton Rouge… that was *Bobby* McGee.)

There was much comment in late August of 1990 when the A's picked up the National League's leader in batting average in a waiver deal just before the September 1 playoff eligibility deadline. Felix Jose was a good outfield prospect (who turned out to be a dud, by the way), but this was WILLIE MCGEE that the two-time defending American League champs had picked up for the stretch run. Adding to the fun was the fact that, by Aug, 29, 1990, McGee had enough plate appearances to qualify for the National League batting championship, and here he was, playing for the best team in the American League. Indeed, McGee's NL average was frozen at .335, and, even though he hit just .274 in the American League, that didn't count. The closest anyone came to .335 in the NL was Eddie Murray at .330… so, the Oakland A's Willie McGee was the 1990 National League batting champ. (And that was without interleague play confusing the issue even more.)

Quite frankly, though, it all was a tempest in a teapot. Willie McGee was not an outstanding offensive force, for either the Cardinals or the A's in 1990. In fact, he was generally below average, despite his gaudy BA. How do we know that? Well, there are many ways to measure offensive production, most of them very complicated. Even some of the simple ones, like OPS are hard to figure out if you don't have both averages in front of you, and also hard to judge as far as the good, the bad and the ugly (The Ordonez Line!) So, here's a really simple means to measure offensive production that anyone can use, and without a calculator. Call it "The Rule of 10."

Thirteen years after Willie McGee was traded, it is hopefully fairly well recognized that the two most important components of offensive production are the ability to get on base, and the ability to get extra bases – extra base hits, that is. Since the beginning of the Rocketball Era (1993), the number of extra base hits, and the number of walks, in relation to total at bats (not plate appearances, but at bats) in the major leagues has remained fairly constant. And, that constant is pretty close to 10%. That is, for the National and American Leagues as a whole, each year there will be roughly one walk or one extra base hit for every 10 official at bats. So, if player X has somewhere close to a tenth as many extra base hits as at bats, and right around a tenth as many walks as at bats, you can figure he's a pretty average offensive player. For example, here are the past three years' figures for both leagues as a whole…

National League

Year	At Bats	Extra Base Hits (% of AB)	Walks(% of AB)
2002	87,794	7565 (8.6)	8921 (10.2)
2001	88,100	8053 (9.1)	8567 (9.7)
2000	88,743	8170 (9.2)	9735 (11)

American League

Year	At Bats	Extra Base Hits (% of AB)	Walks (% of AB)
2002	77,788	7115 (9.1)	7325 (9.4)
2001	78,134	7146 (9.1)	7239 (9.3)
2000	78,547	7377 (9.4)	8503 (10.8)

Over the 10 seasons in question, the NL average for extra base hits has been 8.6% (with a high of 9.2% and a low of 7.8%) of total at bats, and the AL average has been 9%, with a high of 9.4% and a low of 8.2%. In both cases, just a bit below the 10% figure for something on the order of three-quarters of a million ABs. As far as walks go, in the NL the average from 1993-2002 has been exactly 10% (high of 11%, low of 9.2%) and the AL average has been 10.3% (high – 10.9%, low – 9.3%)

Is The Rule of 10 a perfect metric? Of course not. Nothing is. And there are other factors that come into play, most notably pitchers batting in the NL (which means that the average everyday NL player's figures are a little higher than 8.6% and 10%) and the added value of a home run, as opposed to a double. However, The Rule of 10 is a simple one, and one that anyone can do at a glance. Just knock the last digit off a players' at bat total, and compare that to their doubles plus triples plus home runs, and you've got an idea how they fare against the league average. If the two numbers (10% of at bats – which is what you get by removing the last digit of the total – and total extra bases hits) are pretty close, you know they have somewhere near average power. Likewise, for walks, knock the last digit off total at bats and compare that to the number of base on balls. If their walks are less than 10% of their at bats, well, you know plate discipline is not one of their strong points.

Let's apply The Rule of 10 to Mr. McGee at the point in 1990 when he was traded from the Cards to the A's.

	AB	**Extra Base Hits**	**Walks**
Willie McGee/St. Louis	501	40	38

Hmmm… both figures below the 10% mark. Despite his league-leading batting average, McGee was, as far as The Rule of 10 is concerned, a below-average offensive player when he was traded. (Actually, he's a little better than he looks, because extra base hits were only 7.4% of total at bats in 1990.)

Of course, trades to bolster contenders neither began nor ended in 1990. Indeed, one had the impression by mid-afternoon on Thursday,

July 31, 2003 that every mediocre hitter in both the National and American Leagues had been traded in the past week or so. That's right. Of the 18 offensive players movin' out during the Great Trading Frenzy (Frank Lane, where are you now that we need you?), only two, Raul Mondesi and Carl Everett, passed the test of The Rule of 10 for both walks and extra base hits.

Name	AB	ExBaseHits	Walks
Aaron Boone	403	40	35
Aramis Ramirez	375	38	25
Raul Mondesi	361	42	38
Kenny Lofton	339	32	28
Jose Hernandez	326	21	30
Jose Guillen	315	45	17
Shannon Stewart	303	31	27
Robin Ventura	283	22	40
D'Angelo Jimenez	271	23	32
Carl Everett	270	34	31
Roberto Alomar	263	20	29
Alex Sanchez	243	13	10
Bobby Kielty	238	22	42
Jeromy Burnitz	234	36	21
Tony Womack	219	15	8
Shane Spencer	210	18	18
Doug Glanville	195	9	6
Rey Sanchez	174	4	8

As noted, only Mondesi and Everett were above the 10% mark in both extra base hits and walks when they were traded. Guillen and Burnitz are the two power hitters who top just the mark in extra bases, while Ventura and Kielty are also getting well above one walk for every 10 official at bats, though their power leaves something to be desired. As for the other 12 players on the traded list – well, they may or may not have been an upgrade for the players they replaced, but, according to The Rule of 10, they weren't any better than replacement players – in other words, they weren't any more than average offensively.

As to what this all means on the trading front… using this metric, it appears as if the White Sox made out pretty well with Everett and Alomar (who was a little above 10% in walks), and that the D'Backs, if they can keep Mondesi's head on straight, certainly got more offense that they gave up when they shipped Tony Womack off to Colorado. (Why would anyone want Tony Womack?) The Bums of LA also did OK, getting a power hitter in Burnitz and an on-base man in Ventura. Finally, in the most remarked upon "challenge trade" (a deal where the participants trade players that are essentially similar), the Stewart for Kielty deal, it looks as if Kielty's ability to get on base does swing the deal in favor of the Jays, and away from the Twins. Of course, there's always the other side of the coin… never trade for someone named Sanchez. At least, according to The Rule of 10.

CHAPTER 36

August 18, 2003

Item: August 16, 1944 – Eddie "The Walking Man" Yost makes his major league debut (at age 17) with the Washington Senators… he probably drew a walk.

Actually, it's pretty unlikely that the Walking Boy drew a walk in his first major league game. He only picked up one base on balls in 16 plate appearances as a 17-year-old. Nevertheless, Yost soon made up for that deficiency, ultimately becoming an heroic figure, the likes of whom are seldom seen in these parts anymore. An Alexander the Great. A Hercules (if you believe the Disney movie). A Hannibal. A William Wallace. A Richard the Lion Heart. A Jeanne D'Arc. An Abe Lincoln. A Fred Rogers (Yes, Mr. Rogers was a war hero. So was Captain Kangaroo.)

In 2109 games for the Senators, Tigers and Angels, Yost drew 1614 walks, which is nearly as many hits (1863) as he had over the same time. Thanks to eight seasons of between 123 and 151 walks, his modest .254 career batting average was transcended by his .394 career on base average. You see, Eddie Yost was an ID Monster. It is in ID that, unbeknownst to anyone, Max Bishop holds a significant major league record. No one, in the 127-year history of the major leagues, was as good at drawing a walk (relative to his other skills as a hitter) as Max Bishop. Why do you think they called him "Camera Eye?"

From 1924, when Connie Mack bought his contract for the Philadelphia Athletics from Jack Dunn of the then minor league Baltimore Orioles for the princely sum of $50,000, until his final season with the Boston Red Sox in 1935, Max Bishop was the greatest walker of all time. The best ballplayer ever at telling a ball from a strike. Better than Ted Williams. Better than Babe Ruth. Better than Rickey Henderson. Better than Barry Bonds (we'll discuss his case later). In 5776 plate appearances in 1338 games, Bishop drew 1153 walks and, although he never batted more than 497 times in a single season, he had seven seasons of 100+ walks (plus a 97, an 87 and an 82 – and this was before the era of the automatic intentional walk). In 1930, he became the only regular player to ever score more runs (117) than he had hits (111) in a season. But, even those numbers don't tell the whole story, because Maxie Bishop (also known as "Tilly") was the greatest ID Monster of all time. In the history of baseball, no one who came to the plate 5000 times or more ran up a higher career ID than Max Bishop. Here are the Top 25 Career ID leaders, as of the end of the 2002 season:

	OBA	BATTING	ID
1 Max Bishop	.423	.271	.152
2 Gene Tenace	.388	.241	.147
3 Eddie Stanky	.410	.268	.142
4 Eddie Yost	.394	.254	.140
5 Ted Williams	.482	.344	.138
6 Barry Bonds	.428	.295	.133
7 Babe Ruth	.474	.342	.132
8 Mark McGwire	.394	.263	.131
9 Mickey Tettleton	.369	.241	.128
10 Jim Thome	.414	.287	.127
11 Mickey Mantle	.421	.298	.123
11 Roy Thomas	.413	.290	.123
11 Rickey Henderson	.402	.279	.123
14 Eddie Joost	.361	.239	.122
15 Joe Morgan	.392	.271	.121
16 Earl Torgeson	.385	.265	.120
16 Harmon Killebrew	.376	.256	.120
18 Ralph Kiner	.398	.279	.119
19 Harlond Clift	.390	.272	.118
19 Frank Thomas	.432	.314	.118

21 Miller Huggins	.382	.265	.117
22 Elmer Valo	.398	.282	.116
22 Jim Wynn	.366	.250	.116
24 Lu Blue	.402	.287	.115
25 Mike Schmidt	.380	.267	.113
25 Elbie Fletcher	.384	.271	.113
25 Darrell Evans	.361	.248	.113

It's a list that lends itself to several observations, including three basic categories of ID Monsters… Power Hitters, Banjo Hitters and Hybrids.

First, many of the Top 25 in ID were either feared Power Hitters like Williams, Bonds, Ruth, McGwire, Thome, Mantle, Killebrew, Kiner, Thomas and Schmidt, or little Banjo Hitters who drove pitchers crazy trying to get them to swing – Bishop, Stanky, Yost (although he did hit 139 home runs), Thomas and Huggins personify this type of player. Indeed, one of the values of ID is that it can illuminate the offensive contributions of players who may not, at first glance, seem very impressive. This is also true of some of the Hybrid players on the list, guys with a low average, high walk, medium power profile who also traditionally haven't gotten the credit they were due – Tenace, Tettleton, Joost, Torgeson, Valo and Evans come to mind.

Second, although no one has ever identified Connie Mack as being an especially radical or forward thinker, his distant "descendent" as the brains behind the Athletics, Mr. On Base Average, Billy Beane, should admire the Tall Tactician's eye in picking out a player who would take a walk – on this list, Bishop, Valo and Joost were all Athletics, while, among those who just missed the cut, Jimmie Foxx, Wally Schang, Topsy Hartsel and Ferris Fain (his career ID was .134, but, he was less than 100 PA short of the 5000 requirement) also wore the Gothic "A" on their chests. Furthermore, Athletics Eddie Collins, Mickey Cochrane, Indian Bob Johnson, Nap Lajoie, Al Simmons and Pinky Higgins are all also among the Top 200 in career on base average.

Third, among the current or recent players on the Top 25 list (Bonds, McGwire, Thome, Henderson, Thomas), only Rickey Henderson isn't a pure power hitter, and, with 297 career home runs, he's hardly a wimp. A look at 2003's leaders in ID gives the same picture:

1 Barry Bonds .178
2 Jason Giambi .159
3 Adam Dunn .141
4 Larry Walker .139
5 Jorge Posada .133
6 Brian Giles .130
7 Frank Thomas .125
8 Carlos Delgado .124
9 Erubiel Durazo .122
10 Bobby Kielty .118

Once again, only Posada and Kielty aren't big power hitters, and neither one of them is exactly a 98-pound weakling. (In fact, Posada's career slugging percentage is .494.)

Now, Bonds' figure is especially interesting, because it is misleading. National League managers seem to suffer from a collective bad case of Bondsaphobia, which can be described as either the fear of investing in government-backed securities (maybe not a bad idea!), or the fear of pitching to Barry (bad idea!) Take out his 48 intentional walks, and his ID when someone has the guts to actually pitch to him is .127, slightly below his career mark. (Delgado is the only other player on this list with more than 10 IBB, and he only has 16.) Does it make sense to intentionally walk Bonds so often? No, it doesn't. In *The New Bill James Historical Baseball Abstract* the author presents the results of a computer study wherein the greatest player of all time (Babe Ruth), having his greatest season (1921), is put into a lineup of stiffs – Willie Wilson (in a bad year), Al Weis, Gerald Perry, Ruth, Gino Cimoli, Don Wert, Jamie Quirk, Angel Salazar, and Sandy Koufax (as a hitter.) The computer ran that lineup out there for 2000 simulated seasons. When the Babe was allowed to bat normally, he hit an average of .385 with 61 home runs, and the team scored an average of 601 runs over 1000 seasons. Then, for the next 1000 seasons, the Babe got a walk EVERY time he came up. For those 1000 seasons, the team scored an average of 667 runs per season. I mean, Gino Cimoli, hitting fifth, hit .267 with an average of nine home runs, and drove in an average of 151 runs a year![57]

Although the hypothesis that James was testing was to see if there ever was a hitter who should be walked every time he comes up, one by-product of this study seems clear… if you pitch to Barry Bonds every time he comes up, even if he's having an off-the-wall year (such as he's had the last three years at the highly suspicious ages of 37, 38 and 39), he'll get on base a little over half the time. If you walk him intentionally every time, he'll have an on base percentage of 1.000… and that's a lot worse for the opposition.

CHAPTER 37

August 25, 2003

Item: August 25, 1908 – The first place New York Giants beat the second place Pittsburgh Pirates, 5-3, behind Otis "Doc" Crandall, moving two and-a-half games ahead of the Pirates in the National League. "I do not fear Pittsburgh in the least. It is [third place] Chicago we must beat to win the flag," says Giants Manager John McGraw to the *New York American's* William F. Kirk.[58]

The 1908 National League pennant race has gone down in history as perhaps the greatest of its kind. Three fascinating teams – the Chicago Cubs, the New York Giants and the Pittsburgh Pirates, battled down to the wire for a flag that wasn't decided until (technically) after the season was over... when Frank Chance's bear cubs and Muggsy McGraw's J'ints met in the Polo Grounds on Oct. 8 to replay the already-famous "Merkle Game" of Sept. 23.

It wasn't enough that the Oct. 8 game that finally decided the season was a replay of possibly the single most famous (and certainly the most controversial) game in baseball history. It wasn't enough that the Cubs' 4-2 win was pronounced by famed sportswriter Fred Lieb as the number one game of the past 100 years.[59] It wasn't enough that the third team in the race – the Pirates – had been carried bodily to the last day of the season by possibly the greatest single season ANY player (Honus Wagner) ever had. It wasn't enough that the Giants' team doctor, Joseph Creamer, tried to bribe umpires Bill Klem and Jimmy Johnstone with $5000 before the game, saying, "You know who is behind me and you needn't be afraid of anything."[60] (Recall that McGraw was an absolute dictator – he ran everything on the Giants.) It wasn't even enough that the Cubs and the Giants – who happened to represent the two largest cities in the land – hated each other's guts. This was a race for the ages, featuring the best team of all time (at least, as far as total wins over five seasons are concerned), the 1906-1910 Cubs, against the best-known team of the times, the Giants, against the team with the second-best player of all time, the Pirates' Big Honus.

Interestingly, what is less-often remembered is that the American League had an equally good three-team pennant race that year… it's just that the AL didn't have McGraw making all the noise. In fact, up until very late in the year, the AL actually had a four-team race, as Rube Waddell, having his last great season, led the otherwise mediocre St. Louis Browns into contention. With Connie Mack taking a season to re-tool his first Athletics dynasty, the door was opened for the defending champion AL Detroit Tigers, the 1906 World Champion Chicago White Sox and the Nap Lajoie-led Cleveland Indians to stage another fray of epic proportions, with the Tigers beating the Sox 7-0 in Chicago on the last day of the season, and winning the pennant by a half-game over the frustrated Hitless Wonders, who had played (and lost) one more game than the Ty Cobb-led Tigers. There was no provision at the time that a team had to play all its games, or had to make up postponed games. (In 1907, the A's LOST one LESS game than the Tigers, and still finished second because the Bengals WON four MORE games.) The Giants/Cubs Oct. 8 game was a replay (not a playoff) of the Sept. 23 game that was eventually ruled a 1-1 tie because rookie Merkle failed to touch second while the winning run was scoring in the ninth – and was played ONLY because the two teams were tied at 98-55 when the season ended.

While it is certainly possible to bewail the ill-fate that dogged the Giants (and McGraw did bewail it… at great length and volume), Pirates, White Sox and Indians in 1908… there's more to the story than meets the eye. In point of fact, one of the winners and two of the losers of these classic battles have been tortured by the slings and arrows of outrageous fortune almost since Oct. 14, 1908, when the Cubs polished off the Tigers in the World Series, four games to one.

Since that fateful day, the Cubs have not won a World Series. The

Indians have won just twice (in 1920 and 1948) and the White Sox, although they did win in 1917, then proceeded to throw the 1919 Series, and, except for the 1959 affair, they haven't been back. It would seem that all three of these teams are, for want of a better word, "cursed."

Of course, any discussion of baseball curses has to include the granddaddy of all curses, the Boston Red Sox' "Curse of the Bambino." Actually, the Cubs' ills pre-date the Red Sox' (who last won the Series in 1918) woes by 10 years, but the Bambino's Curse is much better known than the Cubbies "Curse of the Billy Goat," which didn't come about until 1945. The Indians' "Curse of Rocky Colavito" just dates from 1960, and, though also less-known, seems just as potent. Then, there are the on-going woes of the Philadelphia Phillies. They've won just one World Series (in 1980) since they stupidly traded Grover Cleveland Alexander (to the Cubs, of all teams) on Dec. 11, 1917 for $55,000 and a case of Patio Diet Cola because they were afraid Alex wouldn't come back from World War I in one piece. So, it would seem that you can rank the Curse of Alex right up there with all the rest.

To briefly re-cap the plagues upon the houses of the Red Sox and the Indians... Boston owner Harry Frazee, who was more interested in producing Broadway plays then he was in the success of the Red Sox, sold Babe Ruth to the New York Yankees on Dec. 26, 1919 (the deal wasn't announced until Jan. 3, 1920) for $125,000 and a $300,00 mortgage on Fenway Park. After which the Babe blasted Frazee in the Boston newspapers. (Contrary to popular belief, Frazee did not use the money to underwrite "No, No, Nanette," his big Broadway hit that actually came a few years later.) Trader Frank Lane, who loved to swap players like Bill Veeck loved fireworks, was the culprit in Cleveland in the Colavito deal. Claiming he was trading hamburger for steak, he dealt the 1959 AL home run champion (and popular idol in Cleveland) to Detroit for 1959 AL batting champion Harvey Kuenn. After which the Cleveland newspapers blasted Lane.

The two Windy City curses are even more interesting. The Cubs' Billy Goat Curse dates from the 1945 World Series, when local tavern owner Billy Sianis tried to bring his pet goat (according to Brian

Walton, the goat's name was "Murphy") into Wrigley Field for a game. (Whassamatta… don't the bars in your town have their own goats?) Sianis, the owner of the Billy Goat Tavern (that's the name of the place… and it's quite famous in ChiTown) was rebuffed in this effort (the Cubs apparently had enough goats on the roster already) and supposedly put a curse on the Cubbies as a result. The Southsiders' curse, as suggested by Rob Neyer in his ESPN.com column, would be the Curse of Shoeless Joe, in memory of the 1919 Black Sox tanking the World Series. (Although, in reality, the Reds had a better record during the 1919 regular season.)

So here you have five major league franchises that have won a total of two World Series since 1920. That's two wins out of a collective 410 seasons. You almost have to think they're cursed, right? Well, maybe they are, but the "curses" are a little more grounded in fact than the interdiction of an annoyed goataphile.

First, the White Sox, Indians and Red Sox. Their problem, from 1921 to 1964, from the mid-1970s to 1981, and since 1996, has largely been the New York Yankees. For instance, the Indians and the White Sox were good teams in the 50s (each winning one pennant), but the Yankees were better. The Indians have also suffered from the same problem recently, as have the Red Sox, both in the past eight years and in the late 30s, early and late 40s, and early 50s.

During most of the other years, all three teams have suffered from bad management. The White Sox, devastated as no team has ever been before or since by the Black Sox purge, were awful up until the 50s as the Comiskey heirs pretended they were the Battling Bickersons. The Red Sox similarly suffered under first Frazee's sell-offs and then poor judgment in the 50s and 60s (notably the lack of having any black players until 1959), while the Indians, a good team until the Colavito trade, shortly thereafter went downhill, due largely to poor personnel management.

The Phillies have simply been the most consistently under-capitalized team in baseball history. (Although the St. Louis Browns and the Athletics have also shared that particular "curse.") Starting with the 1917 sale of Alexander, the team just didn't have the resources to compete, largely under owners William Baker (who bought the team in 1913 and subsequently initiated The Curse of Alex before dying in 1930) and Gerald Nugent (1932-1943). Finally, following William Cox' one-year reign during the 1943 season, the Carpenter family, the scions of the DuPont fortune, bought the team, and the Phillies (who had been pretty good from the mid 1880s until 1917) were eventually able to get back in business. Not coincidentally, the team's periods of greatest sustained success, 1949-1953, 1963-1966, and 1975-1981, were during the years the Carpenters owned the team. Since 1982, the group ownership led by Bill Giles has once again returned to the relatively impoverished days of Baker and Nugent.

The Cubs are a little harder to explain, although, in recent years – since their last (losing) World Series appearance in 1945 – they have played a disproportionate (compared to the rest of the NL) number of games under the hot summer sun, and have typically had a lousy record in September. In other words, they wear out down the stretch. Actually, between 1908 and 1945, the Cubs were good – they just couldn't win the World Series despite pennants in 1910, 1918, 1929, 1932, 1935, 1938 and 1945. And all that happened before the goat man came on the scene. Maybe it's the Curse of John McGraw…

Jumping ahead to 2003, it seems as if maybe the National League Central race is cursed as well. Cursed with mediocrity. (Actually, the AL Central race suffers from the same malady.) In a contest reminiscent of the 1973 National League East bumble-thon, the Cardinals, Astros and Cubs are blundering into September in a race that seems as if none of them deserves to win. At the moment, the Cards and Astros are tied for first at a mild 68-62, while the Cubs lurk a half game back at 67-62. However, somebody has to win… the question is, who?

Right off, let's eliminate the Cubs. No, not because of the Curse of the Billy Goat, more because of the Curse of Wrigley Field and the Curse of Dumb Personnel Moves. As previously noted, the Cubs' futility since 1945 is largely their futility in the month of September. In 56 seasons since 1945, the Cubs have played sub-.500 ball 41 times (plus two seasons at .500) in September. Overall, their September "winning" percentage is 29 points lower than their overall mark.

That record takes in a lot of different teams, managers, lack of managers (the famed College of Coaches) and administrations. However, the current bunch seems determined to perpetuate the Cubs' futility. Normally known as a high-scoring team with deficient pitching (another legacy of Wrigley Field), the Cubs are playing role reversal this year, featuring an excellent group of pitchers, led by young guns Mark Prior and Kerry Wood. However, their offense has been offensive, Sammy Sosa notwithstanding. To try and alleviate this dearth of production, the Cubs have recently traded for such OPS-challenged individuals as… Aramis Ramirez (.781), Kenny Lofton (.764), Doug Glanville (.630), Randall Simon (.743), and, here's the capper, Tony Womack (.555). Wow! (Recall that an .800 is considered good and a .600 is The Ordonez Line.) And, just for good measure, they sent their one young power prospect, Hee Seop Choi (.786 OPS), to the minors, so they could activate Tom Goodwin (.711 OPS) from the DL.

On to the Cardinals. This team, on paper, should be running away with the division. However, only APBA and Strat-o-Matic baseball are played on paper, and the Cards, while they're playing in the field, are stumbling all over it. One would think that a team with Albert Pujols (having a Triple Crown caliber season), Jim Edmonds, Scott Rolen and J.D. Drew, while playing in a weak division, would be preparing for October at this point. Alas, the Cards' problem is the exact opposite of the Cubs – good hit, no pitch. Injuries (Matt Morris, Jason Isringhausen), Steve Blass Disease (Rick Ankiel) and just plain ineffectiveness (Garrett Stephenson, Brett Tomko, Jason Simontacchi, Jeff Fassero, et al) have left Woody Williams as their sole hope of the mound.

While the Cards' team OPS is an outstanding .813 (second in the NL to Atlanta), their opponents are almost as good – .792 (that's 12th in the NL), and the pitching staff carries a collective 4.70 ERA. And, somehow, the acquisitions of Sterling Hitchcock and Mike DeJean haven't exactly whipped up pennant fever on the banks of the Mighty Mississippi. I mean, the Yankees have been trying to dump Hitchcock and his 5.44 ERA forever. Meanwhile, getting pitchers from the Brewers is sort of the opposite of sending coal to Newcastle, maybe like buying refrigerators from the Eskimos.

As to the Astros… they would seem to have the best-balanced team in the race. A Jeff Bagwell/Lance Berkman/Jeff Kent/Richard Hidalgo/Craig Biggio-led offense. Good young starting pitching, fireballer Octavio Dotel setting up, and the Wagner Power Painter closing. And yet, it just ain't happening in Houston. Part of the blame certainly lies with the instability of the starting pitching, as ineffectiveness and injuries have led the 'Stros to use a staggering 12 starters so far this year. Only Wade Miller, Otis Redding and Pat Robertson have made more than 20 starts apiece (OK, Tim Redding and Jeriome Robertson – just wanted to see if you were still paying attention) with only Redding (3.66) having a decent ERA. Meanwhile, an amazing collection of "Who's He" hurlers have rotated through the starting rotation, with such noted names as Scott Linebrink, Jared Fernandez, Brian (Right Rear) Moehler, Jonathan Johnson, Kirk Saarloos (the only player in the majors named after a section of Europe that France and Germany have fought over for centuries) and Pete Munro having combined for 21 starts. And yet, playing half their games in a home run heaven, the Houston staff ERA, at 3.94, is three-quarters of a run better than the Cards'.

Offensively, the Astros present a very mixed bag… well. That is, Bagwell and friends (Berkman, Hidalgo, Kent) are hitting up a storm, and, in part time play, Morgan Ensberg has an OPS over .900. However, the evidence seems to suggest that Biggio, at age 37, is reaching the point of no return. His last three OPS' are .781, .837 and .734, and he's currently struggling at .735. Nevertheless, it's a stretch to lay much fault at Biggio's feet, whether they be at second base or in centerfield. Not when Brad Ausmus (.573), Geoff Blum (.685), Adam Everett (.660), 36-year-old Orlando (is he still around?) Merced (.671), Jose Vizcaino (.644) and Gregg Zaun (.599) all have between 120 and 354 at bats. With such an offensive dichotomy, it's a wonder the Astros can keep any rallies going past the bats of their Big Four. It would seem that their best bet for improving the offense is to offer Ausmus, Vizcaino and Zaun to the Cubs.

However, with their better-balanced roster and the Wagner/Dotel/

Brad Lidge bullpen as their ace in the hole (and unless the Cards' pitching staff takes a quick trip to Lourdes), it looks like the Astros have the edge at this point.

CHAPTER 38

September 2, 2003

Item: August 2, 1972 – Steve Yeager makes his major league debut behind the plate for the Los Angeles Dodgers.

While it might be a stretch to say that Steve Yeager was a direct descendent of famed Dodger catcher Bill Bergen, it's not a stretch to say that Yeager, like Bergen, holds an unenviable record. The Dodgers' semi-regular catcher from 1904 to 1911 (he was with the Reds in 1901, 02 and 03), Bergen holds the record as being simply the worst hitter to play on a regular basis in the major leagues. He hit .170 with a .194 on base average and a .201 slugging percentage – in 3028 career at bats. Yeager, while practically Babe Ruth compared to his predecessor (.228/.298/.355 were his numbers), does nonetheless hold another noxious distinction – he is the only worthless hitter to ever play for more than one pennant winner in the modern era.

Now, that's going to take a little explaining. First, the "modern" era. For purposes of this discussion, we'll consider that to be from the 1920 season (when trick deliveries were outlawed – though not forgotten – and the Babe really geared up his power act) on… a total of 83 seasons. As to "worthless," let's say that any regular (as in someone who was a team's primary player at one position) who has a batting average below .220 without any other redeeming offensive characteristics (i.e., either he could draw walks or hit with power) is a pretty worthless hitter. Given that set of parameters, there have been approximately 48 truly worthless regulars on teams that finished the regular season in first place in the past 83 seasons. (Interestingly, there were NONE between 1920 and 1939.) That breaks down to four in the 40s, four in the 50s, eight in the 60s, 11 in the 70s, 15 in the 80s, four in the 90s and two so far in the 21ˢᵗ Century. By this accounting, 46 different offensive dead weights have failed to keep their teams from the pennant. Only one, Steve Yeager, has ever done it more than once, and he had THREE such years – that is, there were three seasons (1978, 1980, 1983) when the Bums finished first despite their catcher contributing basically nothing to the offense.

You can make all the excuses you want – Dodger Stadium is a terrible hitters park, Yeager must have been a tremendous defensive catcher to stay in the line up, at least he hit a few home runs, his plate discipline was OK – but, there's no getting around the fact that Steve didn't scintillate at the plate in those three years…

	G	AB	R	H	2B	3B	HR	RBI	BB	SO	BA	OBA	SLG	OPS
1978	94	228	19	44	7	0	4	23	36	41	.193	.301	.276	.577
1980	96	227	20	48	8	0	2	20	20	54	.211	.274	.273	.547
1983	113	335	31	68	8	3	15	41	23	57	.203	.256	.379	.635

Ugly. Only in 1983 did he have an OPS above The Ordonez Line (.600), and his 1978 season was, in one sense, historically bad. How bad was it, you ask? Well, only 12 other players since 1920 (actually, since 1945 in this case) have managed to hold down a regular spot on a pennant winner and still hit below .200. The Dirty Dozen (plus one)…

	BA	OBA	SLG	OPS
Skeeter Webb 1945 Tigers	.199	.254	.238	.492
Wes Westrum 1954 Giants	.187	.315	.305	.620
Don Zimmer 1959 Dodgers	.165	.274	.249	.523
Jerry Kindall 1965 Twins	.196	.274	.289	.563
Mike Ryan	.199	.282	.261	.543

1967 Red Sox
Ray Oyler   .135   .212   .186   .398
1968 Tigers
Denis Menke   .191   .368   .270   .638
1973 Reds
Ray Fosse   .196   .241   .324   .565
1974 Athletics
Steve Yeager   .193   .301   .276   .577
1978 Dodgers
Tim Laudner   .191   .252   .389   .641
1987 Twins
Alfredo Griffin   .199   .259   .253   .512
1988 Dodgers
Turner Ward   .192   .287   .311   .598
1993 Blue Jays
Mark McGwire   .187   .316   .492   .808
2001 Cardinals

Now, clearly, one of these seasons doesn't really belong on a "worthless" list. That's the Big Mac's final season, when knee injuries forced him to retire, despite the fact that he could still powder the ball. In fact, McGwire's 2001 season is as unique a campaign as you'll find. On quick review, only another Wes Westrum season (1951) is similar. (By the way, neither of these seasons was counted in The Worthless 48…)

	AB	R	H	2B	3B	HR	RBI	BB	SO	BA	OBA	SLG	OPS
McGwire/2001	299	48	56	4	0	29	64	56	118	.187	.316	.492	.808
Westrum/1951	361	59	79	12	0	20	70	104	93	.219	.400	.418	.818

McGwire had more home runs and strikeouts, and Westrum had more singles, doubles and walks, but, taken altogether, these two exceedingly fluky seasons are remarkably similar.

Then there's a truly historic season, Ray Oyler's incredible 1968 year (a .398 OPS!!! That's Bergenesque!) with the World Series-winning Tigers…

AB	R	H	2B	3B	HR	RBI	BB	SO	BA	OBA	SLG	OPS
215	13	29	6	1	1	12	20	59	.135	.212	.186	.398

When Oyler was in the lineup, Detroit, in effect, had two pitchers batting that year. Even given that this was the Year of the Pitcher, Oyler was so bad at the plate that manger Hold the Mayo Smith replaced him at short with an outfielder (Mickey Stanley) for the Series.

Overall, a pretty rare breed… a man who can have a worthless offensive season and still keep a regular job with a team that finishes first. Of course, some of the individuals who made The Worthless 48 were good players having bad years – Clete Boyer (64 Yankees), Dave Concepcion (72 Reds), Denis Menke and Cesar Geronimo (73 Reds – that gives you an idea of how good the rest of the hitters were on the Big Red Machine), Ray Fosse (74 Athletics), Don Money (81 Brewers), Dave Lopes (81 Dodgers) and George Bell (93 White Sox) come to mind. Other than the 1973 Reds, only two other teams, the 1968 Tigers (with Don Wert joining Oyler) and the 1974 Athletics (add Dick Green to Fosse) were able to win with two of The Worthless 48 in the lineup. Not surprisingly, they are almost all either middle infielders or catchers. And, discarding Big Mac's 2001 season, it's only happened twice since 1993… the Cards' Mike Matheny in 2001 (.218/.276/.304) and the Braves' Keith (How Have You Managed to Stay in the Majors for So Long?) Lockhart in 2002 (.216/.282/.331).

Now, the question is, will some unfortunate soul join this hardy band in 2003?

There would appear to be three pretty good (or pretty bad) candidates for joining The Worthless 48… and two of them are not only on the same team, they share the same position. And, they're not even middle infielders or catchers. It's fair to say that third base has been the Black Hole of Cal Ripken (or is it Cal Cutta?) for the Seattle Mariners during the 2003 season, what with Mark McLemore and Jeff Cirillo standing one-two on their depth chart…

	AB	BA	OBA	SLG	OPS
McLemore	277	.231	.312	.321	.633
Cirillo	257	.206	.282	.272	.554

Cirillo, who was thought to be a pretty decent player when he was in Colorado (more evidence of how playing baseball at altitude warps the game?) isn't even close to The Ordonez Line. He's a lock to get the "worthless" tag if he keeps playing. And McLemore just has to drop another 12 points on his batting average (while getting more playing time than Cirillo) to join The Worthless 48.

Then there's one of the reasons the Astros have struggled, despite playing in the best hitting park this side of Coors Field, and having some pretty fair offensive players (Bagwell, Berkman, etc.) to boot. Catcher Brad Ausmus, the man who gives new meaning to Mike Gonzalez' deathless line about "good field, no hit" is doing just that…

	AB	BA	OBA	SLG	OPS
Ausmus	371	.226	.298	.294	.592

Since he's "da man" behind da plate for da 'Stros, Ausmus just has to drop another seven points off his BA to join our Worthless 48. One other catcher, the White Sox' Miguel Olivo (.233/.283/.361), also has a shot at The Worthless 48, if he goes into a bit of a slump. Of course, none of these four worthies will actually qualify for The Worthless 48 if their respective teams don't finish first – by no means a sure thing in any of the four cases, partly because these guys are playing regularly.

Finally, three more players who will probably not make The Worthless 48 nevertheless deserve special mention. Until Jermaine Dye of the Oakland Athletics had his season put out of its misery by a shoulder injury (meaning he won't have played enough to be considered one of the team's regulars), he was on his way to an historically bad year with a very good team…

	AB	BA	OBA	SLG	OPS
Dye	150	.160	.235	.227	.462

Dishonorable mention should also go to Tony Womack, now with the Cubs, and Henry Blanco, Greg Maddux' most recent personal catcher with the Braves. For some reason that has never been adequately explained, Maddux just will not pitch to regular catcher Javy Lopez except at the point of a gun. This makes Blanco (.200/.255/ .269) the Braves' regular catcher every fifth game. The much-traveled Womack, on the other hand, won't get into enough games with the Cubbies to qualify as one of their regulars, but he certainly is a worthless offensive player (.228/.255/.311).

CHAPTER 39

September 8, 2003

Item: September 7, 1980 – The Phillies' Marty Bystrom makes his major league debut with one inning of relief against the Dodgers.

Is Dontrelle Willis the next Marty Bystrom? Or the next Dwight Gooden? Or the next Grover Cleveland Alexander? Clearly the Marlins (or wherever Willis ends up after the next Florida Fire Sale) hope it's the latter. However, generally-speaking, there are three possible career paths for young pitchers who have remarkable success (literally – success worth remarking upon) right out of the box. Their rookie years might be just a month, like Bystrom's, or a half season, like Von McDaniel's, or an entire year, like Harry Krause's, but, in any case, there are greatly divergent career paths to be followed by these pheeeenoms.

First, there's the Alexander Track – a great rookie season, followed by a Hall of Fame career. Among the practitioners of this fine art were; the aforementioned Alex (28-13, 133, 24), Christy Mathewson (20-17, 138, 20), Tom Seaver (16-13, 122, 22) and Whitey Ford (9-1, 153, 21). Their rookie stats are as follows; won-loss record, adjusted ERA, age.

Then there's the Gooden Track – a great rookie season, followed by a good career, but one that is ultimately disappointing, given the hurler's early promise. As a 19-year-old with the 1984 Mets, Gooden went 17-9 with a 137 Adjusted ERA and 276 strikeouts, the last figure breaking Alexander's rookie mark, it might be added. However, Gooden's 194-112 career record was clearly a disappointment to Mets fans who thought they'd uncovered the next Tom Seaver (or better) in

1984. Don Newcombe also fits this mold, with a 17-8, 130 rookie season in 1949 at the age of 23, as does Dizzy Dean (18-15, 119, 22). However, Newk's career ended in the bottle (149-90, 114), and Diz' reign of brilliance ended with Earl Averill's line drive off his toe in the 1937 All-Star Game (150-83, 130).

And then there are the flameouts. The great rookies who NEVER had another year even vaguely close to their first season. Marty Bystrom. Von McDaniel (57 Cards). Harry Krause (more on him in a minute). Joe Black (52 Dodgers). Bob Bowman (39 Cards). Butch Metzger (76 Padres). Rusty Meacham (92 Royals). Rich Nye (67 Cubs). And the most famous of all, Mark "The Bird" Fidrych. Of these nine sad stories, Bystrom, Krause and Fidrych are the most interesting, because, like Willis, they were all 21-year-old rookies. Here are their numbers…

	W-L	IP	H	W	K	ERA	*ERA
Bystrom	5-0	36	26	9	21	1.50	253
1980 Phillies							
Rest of Career	24-26	399	428	149	236	4.51	
Total	29-26	435	454	158	258	4.26	87
Krause	18-8	213	151	49	139	1.39	172
1909 A's							
Rest of Career	18-18	312	295	97	159	3.26	
Total	36-26	525	446	146	298	2.50	106
Fidrych	19-9	250	217	53	97	2.34	158
1976 Tigers							
Rest of Career	10-10	162	180	46	73	4.28	
Total	29-19	412	397	99	170	3.10	126

Except for Fidrych not having a strikeout pitch and a little better control, and Bystrom's poorer *ERA, their careers actually ended up pretty similar. Bystrom was the National League Pitcher of the Month for September 1980, and the Phillies would not have made it to the

World Series without him. Krause, who had pitched in four games for the Athletics in 1908, led the American League in ERA in 1909, thanks to an incredible stretch of 10 starts (his first 10 starts no less, in a period from May 8 to July 12 – it was tough getting work with Eddie Plank, Chief Bender, Jack Coombs, et al, already in the rotation) where he went 10-0 with six shutouts and an 0.38 ERA. The Bird similarly led the AL in ERA in 1976, and was named Rookie of the Year (as Krause would have been, if the award existed in 1909). So, wha' hoppen? In short, all three had shoulder troubles, starting the year after their rookie campaigns, partly due, no doubt, to Krause and Fidrych throwing a lot of innings at a young age (as did Gooden). Krause's arm was the only one to really come back, thanks to some rest and the Pacific Coast League. Unlike the others, he had the option of making a career in the minors, where he pitched for 16 years, winning 300 games.[61]

Now, Willis clearly doesn't have that option. But, would he need it if it was there? If you took his first 17 starts (11-2, 2.56 ERA), clearly the answer would be "no." However, the season didn't end on Aug. 6. Willis has kept pitching, with somewhat different results.

First 17 starts

W-L	IP	H	W	K	K/W Ratio	ERA
11-2	105	90	33	99	3/1	2.56

Even after shutting down the moribund (to put it politely) Expos yesterday, Willis' post-8/6 stats don't look very good…

Next 6 starts

W-L	IP	H	W	K	K/W Ratio	ERA
1-4	31.2	35	14	24	1.7/1	5.68

And five of those starts have come against offensive powerhouses like the Dodgers, Padres, Expos (aka, Vlad and the Seven Dwarfs) and Pirates (twice). Now, it could be that Willis has just hit the wall, but that seems unlikely, since he's only thrown around 175 innings so far this year… 36 with Double A Carolina and 137 with the Fish. More importantly, at the time of his first meltdown, on Aug. 11 (2 innings, 7 runs) against the inoffensive Dodgers, he had thrown just 141 innings.

Or, maybe, the opposition has caught on to his odd delivery. And yet, that seems unlikely as well. Pitchers with strange deliveries who have anything on the ball tend to have pretty good careers… submariners like Carl Mays, Eldon Auker, Ted Abernathy, Kent Tekulve and Dan Quisenberry, and (more relevantly) back-turners like Luis Tiant, Gene Garber, Fernando Valenzuela and Hideo Nomo come quickly to mind.

Now, this is not to suggest that Willis needs to take a trip back to the minors. At this point, the only thing you can say is that his coronation as The Next Great Pitcher may have been a bit premature. He could still turn into Marty Bystrom.

Item: April 26, 1900 – The New York Giants' George Davis, Kid Gleason and Mike Grady stop at a northern Manhattan apartment building a couple of blocks from the Polo Grounds on their way to their game with Boston.

Is Charles Barkley correct? Is it true that professional athletes are not role models? Actually, there is no one simple answer to that… except to say that some athletes probably should be, and some shouldn't. In the former category, Messrs. Davis, Gleason and Grady certainly were role models on Apr. 26, 1900. As so should be present day Cincinnati Red Sean Casey. And thereby lies a couple of tales.

First, as to what Hall of Famer Davis, Gleason and Grady were doing that day on their way to the Polo Grounds… they were climbing up ladders into a burning building, having been among the first people to arrive at a major fire that left 45 families homeless. Along with New York's Finest (who were apparently just as fine in 1900 as they would be 101 years later), the three Giants rescued several women and children before resuming their journey to the ballpark, where they played a 10 inning, 10-10 tie with the Beaneaters. Even in those days, the New York media chased fires and the like, so the *New York World* had a reporter there and, as a result, a story about the three Giants' heroism was published. "I didn't do much," said Davis.[62]

Jump ahead to late August, 2003 in Cincy. Sean Casey is, just like most of the rest of us, driving to work, when a car ahead of him rams a traffic barrel and flips. Casey stops, pulls the driver out of the car (yes, it was a woman… but, no women driver jokes, please), takes her to his car, gives her some Gatorade and calls 911. He stayed with her until the police arrived and, when she asked him his name, he answered, quite accurately, "Sean," and continued on to whatever the Reds ballpark is called these days.

Now, the only reason this story got out was because one of the cops recognized Casey (who didn't even tell his teammates why he was late), and told the woman, who subsequently e-mailed the Reds to thank Casey. Sean, you may not be a Hall of Famer on the field, but, you make a pretty good role model.

CHAPTER 40

September 15, 2003

Item: September 10, 1940 – Hughie "Losing Pitcher" Mulcahy loses his 20th game of the season, 11-3 to the Pirates.

Everyone seems to have an opinion on 20 game losers. And they mostly revolve around the musical question as to whether or not they are what they appear to be. Certainly, major league managers over the past 23 years have treated the subject as if a 20 game loser is indeed a "loser," and have generally avoided putting pitchers in the position of losing 20. However, Alan Trammel of the Tigers, either through True Grit or a lack of other options (how many do you have on a team with 110 losses?), refused to buckle under to this recent superstition when he sent Michael Warren Maroth to the mound on Sept. 5 to face the Toronto Blue Jays. The 6-19 Mike Maroth who, true to his record coming into the game, gave up eight runs in three innings on the way to an 8-6 Bengal Beating, and thus became the first 20 game loser since Brian Kingman with the 1980 Athletics.

While Maroth's 5.55 ERA (it's 6.30 away from the pitcher-friendly confines of Comerica Park) would certainly seem to indicate he deserves his fate, the long term question is, what will his fate be after the 2003 season drags to a close in Detroit? In other words, is Mike Maroth a loser just because he lost one more game than Omar Daal or Bobby Jones or Scott Erickson or Jose DeLeon (all of whom lost 19 in the years between 1980 and 2003)? Obviously, the quick answer to that is, of course not. What's one more loss, when you've already got 19?

And yet, a lot of somebodies out there must think so, since there's no question that the 20th loss has been avoided like the plague for more than two decades. However, that wasn't always the case. The Phillies' Losing Pitcher Mulcahy picked up that nickname only because he did it with such stunning regularity, losing 18, 20, 16 and 22 games in consecutive years (1937 to 1940) before he became the first player drafted prior to World War II. (He probably welcomed the army at that point. In fact, he probably secretly enlisted.) Indeed, in the 1939 season, the two Philadelphia teams between them employed Losing Pitcher Mulcahy, the onomatopoetic Boom-Boom Beck (who had lost 20 for the Daffiness Boys in 1933) AND Lynn "Line Drive" Nelson… all at the same time. So, losing pitchers have been with us for a long time.

If we just go back to the start of the Expansion Era (1961), we find that a total of 25 pitchers lost 20 or more games in a season 30 times in the 20 seasons between 1961 and 1980. (That's right, five poor souls – Roger Craig, Al Jackson, Dick Ellsworth, Wilbur Wood and Phil Niekro – did it twice apiece.) The Mets lead the parade, with seven 20 game losers, followed by the Cubs with four and the Padres and White Sox with three each. Of more significance, though, is how these 25 "losers" can be grouped. Essentially, there were five types of 20 game losers in the period 1961-1980…

Expansion Team Pitchers – Jack Fisher, Turk Farrell, Roger Craig, Al Jackson, Tracy Stallard, Clay Kirby, Steve Arlin

The most common type of 20-game loser, these guys didn't have much hope, pitching mostly for the horrible early Mets teams (Fisher, Craig, Jackson, Stallard) and the almost as bad early Padres (Kirby and Arlin). Trouble was, they were mostly expansion-quality pitchers, that is, guys who maybe wouldn't have been in the majors that year except for expansion. Good relievers Farrell and Craig – who were forced into starting roles – are the exceptions here.

Aces Having Bad Years, or Suffering from Poor Support – Steve Carlton, Jerry Koosman, Luis Tiant, Larry Jackson

Four notable examples of managers sticking with quality pitchers even in an off year. These four guys averaged 243 wins for their careers.

Pitchers With Heavy Work Loads that Piled Up a Lot of Decisions – Phil Niekro, Wilbur Wood, Stan Bahnsen, Mickey Lolich

That's how knuckleballers, Niekro and Wood, managed to lose 20 twice… they averaged 39 decisions for those four years, and both of them had a season where they were 20 game winners AND losers.

Youngsters – Steve Rogers, Randy Jones, Dick Ellsworth, Mel Stottlemyre (and Clay Kirby again)

Oftentimes, such as was the case this year with the Tigers' Jeremy Bonderman, you throw a young pitcher into the fire. Sometimes, you leave him there long enough to lose 20. These five averaged 23 years of age. Interestingly, the experience didn't totally destroy any of them. Except for Kirby, they all ended up winning at least 100 games.

Mediocre Pitchers Exposed – Orlando Pena, Brian Kingman, Bill Bonham, Clyde Wright, Pedro Ramos (and Tracy Stallard again)

Sometimes, you have to throw to the wolves a "proven" pitcher who is clearly in over his head, mainly because what he's proven is that he's not real good. These six pitchers averaged just 67 wins for their careers, and all had losing records to boot.

The one exception to all of these categories is Denny McLain's bizarre 1971 season with the Senators, when he went 10-22 three years after winning 31. No longer an ace at that point, he doesn't really fit well anywhere.

Now, does anyone think that Hall of Famers Carlton or Niekro were losers? How about Tiant, who should be in the Hall? Or fellow 200 game winners, Koosman and Lolich? Yeah, Larry Jackson lost 183, but he also won 194 (and would have gone over 200 if he hadn't retired rather than pitch for the 1969 Expos). Wouldn't you say Steve Rogers and Mel Stottlemyre had pretty good careers? In the past 40+ years, some pretty good pitchers have lost 20.

However, there's not much at this point to suggest than Maroth will become one of them. Since he is pretty clearly not an expansion team pitcher (although the Tigers are WORSE than almost all expansion teams), nor an ace, nor carrying an exceptionally heavy work load (30 starts, 177 innings, and less than 90 pitches per start), that leaves just two comparative groups for him... he's either a youngster (in other words, a pitcher in his first three seasons in the majors) or he's irredeemably mediocre.

Maroth turned 26 on Aug. 17, 2003. However, it's only his second season in the majors, following a 6-10, 4.48 ERA rookie season in 2002. That ERA, by the way, comes out to a 94 Adjusted ERA (ERA*), just 6 percent worse than the average AL pitcher in 2002. And, since 1961, eight pitchers in either their rookie, second or third seasons have lost 20. Here they are...

	Record	**ERA***	**Age**
Brian Kingman	8-20	98	25
Steve Rogers	15-22	86	24
Randy Jones	8-22	80	24
Steve Arlin	10-21	91	26
Clay Kirby	7-20	93	21
Dick Ellsworth	9-20	81	22
Mel Stottlemyre	12-20	88	24
Al Jackson	8-20	95	26

Kirby and Jackson were rookies, Ellsworth and Stottlemyre were third-year pitchers, and the rest were second-year pitchers. Note that all were between the age of 21 and 26 and all had an adjusted ERA below the league average. Of more interest are their respective career records...

	Record	**ERA***
Brian Kingman	23-45	92
Steve Rogers	158-152	116
Randy Jones	100-123	101
Steve Arlin	34-67	78
Clay Kirby	75-104	92
Dick Ellsworth	115-137	100
Mel Stottlemyre	164-139	112
Al Jackson	67-99	91

Kingman, Arlin, Kirby and Jackson actually had a better ERA* in their 20-loss seasons than they had for their careers.

Overall, the Unfortunate Eight had a total record of 736-866 (or 92-108 per pitcher), a .459 winning percentage. That's not very good, but the numbers are dragged down by the four worst pitchers (in terms of ERA*); Kingman, Arlin, Kirby and Jackson. In fact, what you have here are four pretty good pitchers (the other four), three mediocre pitchers and one really bad pitcher who quickly went on to dentistry (Arlin). So, maybe Maroth has a 50-50 chance of either lasting long enough in the majors to become a mediocre pitcher, or a pretty good pitcher.

It is also interesting to note that the two 20-game losers as rookies – Kirby and Jackson – were the worst of the Unfortunate Eight (again, excepting Dr. Arlin). The Tigers' Bonderman was going to be part of this discussion, however, Trammel pulled him from the Tigers' rotation on Sept. 3, possibly because he didn't want the 20-year-old pitcher to be irredeemably scarred by losing 20 in addition to the beatings he has already suffered. Very, very few pitchers go on to good careers after getting beat up as bad (6-18, 5.49 ERA) as a very young rookie as Bonderman has been. Oddly enough though, the two most prominent exceptions to that trend are still hanging in there – Tom Glavine (he was 7-17 with an 81 ERA* at age 22) and Greg Maddux (6-14, 76, 21).

Now, while Bonderman has been promoted as a hot prospect ever since he was drafted, you have to wonder if jumping him all the way to the majors from Single A was such a hot idea. There have been a lot more David Clydes and Clay Kirbys and Steve Arlins than there have been Tom Galvines or Greg Maddux (what's the plural of Maddux?) On the other hand, the experience didn't ruin Rogers, Jones, Ellsworth or Stottlemyre. Of course, they weren't quite so young, either. Either way, we may still get a chance to develop this story further this year, since Trammel has indicated he's going to put Bonderman back in the rotation. (What the heck, they've already lost 110 games, what does it matter at this point?)

Finally, let's look at one other measure in trying to determine the fates of Maroth and Bonderman. Noting that strikeout rate is a better indicator of a pitcher's future success than any other statistic, here are their numbers to date for 2003...

	IP	W	K	K/W	K/9IP
Bonderman	156	57	104	1.82	6.01
Maroth	177	46	78	1.7	3.97

Clearly, Bonderman is a better strikeout pitcher than Maroth, with both a better strikeouts/walks ratio and more strikeouts per nine innings. Maroth's figure in the latter category is awful... less than four Ks per nine innings... or 42nd out of the 44 American League pitchers who have thrown enough innings to qualify for the ERA crown (he's 42nd in that list, too, one place ahead of Bonderman.)

In any case, in the past 20 years, there haven't been any Mike Maroths. A tip of the *Baseball: 1862 to 2003* cap to the first 20-game loser in 23 years. Good luck, Mike (you might need it... and so might Jeremy.) If a prediction has to be made as to whether either or both of them will be a "loser," we'll consign Maroth to mediocrity and leave Bonderman in the "wait and see" category.

CHAPTER 41

September 23, 2003

Item: September 23, 1908 – Fred Merkle fails to touch second base.

Baseball is a game of feet. In this case, 19-year-old first baseman Fred Merkle's feet. The feet that didn't touch second base and thereby cost the New York Giants the flag in the most dramatic pennant race ever staged. Right?

Wrong. Yes, the Cubs won the 1908 National League crown after a three-way fight with the Giants and the Pirates (this was back when major league baseball was still being played in Pittsburgh), and went on to demolish the Tigers (see previous comment on Pittsburgh) in the World Series, but, no, Merkle's failure to run to second base on a "game-winning" single by Al Bridwell did not cost the Giants the pennant. Says who? Well, John McGraw, among others. The Giants' manager never blamed Merkle for the loss of the diadem (one of those great terms early 20th century sportswriters liked to use). And, for that matter, history itself also fails to support what came to be called the Merkle Boner as the primary cause of the Giants' fall.

After all, the Giants were in first place when the Merkle Game started on Sept. 23, 1908, and they were in first place when the game more-or-less ended as a 1-1 tie. And, they remained in first place the next day, after beating the Cubs 5-4. In fact, McGraw himself never blamed Merkle for losing the pennant, saying instead that the Giants had lost several games they should have won after the Merkle game. Since the season finally came down to a single game – the replay of the Sept. 23 tie – clearly, the Giants' five losses in the interim (they were

11-5 between the Merkle game and its Oct. 8 replay) were crucial. In fact, if you want to blame a single individual for the Giants' failure to win, let's nominate Harry Coveleski, who wasn't even a Giant, for goodness sakes.

First, though, let's try to decipher exactly what happened at the Polo Grounds on Wednesday, Sept. 23, 1908. As is the case with many historical events, the most definitive sources as to what happened are contemporary accounts – in this case, the newspaper stories of the next day. Thanks to G.H. Fleming's remarkable compilation of the day-by-day accounts of the 1908 National League season, *The Unforgettable Season*, we have all the important words that were written for publication on Sept. 24, 1908 in one place.

To set the scene… the score was tied 1-1 as the Giants came to bat in the bottom of the ninth against Jack "The Giant Killer" Pfiester. (An unusual nickname, though one that would become more common in a couple of weeks.) Cy Seymour grounded out to shortstop Joe Tinker. Art Devlin singled, but was forced at second by Moose McCormick. Two outs, man on first. Enter Merkle, who was playing only because regular first baseman Fred Tenney had a bad back (this was the only game all year that Tenney would miss). He drove a long single to right, and McCormick went to third. First and third, two outs. Al Bridwell was up. He hit a line drive up the middle, causing base umpire Bob Emslie to dive for cover. McCormick waltzed home with the winning run under the watchful eye of home plate umpire Hank O'Day.

Or was it the winning run? Merkle started for second but, when he saw the ball land in the outfield, he took a right turn toward to Giants' clubhouse in deep center field, wishing to beat the hordes of fans that typically swarmed the field at the end of a game. Cub second baseman Johnny Evers, seeing Merkle leave the bases, pitched a royal fit (he was good at that) and called for centerfielder Circus Solly Hofman to throw him the ball.[63]

(It should be noted at this juncture that the exact same situation had happened to the Cubs on Sept. 4, 1908 in a game against the other NL contender, the Pirates. With men on first and third, Pirate rookie Warren Gill didn't run to second base after a "game-winning" single.

At the time, the umpire disallowed Evers' protest, saying he didn't see Gill's misdeed. The umpire? Hank O'Day.)[64]

Hofman corralled the ball, and threw it in the direction of Evers. Now, things get murky. The general consensus is that Iron Man McGinnity, who was coaching third base, figured out what Evers had in mind, and, in some fashion (very possibly after a scuffle with several Cubs), got his hands on the ball before Evers did. This is known as interference, and, right there, Merkle is out, due to the Iron Man's actions. What does seem certain is that McGinnity, wishing to get rid of the evidence, threw the game ball in the direction of the left field stands. And yet, somehow, Evers ended up with a ball in his hands, standing on second base, and screaming for justice at the top of his lungs. (He was good at that, too.) In this case, justice meant a simple – well, maybe not that simple – force play on Merkle, that would become the third out and nullify McCormick's winning run.[65]

The next question is… how did Evers get the ball? And, was it the original ball that Bridwell hit? There are actually two scenarios here. One, is that Joe Tinker and third baseman Harry Steinfeldt (the non-rhyming member of the infield) went and retrieved the game ball the Iron Man tossed toward the stands.[66] Perhaps more plausible is Charles Dryden's account from the *Chicago Tribune*. (Not only was he NOT a New York reporter who was looking for a way to disavow the Cubs' claims, but he was also one of the era's best sportswriters.) Dryden wrote that Cub pitcher Floyd Kroh (he wasn't in the game, either) retrieved the ball from a bunch of spectators (or potato bugs, as Dryden referred to them… fans were generally called "bugs" in this era) and passed it to Steinfeldt who gave it to Tinker, who gave it to Evers. Still another theory has it that Kroh took a ball off the Cubs' bench and got it to Evers. Either way, this is also interference on Kroh's part, but, at this point, who's counting?

However, if you're scoring at home, that's Hofman to Kroh to Steinfeldt to Tinker to Evers… and there's no chance a play like that ever happened again. Remembering that it took place almost two years before Franklin P. Adams wrote the Tinker-to-Evers-to-Chance poem, Dryden's account of the play is practically eerie (in addition to being pretty funny...)

"Some say Merkle eventually touched second base, but not until he had been forced out by Hofman to McGinnity to six potato bugs to "Kid" Kroh to some more Cubs, and the shrieking, triumphant Mr. Evers... There have been some complicated plays in baseball, but we do not recall one like this in a career of years of monkeying with the national pastime."[67]

Monkeying, indeed. The monkey business wasn't over, as practically all the writers had a slightly different account of umpires' actions after Bridwell's hit. It does seems pretty clear that Emslie – as the base umpire, it was initially his call – didn't see the play, either because he was flat on the ground, or because the "bugs" got on him so quickly that he couldn't tell what happened. Furthermore, Hank O'Day, having had the exact same scenario presented to him just 19 days before by the same player (Evers), ran out toward second base to follow the action. And, it was O'Day, well after the action subsided, who made the fateful call (apparently from underneath the stands) that Merkle was out and McCormick's run didn't count – thus rendering the game, in effect, a 1-1 tie.[68]

It took until Oct. 6 for the National League office to uphold what, at this point, 95 years later, seems to be the correct decision (if for no other reason than because of McGinnity's interference) by the umpires – the Sept. 23 game was a tie.[69] This belated judgment came while the Giants were in the midst of sweeping three games from Boston, to come from behind and tie the Cubs for first. When that series concluded on Oct. 7, and with the regular season at a close, the Giants and Cubs were once again tied for first. Another part of the Oct. 6 ruling was that the tied Merkle Game was to be replayed at the Polo Grounds, ASAP, or, in this case, Oct. 8. Note that this replay game (won 4-2 by the Cubs, and finally giving them the pennant by one game) was not a playoff game, but a replay of the Sept. 23. Although there was no provision in the rules for unplayed games to be made up, the Sept. 23 game was a tie game, and it had to be replayed.

But, wait a minute. How did the Giants fall behind the Cubs? Why did they have to win three straight against Boston just to get back into a tie? They'd been 3 ½ games up on Sept. 21, and they were still a game and a half ahead after the Sept. 24 win… with no more games scheduled against the Cubs. What if they had won just one more game between Sept. 23 and Oct. 7? Then, they would have had a one game lead after sweeping the Braves, and the Cubs would have only tied the Giants for the lead (necessitating a three-game playoff) on Oct. 8.

Enter another Giant Killer, 22-year-old Phillies' rookie pitcher Harry "The Giant Killer" Coveleski. Prior to beginning eight straight games against them on Sept. 28, the Giants had gone 11-3 against the Phillies in 1908, However, the Giants went just 5-3 in those games – good, but not good enough. And, all three losses came at the hands of Coveleski… 7-0 in the second game of a Sept. 29 doubleheader, 6-3 in the second game of an Oct. 1 doubleheader, and, the "killer," 3-2 over Christy Mathewson on Oct. 3. The shutout knocked the Giants into second place and Matty's loss to Coveleski put the Giants a game back. Look at the standings before the New York/Philadelphia series, and after The Giant Killer's last win (which was also before the New Yorkers' series with Boston …

Sept. 28

NY	90	52	1/2
Chi	93	54	—
Pitt	92	55	1 [70]

Oct. 5

Chi	98	55	—
Pitt	98	56	1/2
NY	95	55	1 ½ [71]

During this key stretch, the Giants had gone 5-3, but the Cubs had gone 5-1, to open a game-and-a-half lead. Hence, if the Giants can just beat Coveleski once in those three games, they finish the Boston sweep

99-54, with a game lead. If they win two of Coveleski's games, then they're 100-53 and NL champs.

It seems as if a lot of close pennant races come down to a key series or two. Certainly, the American League Central had one from Sept. 17 to Sept. 19, when the White Sox went into Minnesota, trailing the first place Twins by a half game, and promptly got swept, 5-2, 4-2, 5-3, starting a full tilt flop that left them, as of yesterday (Sept. 22), five and-and-a-half games out and clinically dead. No wonder Jerry Manuel has been on heavy doses of Tums… the surest way to lose a close pennant race is in head-to-head competition with your top rival.

Although this year's AL Central race has hardly featured teams of the quality of the 1908 Cubs, Giants and Pirates, it certainly has been interesting and, until last week, close. The combination of the Cinderella Royals, last year's Cinderella Twins, and the underachieving Sox has made for excellent theater. Even after the inevitable collapse of the Royals' oft-injured pitching staff – 15 different pitchers have started games, no one has won in double figures, and only Darrell May has pitched enough innings with KC to qualify for the ERA title – just after Labor Day, it was a good two-team race until the Sox wandered into the world's largest Glad Bag…

Aug. 24

Chi	69	61	—
KC	67	61	1
Minn	66	63	2 ½

Aug. 31

Chi	72	64	—
KC	70	63	½
Minn	71	64	½

(Here's where the Royals fell back… going 2-6 for the week and giving up six runs twice, seven runs twice and eight runs once in five of the losses in that eight game stretch. Maybe Harry Coveleski would have helped… although he hurt his arm in 1909, and went back to the minors before re-surfacing as the Tigers' ace in 1914 and going 65-36 over the next three years. Of course, he also threw 940 innings in those three years, and permanently wrecked his arm in the process.)

Sept. 7

Chi	75	66	—
Minn	75	66	—
KC	72	69	3

Sept. 14

Chi	79	69	—
Minn	79	69	—
KC	75	72	3 ½

Sept. 22

Minn	87	69	—
KC	81	74	5 ½
Chi	81	74	5 ½

And that, folks, is all she wrote for the AL Central.

CHAPTER 42

September 29, 2003

Item: September 29, 1964 – The Philadelphia Phillies lose 4-2 at St. Louis, their ninth consecutive loss.

With the 2003 regular season at a close, let's remember the teams that didn't make it. Not this year's Tigers and Padres and Pirates… teams that never had a chance… but the teams that came oh so close, and fell short. While the 1964 Phillies may be the best-known example of a team losing a lead late in the season, they are hardly the only example. Teams have been falling short ever since the 1877 Louisville Grays literally tanked the last two weeks of the season… deliberately blowing their lead at the wire and finishing second to the Boston Red Caps. While it may be clear as to what happened in the 1877 National League race, there is a serious misconception about the 1964 National League race that needs to be cleared up. To wit… Phillies Manager Gene Mauch has gotten a bum rap over all these years – he did not panic and blow the season by over-working aces Jim Bunning and Chris Short down the stretch. Yes, he did start them on short rest, but he had very little choice in the matter. And, in reality, it's a miracle that Mauch got the 1964 team as close to the pennant as he did. In point of fact, that team played over its head all year.

The Phillies had finished fourth the year before, and that's just about where they deserved to be. The offense (third in runs scored) was carried by just two players having outstanding years, Rookie of the Year Dick Allen and could-have-been MVP Johnny Callison. Besides Allen (.939) and Callison (.808), only platoon outfielder Wes Covington (.803) among the regulars had an OPS over .800 (in fact, among the others, only leftfielder Tony Gonzalez was even above .700), and he only batted 339 times because he couldn't hit lefties. The rest of the infield was so bad that Golden Glove shortstop Ruben Amaro, Sr., had to play 58 games at first that year. The two previously mentioned starters; Bunning (2.63) and Short (2.20) pulled an otherwise remarkably mediocre pitching staff to the fourth spot in league ERA… although it is true that relievers, Jack Baldschun and Ed Roebuck, both had excellent years.

So, who were Mauch's other choices for starters as the season was closing? The number three starter was Dennis Bennett, who was actually a pretty fair pitcher, and who made MORE starts (32-31) than Short over the course of the year. In fact, Bennett was the Phillies' opening day starter in 1964 (yes, ahead of Bunning). So, why was Mauch afraid to use Bennett as the season wound down? The answer goes back to Sept. 11 and Sept. 15, when Bennett threw back-to-back 1-0 shutouts against the Giants and the Astros. Unfortunately, he hurt his left shoulder in the latter game, ultimately derailing a promising career and leading to his trade to Boston (for Dick Stuart!) in '65. The number four starter was Art Mahaffey. He had been their ace from 1960-1963, but he had an even worse arm (he only pitched 71 innings the next year, and 35 in 1966, ending his career) than Bennett. Once a feared strikeout pitcher – he fanned 17 Cubs in a game in April 1962 – Mahaffey had lost his fastball to an arm injury in 1963, and was getting by on guile. Then there was Ray Culp, who had made the All-Star team as a rookie in '63. He was, in effect, the number five starter, but he made only 19 starts all year, and most of those were early in the year. He was only 22 years old and wilder than Ryne Duren – who pitched two games for the Phils in '64 – without his glasses. He also would have a history of arm trouble throughout his career, possibly as a result of having thrown 203 innings as a 21-year-old in 1963.

In reality, Mauch had used a four-man rotation throughout the year... Culp was a fill-in, as was the number six starter, Rick Wise, who was all of 18 years old. And, those were all the starters they had... they made 158 starts between them. (John Boozer made three and Calvin Coolidge Julius Caesar Tuskahoma McLish, on July 14, made one).

Mauch's only other choice would have been to call Bitsy Bobby Shantz out of the bullpen to start (they had picked him up late in the year, and he pitched well in 14 games in relief), but, he'd been a primarily a reliever since 1958, and was 38 years old.

Given the hand that GM Bob Quinn (the real villain in the play… the Phillies' only other pick-up down the stretch was washed up first baseman Vic Power) had dealt him, what was Mauch going to do, throw pitching coach Al Widmar out there? Well, he didn't, and here's who did start (courtesy of the amazing www.Retrosheet.com website). Note that the first time one of the two aces (Bunning) started on short rest was in place of Mahaffey on Sept. 16. (The day I started seventh grade, in case you're keeping score.) It certainly seems that Mahaffey was seriously hurting at that point.

Date	Result	Phils' Starter	Opponents' Starter	Winner
9- 9-1964	Vs STL N L 5-10	Jim Bunning	Curt Simmons	Bob Humphreys
9-10-1964	Vs STL N W 5- 1	Chris Short	Ray Sadecki	Chris Short
9-11-1964	At SF N W 1- 0	Dennis Bennett	Juan Marichal	Dennis Bennett
9-12-1964	At SF N L 1- 9	Art Mahaffey	Gaylord Perry	Gaylord Perry
9-13-1964	At SF N W 4- 1	Jim Bunning	Dick Estelle	Jim Bunning
9-14-1964	At HOU N W 4-1	Chris Short	Bob Bruce	Chris Short
9-15-1964	At HOU N W 1- 0	Dennis Bennett	Ken Johnson	Dennis Bennett
9-16-1964	At HOU N L 5- 6	*Jim Bunning	Don Nottebart	Hal Brown
9-17-1964	At LA N W 4- 3	Rick Wise	Don Drysdale	Bobby Shantz
9-18-1964	At LA N L 3- 4	Chris Short	Pete Richert	Bob Miller
9-19-1964	At LA N L 3- 4	Dennis Bennett	Larry Miller	Phil Ortega
9-20-1964	At LA N W 3- 2	Jim Bunning	Jim Brewer	Jim Bunning
9-21-1964	Vs CIN N L 0- 1	Art Mahaffey	John Tsitouris	John Tsitouris

Date / Result	Phillies Pitcher	Opposing Pitcher	Pitcher of Record
9-22-1964 Vs CIN N L 2- 9	Chris Short	Jim O'Toole	Jim O'Toole
9-23-1964 Vs CIN N L 4- 6	Dennis Bennett	Billy McCool	Billy McCool
9-24-1964 Vs MIL N L 3- 5	Jim Bunning	Wade Blasingame	Blasingame
9-25-1964 Vs MIL N L 5- 7	*Chris Short	Hank Fischer	Clay Carroll
9-26-1964 Vs MIL N L 4- 6	Art Mahaffey	Denny Lemaster	Blasingame
9-27-1964 Vs MIL N L 8-14	*Jim Bunning	Tony Cloninger	Tony Cloninger
9-28-1964 At STL N L 1- 5	*Chris Short	Bob Gibson	Bob Gibson
9-29-1964 At STL N L 2- 4	Dennis Bennett	Ray Sadecki	Ray Sadecki
9-30-1964 At STL N L 5- 8	*Jim Bunning	Curt Simmons	Curt Simmons
10- 2-1964 At CIN N W 4- 3	Chris Short	Jim O'Toole	Ed Roebuck
10- 4-1964 At CIN N W 10- 0	Jim Bunning	John Tsitouris	Jim Bunning

With Culp (who hadn't started since Aug. 15) and Wise as fill-ins, Mauch had been going with a Bunning/Short/Bennett/Mahaffey rotation for most of the Summer, while the Phillies built a 6 ½ game lead (on Sept. 20… and that was after Bunning first pitched on two days rest) in their battle with (primarily) the Giants for first.

The five games that are asterisked are the only times Bunning and Short started on two days rest – and four of those were during the 10-game losing streak. In effect, what Mauch did from Sept. 24 on was go with a three-man rotation, with first Mahaffey (on five days rest) and then Bennett (on six days rest) alternating as the third man in an effort to conserve their arms.

In hindsight, neither Short nor Bunning pitched very well during the losing streak, but, on the other hand, Bennett had hurt his shoulder on Sept. 15 and Mahaffey hadn't won since a 10-8 game on Aug. 29 in Pittsburgh. Also note that, thanks in part to the days off on Oct. 1 and Oct. 3, both Bunning and Short also pitched twice on their regular three days rest during the last 12 games. Furthermore, leaving out the Sept. 27 game, the Phillies averaged a mighty 2.9 runs during the 10 game losing streak – and it's pretty hard to win with any kind of pitching under those circumstances.

Since the Phillies finished one game behind the Cardinals, it's easy to say after the fact that Mauch would have been better to, let's say, push Bunning's Sept. 27 start against Milwaukee (the 14-8 loss where Callison hit three home runs) back a day – to both give him three days rest and to face Bob Gibson and the Cardinals, who were in third, a half game back of the Phillies. However, Sept. 27 was also the day the Reds went into first place, and, after six straight losses, Mauch clearly felt he had to throw his best against the Braves to stop the slide.

It didn't work out, but, that's what Mauch was doing, going with his best (and practically only) options.

Mauch was hardly alone in his fate. Certainly the Red Sox coughing up a whopping 14 game lead over the Yankees in 1978 deserves dishonorable mention. (Remember the "Boston Massacre?" Four Yankee wins by a combined 42-9 score.) For that matter, so do the Yankees for losing a 12 game Fourth of July lead to the Red Sox in 1949 – a faux pas that was largely forgotten after the Yankees won the last two games of the season against the Sox and still took the pennant. And, of course, who can forget the Dodgers blowing a 13 ½ game lead in August 1951 to the Giants, prior to losing a 4-1 lead in the ninth inning of the third playoff game. (The Giants win the pennant! The Giants win the pennant! The Giants win the pennant! Etc., etc.)

Another famous flop was pulled off by those same Chicago Cubs who just benefited from a swoon by the Houston Astros. The Cubbies had a 5 game lead on the Mets on Sept. 4 of that fated Summer of 1969, only to finish an incredible eight games back… the Mets having gone 19-5 while the Cubs went 6-14. Nice job, Leo. And, in 1995, the Mariners were six games in back of the Angels on Sept. 8, and still made it to a playoff that they won.

Well, you get the idea. It does happen. And, by George, it happened again (in a slightly less dramatic version) this year, this time to the Astros. Now, typically, the 'Stros go belly up in October, AFTER the playoffs have started. In 2003 though, someone turned off the juice at Minute Maid a little early. Still holding a game-and-a-half lead on the

Cubs at the end of play on Sept. 19, the Astros (then 84-69) managed to go 2-6 over the next eight games while the Cubs (83-71 on Sept. 19), who have made a history of September Swoons, went 5-2 at the same time. That gave the Cubs a two game lead with one game left, and the NL Central crown… much to the surprise of Houston fans and much to the distress of St. Louis fans.

So what happened? Well, it didn't help the Houston cause any that the first five of those games were against two pretty good teams – the Giants and the Cards… any more than it helped the 1964 Phillies to play eight of their last 12 games against the Reds (who finished tied for second) and the eventually pennant winning Cards. However, the Astros have no excuse for blowing two straight games to the downtrodden Brewers when the chips were down, or for averaging less than 3.4 runs per game over that crucial eight game stretch.

On the other hand, the Cubs were fortunate enough to finish their season against the wretched of the earth, aka, the Pirates and Reds… both of whom had long since thrown in the towel for 2003. So, maybe the moral of the story is, if you're planning a pennant race in September, load your schedule with patsies at the end… sort of the opposite of college football and basketball.

Now, as to the innumerable teams that actually did make the playoffs… here's how *Baseball: 1862 to 2003* sees the first round going…

National League

San Francisco vs. Florida – a no-brainer. The Marlins are a fluke (Marlins… fish… fluke, get it?) that got hot at the right time of the year. Although the Giants do not present an imposing lineup behind Barry Bonds, they took five out of six from Florida during the season and will rough up the Marlins' inexperienced starters. Offensively, the Flukes look more like last year's Angels (8th in NL OPS) than a Great White Shark.

Chicago vs. Atlanta – ditto. The Cubs remember who they are and their long and undistinguished history of late season play since 1945 and go quietly. As usual, the Braves get lucky and draw a patsy… Cubs' offense is so wimpy (11th in NL OPS) that it won't be able to take advantage of the Braves' awful pitching.

American League

Minnesota vs. New York – are you kidding? The Best Team That Money Can Buy wins in a walk over the winner of a weak division.

Boston vs. Oakland – clearly the best (and maybe the only good) series of the four. The Boston offensive juggernaut brings back memories of the 1950 team – 960 runs (almost 200 more than the A's) and a .492 TEAM slugging percentage. Can Hudson and Zito hold them back in Mulder's absence? Will Ted Lilly end up holding a lily? Will good pitching stop good hitting? Can the Sox get enough pitching behind Pedro (who figures to start twice in the series)? Will Byung-Hyun Kim self-destruct in October again? What about the rest of the Sox bullpen? Is Bill James a better in-series analyst than Billy Beane, and, will the Sox listen to him? This may be the first series ever decided off the field by a couple of sabrmetric geniuses. Let's give the nod to Boston and James (assuming his Internet connection to Old Towne doesn't get the Microsoft Blaster virus.)

Item: September 7, 1993 – St. Louis Cardinal Mark Whitten (Mark Whitten?) hits four home runs in the second game of a doubleheader at Cincinnati.

It would be truly unfair to Carlos Delgado to allow his four home runs of Sept. 25 to go unnoticed in the fuss stirred up by the end of the regular season. In fact, it's also unfair to compare Carlos Delgado to Mark Whitten. However, Whitten previously held the record for the latest (in the season) four home run game, so his name comes up in the timeline.

Delgado became the 15th player in major league history to hit four dingers in one game when he helped lead the Blue Jays to a 10-8 win over Tampa Bay (alright, so maybe it wasn't a major league game.)

Now, what does this say about Carlos Delgado? At least, in comparison to Mark Whitten or the other 13 players to hit four long flies in a game? Certainly, excellence in a single game does not a star, or Hall of Famer, make. If that were the case, Don Larsen, Charlie Robertson, Bill Wambsganss, Ron Hansen, Jim Bottomley and various others would be so enshrined in Cooperstown, N.Y. (What's that? Bottomley IS in the Hall of Fame? Oh well, another mistake by the Veterans Committee.) Actually, 12 of the previous individuals to score four in a game can be nicely pigeon-holed into three categories… Hall of Fame Home Run Hitters, Top Notch Home Run Hitters, and Flukes. Leaving out for the moment Mike Cameron and Shawn Green, who are still active, here are the first 12 to perform this rare feat…

May 30, 1894	Bobby Lowe (Boston NL)
July 13, 1896	Ed Delahanty (Phila NL)
June 3, 1932	Lou Gehrig (NY AL)
July 10, 1936	Chuck Klein (Phila NL)
July 18, 1948	Pat Seerey (Chi AL)
Aug. 31, 1950	Gil Hodges (Brklyn NL)
July 31, 1954	Joe Adcock (Mil NL)
June 10, 1959	Rocky Colavito (Clev AL)
Apr. 30, 1961	Willie Mays (SF NL)
Apr. 17, 1976	Mike Schmidt (Phila NL)
July 6, 1986	Bob Horner (Atl, NL)
Sept. 7, 1993	Mark Whitten (StL NL)

Gehrig (493), Mays (660) and Schmidt (548) are the Hall of Fame Home Run Hitters, with 15 home run crowns (and three spots in the Hall of Fame) between them. Certainly, no one would deny that Delahanty, Klein, Hodges, Adcock and Colavito were major stars. The first two are in the Hall of Fame, and, collectively, they won seven home run crowns. Leaving out Dead Ball Era slugger Delahanty, the other four averaged 345 home runs.

However, Lowe, Seerey, Horner and Whitten are just flukes – four of the strange things that have happened over the past 110 seasons.

None of them ever led his league in home runs, and they totaled fewer home runs altogether (480) than Gehrig had by himself. Seerey only hit another 82 home runs in a career more marked by strikeouts (he led the league in that all four seasons he was a regular) than home runs. Whitten barely hit another 100 home runs (career total – 105) during the rest of his major league tenure. Horner, though he hit 218 home runs for his career, only ranked as high as second in the National League once, and that was in 1980, when he trailed Schmidt by a whopping 13. And Lowe (71 home runs for his career), though he did hit all four of his over the fence, was taking aim at the very short (250 feet) fence at Boston's little Congress Street Grounds, where the Beaneaters were playing after their park, the South End Grounds, burned down. (A common problem in 19th Century baseball.)[72]

Some other oddities on this list… There is some disagreement on Delahanty's feat. Most sources place it in Chicago, and many have him hitting four inside-the-park home runs in one game. However, you'll also see it stated that he hit two over the fence and two inside-the-park. And, famed sportswriter Fred Lieb, who actually was an eight-year-old boy when Delahanty connected, claims in *Baseball as I Have Known It* that Del hit all four out of Philadelphia Park (later known as Baker Bowl.) However, Lieb (in the same story) also says that an older friend of his, who said he saw the game, claimed that the last one reached the bleachers on top of the centerfield clubhouse[73] … something no one ever did in the park's 51-year history. It should be noted that Lieb sometimes didn't let the facts get in the way of telling a good story.

Four home run games, at least in the first 80 or so years of their history, have followed the Philadelphia teams around. Phillies Delahanty, Klein and Schmidt all did it, and Gehrig and Seerey had their four home run games against the Athletics… which may or may not say something about the Phillies' hitters and the Athletics' pitchers.

Also note the 36-year gap between Delahanty's feat and Gehrig's four blows. Think Old Biscuit Pants made all the headlines in the New York papers on June 4, 1932? Guess again. June 3, 1932 also happened to be the day John McGraw retired after 30 years as manager of the Giants, and Lou took a back seat once again.

Finally, let's try to see where the last three home run heroes will actually find their respective places in history. Once again, we'll turn to Bill James' Favorite Toy to try and predict how many home runs Cameron, Green and Delgado will end up with for their careers. Conveniently, all three will be 31 years old by the start of the 2004 season, making the comparison more relevant. If we set 500 home runs as the mark for a Hall of Fame Home Run Hitter (Gehrig, by the way, had a 55% chance of reaching 600 home runs before ALS struck him down), then we find that Delgado (currently at 303 home runs) has a 54% chance of reaching that plateau, and Green (253 home runs) a 19% chance. Cameron, with just 131 career home runs at the end of 2003, has no chance. If 300 is a good number to define a Top Notch Home Run Hitter, then Delgado is already there, Green is a lock for that level, and Cameron has just a 19% chance of reaching 300. Actually, Green's numbers have been skewed by his playing with a shoulder injury all year. He only hit 19 home runs in 2003, after hitting 49 in 2001 and 42 in 2002. If, for instance, he bounces back with a 47 home run campaign in 2004 (a not unreasonable number if he's healthy), that jumps his chances for 500 home runs back up to 38.5%.

So, at this stage of the game, it looks like the jury is still out on Green, although the most likely course for him is to become a Top Notch Home Run Hitter. Cameron's feat was clearly a fluke, and Delgado has a better than average chance of becoming the fourth Hall of Fame Home Run Hitter to hit four in one game.

CHAPTER 43

October 6, 2003

Item: October 5, 1941 – "A little wet slider" gets by Dodgers catcher, Mickey Owen, starting 15 years of angst for Brooklyn fans.

Maybe the Brooklyn Dodgers didn't have a curse to call their own, but, there's no doubt that fans in the Borough of Churches must have wondered just what was going on from 1941 to 1956. Ten times… 10 (count 'em, 10) times in 16 years, the Bums either; A) lost in the World Series, B) lost in a playoff for the National League pennant, C) lost the final game of the regular season and missed a playoff by one game, or D) came up two games short of a playoff. And, no, that's not multiple choice… they managed to pull off ALL of those feats during a period when they were unquestionably the best team in the National League. Running it down year-by-year…

1941 – Dodgers lose to the Yankees, 4-1, in the World Series (and thereby hangs a tale)

1942 – Dodgers blow a 10 game mid-summer lead (and a 7 ½ game lead with five weeks to go) and finish two games behind the Cardinals

1946 – Dodgers lose to the Cardinals in the first-ever National League playoff series, 2-0

1947 – Dodgers lose to the Yankees, 4-3, in the World Series

1949 – Dodgers lose to the Yankees, 4-1 in the World Series

1950 – Dodgers lose 4-1 to Philadelphia in 10 innings on the last day of the season, and thereby miss a playoff with the Fightin' Phils

1951 – Dodgers blow an even bigger lead (13 ½ games in August),

and lose the second-ever National League playoff to the Giants, 2-1
    1952 – Dodgers lose to the Yankees, 4-3, in the World Series
    1953 – Dodgers lose to the Yankees, 4-2, in the World Series
    1956 – Dodgers lose to the Yankees, 4-3, in the World Series

What a stunning resume of futility when the chips were down. Yes, thanks to a shutout by Johnny Podres, the Dodgers did manage to beat the Yankees four games to three in the 1955 World Series. But, that's still 10 blown opportunities out of 11 in 16 years. Hard to believe, isn't it? (Unless you're a Braves fan…) And, it all began in the fourth game of the 1941 World Series, on Oct. 5, 1941…

The Dodgers were playing in their first World Series since losing the 1916 and 1920 contests. Red Ruffing had beat Curt Davis 3-2 in the first game. The Dodgers' Whit Wyatt had returned the favor, 3-2, in the second game. The third game went to the Yanks, 2-1, when Yankee pitcher Marius Russo literally knocked Dodger starter Fred Fitzsimmons out with a line drive off his knee… eventually breaking up a scoreless, seventh-inning tie against Dodger reliever Hugh Casey.

The key game four, with the Dodgers now down two games to one, continued with an anti-Dodger pattern, as Kirby Higbe was knocked out early and the Yankees took a 3-0 lead. But, miracle of miracles, the Bums came back to take a 4-3 lead into the top of the ninth at Ebbets Field, thanks in part to the relief pitching of Larry French, Johnny Allen and Casey (who came on in the fifth, after pitching two innings and getting the loss in game three.) John Sturm was the first batter in the Yanks' ninth. He grounded out to second. Then Red Rolfe tapped one back to Casey. Two outs. The Dodgers were one out away from tying the series. Tommy Henrich, a dead fastball hitter, was the batter. With two strikes on Henrich, Casey certainly wasn't going to give him a fastball. Instead he threw what Dodger shortstop Pee Wee Reese described as "a little wet slider." Henrich swung and missed (by about a foot) for strike three, but, catcher Mickey Owen didn't get any leather on the ball (both Henrich's and Owen's misses are quite obvious from the photographs of the play) and it went all the way to the backstop as Henrich reached first base.

Now, Casey and Owen always denied that the final pitch to Henrich was a spitter, however, while writing *Bombers: An Oral History of the New York Yankees*, author Richard Lally had a chance to interview Pete Coscarart, who was playing second base (because Billy Herman was injured) that fateful day. According to Lally, "Coscarart claims that Casey definitely threw 'the darndest spitball you will ever see' for the pitch that eluded Owen. Tommy Henrich told me that Mickey Owen always denied that it was a spitball, but Coscarart was adamant that no other pitch in Casey's arsenal could have broken that abruptly. Henrich, who accepted Owen's denial, also said that the ball [did] seem to keep breaking in a pattern so funky, [that] he was hoping that the catcher would not be able to handle it… which is why Henrich got such a quick start out of the batter's box."

The story of "Mickey Owen's Dropped Third Strike" is one of the most famous in baseball's long history. And yet, as is often the case in baseball, the story isn't as simple as some people may think. In reality, Owen didn't cost the Dodgers the game (and the Series) any more than Fred Merkle cost the Giants the 1908 pennant. And, while Owen may have been a contributing party to Brooklyn's 15 years of angst, there is plenty of blame to go around, starting with Dodger manager Leo Durocher.

First and foremost, all that resulted from the dropped third strike (which wasn't a drop, since it appears from the photos that Owen may never have touched the ball) was a man on first with two outs and a 4-3 Dodger lead. True, the next hitter was Joe DiMaggio, but, if Casey gets him out, no one will remember Henrich getting on first. And even DiMaggio, in 1941, only got on base 44% of the time. Alas for the Bums, the pitcher was Hugh Casey – the same Hugh Casey who would later fight an unscheduled, drunken midnight boxing match in Havana with Ernest Hemingway,[74] and who wasn't exactly a teetotaler the rest of the time,[75] and who would shoot himself to death in 1951 (in Atlanta, of all places).[76] This is also the same Hugh Casey who was in his fifth inning of relief (admittedly, a more common practice in those days) after losing the previous game of the Series and pitching in the first game as well.

Soooo… DiMaggio singles. Still, there are just two on and two out. The Dodgers still lead 4-3. Does Durocher figure Casey might be a little rattled? Who knows? Casey stays in. Now Charlie Keller–who was a forgotten key player in this whole sequence – comes to the plate and doubles in both Henrich and DiMaggio, and the Yankees lead 5-4. It's still a one run game. Does Durocher pull Casey? No. Bill Dickey walks, and Joe Gordon doubles in both Keller and Dickey. Now, then game is gone, 7-4. Does Durocher pull Casey? No. Phil Rizzuto walks. Now does Durocher pull Casey? No. Casey finally gets the third out. The Bums are dead, and lose 3-1 in the next game, beginning 15 years of angst.

Clearly Casey, for crossing up the best catcher in the National League (Owen had made ZERO errors in 1941) with a spitball, and then blowing up, and Durocher – for not pulling Casey – deserve far more blame for this disaster than Mickey Owen.

Now, who's to blame for the Braves' similar litany of failure? After all, the Bravos just broke their playoff flop tie with the Dodgers, blowing their 11th playoff series in 12 tries. However, before laying the blame for this year, let's correct a common misconception regarding the major league team in Atlanta. Contrary to what most people seem to think, the Braves HAVE NOT, repeat, HAVE NOT, won 12 straight division titles. Let's try to make this as simple as possible…

1991 – Braves win NL West
1992 – Braves win NL West
1993 – Braves win NL West
1994 – Braves move to NL East. When the season ends in August, the Montreal Expos are in first place, and pulling away. In fact, they have a 74-40 record, the best in the National League. Braves finish second at 68-46, and the Expos win the NL East.
1995-2003 – Braves win NL East (that's nine seasons, in case you're counting)

Got it? As has been the case since 1871 when the Philadelphia Athletics just nosed out the Chicago White Stockings, the team at first place when the regular season ends is declared the "winner" (at least for that league or division.) Doesn't matter how that winner is decided (W-L percentage, number of wins, etc.), or if the season is cut short (no one told the Cubs and Red Sox they weren't the NL and AL winners when the 1918 season was cut short due to WW1), or if there wasn't a World Series (ditto the 1901 and 1902 Pirates, the 1901 White Sox and 1902 Athletics.) It also doesn't matter if one team is rooked because they played fewer games (as happened in the American League in 1972 and in 1908, by the way.) First place at the end of the regular season is still first place. And, since the Braves moved from the NL West to the NL East in 1994, you can't even give them credit for keeping the 1993 NL West crown by default in 1994... because they were in the East at that point. So, let's get it straight people... this is not rocket science. "Giving" the Braves 12 straight is the same as saying the 1994 season didn't exist. And, it did.

Now, as to the Braves' actual results since 1991...

1991 – Braves lose to the Twins, 4-3, in the World Series
1992 – Braves lose to the Blue Jays, 4-2, in the World Series
1993 – Braves lose to the Phillies, 4-2, in the NLCS
1996 – Braves lose to the Yankees, 4-2, in the World Series
1997 – Braves lose to the Marlins, 4-2, in the NLCS
1998 – Braves lose to the Padres, 4-2, in the NLCS
1999 – Braves lose to the Yankees, 4-0 in the World Series
2000 – Braves lose to the Cardinals 3-0, in the NLDS
2001 – Braves lose to the Diamondbacks, 4-1, in the NLCS
2002 – Braves lose to the Giants, 3-2, in the NLDS
2003 – Braves lose to the Cubs, 3-2, in the NLDS

To give the National League version of the Evil Empire its just due, the Braves did manage to defeat the Indians, four games to two, in the 1995 World Series. Still, that's 11 flops out of 12 for unquestionably the best team in the National League over the past 13 years.

Although the two teams' records are amazingly alike, there are some key differences. First, the Dodgers mainly suffered at the hands of the Yankees, losing to the Hateds six times. The Braves have spread the wealth around. With the exception of the Expos and the Brewers they've played every single NL team in the playoffs over the past 13 years, losing to seven different teams in seven years. They've also managed to lose to three different AL teams in the Series, just for good measure.

Second, while the Dodgers got stronger during their 16 years of futility, playing in four out of five World Series and winning one toward the end of their run, the Braves are getting worse. "Hotlanta" hasn't been to the Series since getting swept in 1999, and they've lost in the Division Series, for goodness sakes, three out of the last four years. What's worse, they just lost to the Cubs... marking the first time in 95 years that the Cubbies have beat ANYBODY in the postseason.

Thirdly, the Dodgers always went with the same formula – a tremendous offensive powerhouse (Robinson, Snider, Campanella, Hodges, Furillo, et al) that never had quite enough pitching. The Braves, on the other hand, used to be known for their tremendous rotation and a cobbled together bullpen (with seemingly a different cast of characters each year). However, for 2003, they reversed the pattern, running out the best offense in the National League and a motley crew of starters, backed up by the same patched together bullpen.

And, maybe fourth, there is really no seminal event with which to begin the Braves run... no one to hang the goat horns upon... unless you count Lonnie "Skates" Smith slipping on the bases while representing the potential lead run in game seven of the 1991 World Series. While he may not be as famous as Fred Snodgrass (1912 New York Giants) or Mickey Owen, there is something to be said for Skates' place in history.

Naturally, over a 13- or 16-year period of time, the average major league team will have a lot of turnover. The only person wearing the Bums' uniform who appeared in every playoff (or near playoff) game for the Dodgers from 1941 to 1956 was Hall of Fame shortstop Pee Wee Reese. And, although John Smoltz has been on the Braves roster since 1988, he missed the entire 2000 season after elbow surgery.

However, another key figure in the Braves' regular season run has been Greg Maddux. Although he only came to Atlanta as the team's ace in 1993, his post-season record has not been one to boast about… and that includes losing the key third game to the Cubs on Friday. Overall, this sure Hall of Famer is now 11-14 in the postseason with an ERA about a third of a run higher than his regular season ERA. As such he's sort of the anti-Curt Schilling.

And, of course, Braves Manager Bobby Cox has been at the helm since 1991… makes you wonder, doesn't it?

As to what happened this year… well, that's pretty easy to explain. The Braves' vaunted regular season offense (there's a term you didn't see much from 1991 to 2002) was, in reality, an anomaly as much as anything. If there's anyone out there who thinks that Javy Lopez, Vinny Castilla, Marcus Giles, Julio Franco, Robert Fick and Rafael Furcal will collectively match 2003's numbers in 2004, not matter where they're playing – Atlanta, Japan, Baltimore, Mexico, etc… well, I have a bridge for you that the Dodgers left behind when they went they went to L.A.

(Interestingly, just as the Dodgers fled Brooklyn shortly after their Reign of Error ended, there's a hot rumor going around that AOL Time/ Warner is thinking of selling the Braves. Wouldn't it be appropriate if Asian interests, such as already own the Seattle Mariners, bought the club, and moved them to the Philippines, where they could be re-named the Manilla Folders?)

More importantly, the Braves' offense fell flat when it mattered the most. After setting franchise records with 235 home runs and 907 runs scored, the Braves scored all of 15 runs in the five games against the Cubs, as the erstwhile heart of the offense, outfielders Gary Sheffield, Chipper Jones and Andruw Jones combined to hit .122. Just as bad, Lopez, coming off a season where he set the record for home runs by a catcher, had a Hat Trick – zero home runs, zero walks and zero RBIs. Meanwhile, the wimpy Cubs offense only scored 19 runs against the Braves' shaky pitchers, but that was enough… because it's also true that some blame does need to go to the Braves' pitching. After all those years of dominant starting pitching, the Braves didn't have an ace to go against Kerry Wood and Mark Prior. In 2003 at least, Maddux no longer deserved that title. Not after posting a 3.96 ERA and giving up 225 hits in 218 innings. Twenty-one game winner Russ Ortiz? Puhleeeze! He led the NL in walks and had a 3.81 ERA. Mike Hampton, maybe? Maybe not. Hampton walked 78 and only struck out 110 to go with a 3.84 ERA. As a result, the Cubs won the three games that their two aces started.

However, with Sheffield, Maddux and Lopez all in the last years of their contracts, and AOL Time/Warner most likely poised to keep costs down, we may not get a chance to re-run this story at the end of 2004. The Dodgers' streak of postseason futility lasted 16 years. Is the Braves' over at 13?

CHAPTER 44

October 13, 2003

Item: October 6, 1882 – The Cincinnati Reds, behind pitcher, Will White, shut out the Chicago White Stockings, 4-0, in the first-ever postseason game between first place teams from opposing major leagues.

You have to be real careful in how you present the Cincinnati/ Chicago contest of Oct. 6, 1882. The above statement is literally correct… to call this exhibition game (for that's what it was) anything else, including a "World Series Game," would be as inaccurate as calling the contests that transpired over the last two weeks the World Series. The postseason games of 2003 are, to date, merely a prelude to the real action, brought about by the existence of expansion and the Mild Card. On the other hand, the two 1882 postseason contests between the first place teams from the National League (Chicago) and the American Association (Cincinnati) were merely part of a series of exhibition games designed to raise a little extra money for the participants.

However, the 1882 games were certainly interesting, and far more historic than the NLDS or the ALDS or the NRA, the USSR or a CPA or certainly the GOP. And, thanks to Jerry Lansche's highly-informative 1991 book, *Glory Fades Away*, we have a detailed account of all of baseball's 19th Century post-season activity… an account that does indeed bring back to life a largely-forgotten piece of baseball history. With thanks to Mr. Lansche for his work, we will proceed…

To set the stage… following its 1876 founding, the National League pretty much had the run of the field in terms of being what we would now call a "major" league. While there certainly were other professional leagues in existence, and their level of play was often quite comparable to that of the NL, the "big" league generally (though not always) had the bigger cities, was more geographically diverse and had the pretensions of grandeur as the nation's premier sporting organization. Besides, the National League DID eventually grow up to become the fine organization it is today – the only baseball league in existence that doesn't use the designated hitter.

However, real "major league" competition reared its ugly head in the winter of 1881-82, in the birthplace of professional baseball– Cincinnati. Seems as if the Queen City was not one of the teams in the NL at that time, having been summarily booted out (in other words, contracted… it happened a lot in the 19th Century – those were the good old days) after the 1880 season for selling liquor in its ballpark. Thanks to the work of Justus Thorner (president of the 1880 NL Reds) and sportswriter O.P. Caylor (a seminal figure in early baseball who probably belongs in the Hall of Fame in some capacity), the American Association was formed to start the 1882 season. What marked this league as another "major" league were three key factors – the six teams that signed up to start the 1882 season (Cincinnati, St. Louis, Philadelphia, Louisville, Baltimore and Pittsburgh) represented a population base comparable to that of the eight 1882 National League cities (which at the moment included Troy, NY and Worcester, MA), they actively raided the National League teams for players, and they proclaimed themselves the equal to the National League.

But, were they really equals? The AA forbid its teams from playing NL teams. So, it seemed as if there wasn't any way to tell. Nevertheless, good old American enterprise found a way, and two games between Cincinnati and Chicago did take place after the conclusion of the regular season. In the case of the Reds, Thorner released his entire team after the season, and had them all re-sign with, in effect, a dummy corporation so they could play against Chicago as the "Reds." (Some reports have Albert Spalding's White Stockings doing the same thing, due to an NL prohibition against games with AA teams.)

Why just two games? Well, there are two versions of that story as well. One had it that AA President Denny McKnight threatened to expel Cincy from the AA after two games (What would Thorner have done in that case, start a third league? Actually, he did, the Union Association in 1884.), so the series was abandoned. Another tale has it that only two games were scheduled in any case, because both teams had other exhibitions lined up afterwards, and they didn't have the time to play more games, even if they had wanted to. And, indeed, both teams did play further exhibitions after their two-game "World Series."

This second scenario is certainly more in keeping with the highly informal nature of ALL 19th century postseason play… which tended to be organized along the lines of two bunches of kids tossing a bat in the air, and grabbing at the handle to see who hits first. (One, two, three… shoot! OK, I've got odds, I take Bobby Umbarger first.) Of course, it's also possible that, after McKnight laid down the law to the Reds; Thorner, et al, decided, after the fact, to schedule more exhibition games to make more money.

In any case, only two games were played. And, despite overwhelming sentiment that the Reds were terribly outclassed by the mighty White Stockings (who were coming off three straight NL pennants) of Cap Anson, Ned Williamson and Larry Corcoran (the first pitcher to throw three no-hitters), the two teams split a pair of well-played games at Cincinnati's Bank Street Grounds, an event most fans deemed as unlikely as a call-in radio talk show host acting as an analyst on ESPN. What!? That's happened?! What a world…

Pitcher Will White was indeed the star of the first-ever major league postseason champions' game. In fact, White and his catcher/brother James "Deacon" White (they were also briefly the first brother battery) were an interesting enough story to merit their own book. Will, who threw an eight-hit shutout at Chicago on Oct. 6, 1882, was the first major league player to wear glasses and won 227 games in Cincinnati.

And, Will wasn't even the most unusual member of the family. Deacon (he was a non-smoking, non-drinking church deacon) began playing against the 1869 Cincinnati Red Stockings, and was probably the best bare-handed catcher of all time, playing all the way up to the Brotherhood rebellion that formed the Players League in 1890. And that wasn't the half of it… along with all of his other remarkable accomplishments, Deacon White truly believed the earth was flat. Perhaps you're not too familiar with the level of scientific and cultural sophistication of late 19th century America… in which case, White's belief may not seem that strange for the times. Not true. Deacon White professing publicly that the earth was flat in 1882 was about as odd as… oh, let's think of a social theory that is really out in right field… a famous media figure in 2003 proclaiming that an NFL quarterback is overrated because he's an African-American, and the NFL wants him to look good. Oh, you say that happened, too? Well, just goes to show…

Anyway, to get back to Oct. 6, 1882 – the underdog Reds were essentially a good field, poor hit team that revolved around pitcher White (that one who didn't think the earth was flat), second baseman (and future Hall of Famer) Bid McPhee and possibly the best-ever left-handed infielder (not counting first basemen, of course), Hick Carpenter. And, true to form, White and his mates held the Mighty Whiteys scoreless through six innings that day, much to the delight of the 2,700 Cincinnatians in attendance. Trouble was, Chicago's Corcoran hadn't given up anything either as the Reds came to bat in the seventh (they were batting first that day). With one out, Carpenter got things started with a single. Then first baseman Dan Stearns followed with another single, moving Carpenter to third. Shortstop Chick Fulmer then singled just in front of Chicago centerfielder George Gore, and the Reds had drawn first blood. It was still a 1-0 game with one out and two on… and, if Corcoran could coax a DP, Chicago was still in the game. However, the next batter was Cincy's favorite second baseman prior to Joe Morgan… and McPhee tripled to right center to break the game open. (And was wild-pitched home moments later.) Although the White Stockings threatened in each of the last three innings, White shut the door, the final two outs coming when Anson flied to centerfielder Jimmy Macullar, who then threw Abner Dalrymple out at the plate trying to score on the play… one of the dumber base-running plays of the year.[77] Thus, in the first-ever postseason game between reigning league champions, the Chicago White Stockings (the team now known as the Cubs… and that's definitely the same story) had been Chicagoed (the term for a shutout in those days) by Cincinnati.

Now, what does that tell us about the 2003 postseason to date? Well, in the words of a noted baseball philosopher, in baseball, you don't know nuthin.

That was certainly true in 1882, when the lightly-regarded Reds shut out Chicago (prior to Corcoran and the White Stockings coming back with a 2-0 shutout the next day), and it was just as true in the National League in 2003, when the teams with two of the three best records in baseball both fell to ostensibly inferior squads in the first round of the playoffs. Who woulda thunk it?

However, it is also true that the American League Division Series went pretty much according to form. The Yankees took a game to wake up, and then had little trouble with the Twins, a team whose young starting pitchers have gone backwards over time (with the possible exception of Johan Santana) and whose offense is greatly lacking any outstanding characteristics. Indeed, the only outstanding characteristic of the Twins' offense is a lack of power. With 155 homeruns in the year, they were ninth in the AL, and just six dingers short of the 12th place spot.

Only three regulars – none of whom will ever make anyone forget Harmon Killebrew – Corey Koskie (.845), Doug Mientkiewicz (.843) and A.J. Pierzynski (.824) had an OPS over .800, and they were "balanced" by dead weights Luis Rivas (.689) and Christian Guzman (.676). All in all, not an offense to throw a scare into a pitching staff headed by Mike Mussina and Roger Clemens.

Meanwhile, back by the bays… the Red Sox and Athletics were duking it out in what indeed turned out to be far and away the most exciting series, and not just because of the re-discovery of the squeeze bunt and Derek Lowe's actions. Any series featuring a team with a .491 slugging percentage is bound to produce some fireworks, especially against a team that is down an ace. Although the A's have been ripped for once again failing in the postseason, it is hardly fair to call them a failure – particularly this year, when the strongest part of the team, the starting pitchers, were a man short to start with, due to the injury to Mark Mulder. Then, when Tim Hudson had to leave game four after one inning (the key moment in the series)… well, even with the series lead, at that point a large Nordic female started warming up her vocal cords in the bullpen. Give Mulder a start, or let Hudson stay in game four, and you might well have a different end game.

Now, as for the National League… maybe some brave souls outside of the Windy City picked the Cubs, given the Braves' grisly record in postseason play since 1991, and given the fact that the erstwhile 19th Century White Stockings had two aces in their hand (Prior and Wood) as opposed to the Braves' busted flush. But, this was a team that hadn't won a postseason series since Roosevelt was president… Teddy Roosevelt, that is. And, there is really no good reason why the Giants went belly-up against a team with erratic young pitchers (Exhibit "A" – Willis, Dontrelle) and exactly three good hitters (Lowell, Lee and Pudge), except that maybe momentum is a bigger factor in baseball than sabrmetric types are willing to give it credit for. (As is the fact that anything can happen in a short series… see the 1906 World Series for reference.) The Marlins went into the Division Series hot, and stayed that way. They are, in a word, a fluke. Even Barry Bonds' annual playoff swoon (like the Braves, he's had one good playoff season since 1991) can't explain the S.F. Giants playing like the Singer Midgets in the last three games of the NLDS. While some of the blame can be placed on Sir Sidney Ponson melting down in game two, that really shouldn't be too much a shock, since Sir Sidney is by no means the ace that he seemed to be with the Orioles in the first part of 2003. Prior to 2003, his career ERA was 4.74… somewhat above the AL average for the same years (1998 – 2002) of 4.57.

So, if the Flukes have three good hitters, what about the rest of their more-or-less regular lineup?

	OPS	BA	W	K	Previous OPS
Miguel Cabrera	.793	.268	25	84	N/A
Luis Castillo	.778	.314	63	60	.710
Juan Encarnacion	.759	.270	37	82	.759
Alex Gonzalez	.756	.256	33	106	.656
Juan Pierre	.734	.305	55	35	.727

Hmmmm… where have we seen numbers like this before? Remember the 2002 Angels? A high-average, low walk, middling power (the Flukes had 157 home runs this year… 11th in the NL) offense… remember what happened to that offense in 2003? Basically, an offense like this is like a blind pig… every once and a while, they'll find an acorn… but, don't count on it happening regularly. Well, the latter half of the 2003 season, and the NLDS, were the Flukes' acorn.

To take the five above-mentioned Marlins and look back at their records leaves an inescapable conclusion that Florida (like Anaheim in 2002) was lucky. Unless Cabrera improves that W/K ratio, he'll turn into Juan Samuel. Although Castillo clearly had a better year than expected, he was also 27 years old, the age at which field players tend to peak. Encarnacion exactly matched his career OPS, and he has a lousy W/K ratio as well. Gonzalez hit way over his head, and his W/K ratio is the worst of all… he IS Juan Samuel, except he doesn't steal bases. (Which brings up another point… the Marlins got a lot of credit for playing small ball and stealing bases… another offensive scenario that doesn't hold water for very long, at least in terms of overall success.) Finally, Pierre essentially matched his career OPS, and he's still a lousy top of the order hitter – those 55 walks came in 668 at bats. If you follow The Rule of 10, you know that he needed 67 walks to just be around average in terms of plate discipline.

However, a hot streak can only last so long, and, hence, we can state with absolute certainly that the Cubs will, at the very worst, take three of the first five games against the Flukes in the NLCS. What? That's happened as well? Well, whadda know about that!?

CHAPTER 45

October 17, 2003

Item: October 12, 1929 – The Philadelphia Athletics drop a 10-spot on the Chicago Cubs in the seventh inning of game four of the World Series, thus beginning 74 years of true angst in the Windy City.

"That's the rottenest thing in this life, isn't it? The best team doesn't always get to win." (*New York Tribune* sportswriter Roger Kahn to Duke Snider following the sixth and final game of the 1953 World Series, as quoted in *The Boys of Summer*.)[78]

"The Marlins have pulled off another national disgrace, winning the NL pennant. After spending 162 games proving themselves not to be the best team of 5, it is nothing but a tribute to the small sample size garbage of October that they can call themselves the best of 16." (Lee Sinins, October 15, 2003, in *ATM Reports*.)

All true. And, although beauty, rottenness and disgrace may be in the eye of the beholder, you have to feel sorry for Cubs fans (this one's for you, Mark Dicken and John Schlickman.) Fifty-eight years is a long time. No other major league team has ever gone 58 years between World Series appearances. It's been 44 years for the Second City's second team, the White Sox. The Phillies' longest dry spell was just 35 years. The Braves' 34 and the Pirates' 33. The Angels made it in their 41st year. The Browns spent their first 42 years in the wilderness, but even they made it in 1944. It was 41 years for the Indians. The combined Senators/Twins' longest stretch was 32 years, the Athletics'

(Philadelphia, K.C. and Oakland) 41 years and the Senators/Rangers' 42 years. Even the Astros (41 years – that seems to be the magic number, doesn't it?) and the Expos (34 years) haven't suffered for that long. And now, for the Cubs, it's going to be at least 59 years.

Actually, the real sorrow in Chicago began 74 years ago, on that afternoon in Shibe Park in 1929. Prior to that, the Cubbies had been a power in the National League from its very start in 1876, winning pennants in 76, 80, 81, 82, 85, 86, 06, 07, 08, 10 and 18… and winning two of the official five World Series they played in. However, after dropping the 1929 Series to the Athletics, they proceeded to stumble over the next 16 years, getting flattened in the 1932, 1935 and 1938 Series, before taking the Tigers to seven games in their last appearance in 1945.

You know, I really don't believe in curses, whether they be at the behest of the greatest baseball player of all time or an aggrieved goat owner. And yet… and yet… you could see this one coming. At least, you could see it coming on the evening of Oct. 14, 2003. Almost 74 years to the day from the biggest disaster in World Series history, the 2003 Cubs saw history repeat itself… blowing a shutout, and a seemingly safe lead, late in a key postseason game. Even worse, blowing said lead by getting absolutely squashed by a steamroller that was rolling mainly through improbable circumstances. (Of course, it doesn't help to have Dusty Baker deciding when and when not to change pitchers.) Once that 8-3 game was in the records, you could book it… the Cubs were crushed… they were toast. Because… 74 years ago, in the bottom of the seventh, Charlie Root had the A's just as much under control as Mark Prior had the Marlins. With an 8-0 lead, and just nine outs to go before the Cubbies would even the Series at two games apiece, Chicagoans were looking forward to the Series coming back to the Windy City.

Then, Al Simmons stepped up to the plate to lead off the home seventh, and hit a rocket onto the roof of the left field stands at Shibe Park. Simmons thought he'd wasted a home run. But Jimmie Foxx singled, and Bing Miller stepped to the plate. And, for the first time, fate (or something) took a hand in the lives of the Chicago Cubs. Was it the same fate that put Steve Bartman along the left field foul line to keep Moises Alou from catching that foul ball on Oct. 14, 2003? Was it the same fate that had Alex Gonzalez – a fine defensive shortstop – blow a double play ball that would have ended 2003's fatal inning at 3-1, Cubs? Was it the same fate that had the wind blowing out – thus erasing the Cubs' biggest advantage, pitcher Kerry Wood – on Oct. 15, 2003? Who's to say?

Miller lined a ball at centerfielder Hack Wilson, who lost it in the sun, whereupon the ball dropped for a single. Now, Hack Wilson wasn't a great centerfielder by any means. But, he was a darn site better in the outfield than Chipper Jones, or Ryan Klesko, or Smead Jolley, or Lou Novikoff, or Babe Herman or Glenallen Hill or Greg Luzinski or any of the other hundreds of others who have played out there in baseball's glorious history. And, this time, he just lost a catchable ball in the sun. And so, James J. Dykes came up next with two on and none out, and singled for another run. 8-2. Now, shortstop Joe Boley was the batter. Maybe you've never heard of Joe Boley. He was sort of the 1929 version of, let's say, Mike Mordecai. Here are their key career batting figures…

	OBP	SLG	OPS
Mordecai	.305	.368	.673
Boley	.323	.354	.677

Get the picture? Joe Boley playing a key hitting role on Oct. 12, 1929 is just as strange as Mike Mordecai getting a three-run double in the Marlins' eight-spot of Oct. 14, 2003. Connie Mack called Boley over before he went up to hit, and told him that Root is losing it, and that he should swing at the first pitch,[79] on the theory that Root would just try to get one over on a weak hitter. Boley singled to right and now it was 8-3 with two on and still no outs. George Burns then pinch hit for pitcher Eddie Rommel, and popped up, and the Cubs finally had an out. However, Camera Eye Max Bishop didn't need his record-setting ID as the next batter. He almost removed Root's head with a line drive, and made the score 8-4, with one out and still two on. Root took a shower, and Art Nehf came in to protect what still could have been a pretty safe four run lead. One ground ball to the infield, and the Cubs are out of the inning.

But, it was not meant to be, and now came the key moment in the game, the 1929 Steve Bartman moment when the theme from *The Twilight Zone* was first heard in Chicago. The batter was "The Donk" (as his teammates called him), Mule Haas. He ripped a line drive right at Wilson in center, and Hack lost this one in the sun as well, breaking in and having the ball go over his head. The centerfield fence in Shibe Park in those days was practically out by Broad Street (which was actually some six blocks away, but, you get the picture… actually, the fence was 468 feet at this time),[80] and Haas easily circled the bases for an inside the park home run. So, instead of being out of the inning with five run lead (for, if Wilson had caught Miller's and Haas' hits, there would have been three outs at this point, and only three runs would have scored), it was now an 8-7 game with only one out.

Nehf, rapidly coming unglued like the rest of the Cubbies, then walked Mickey Cochrane. Joe McCarthy figured he'd seen enough of Artie, and brought in Sheriff Blake to arrest the Athletics' (I've always wanted to use that line) rally. And so, Al Simmons, batting for the second time, bounced a single over third, and Double XX followed with another single to tie the game at 8. McCarthy, clearly desperate, then brought in his ace, 22-game winner Pat Malone, who was scheduled to start the next game, to pitch to Miller. Didn't make a bit of difference. McCarthy could have brought in Three Finger Brown and it wouldn't have mattered (in fact, Dusty Baker could have pitched the ghost of Three Finger Brown in game seven Wednesday and it wouldn't have mattered)… even his ace was rattled… he hit Miller with a pitch to load the bases, and bring up Dykes for the second time. And, for a third time in one inning, the now inexorable fate of the Chicago Cubs took a hand. Dykes – having lost track of the score in the offensive explosion, thought the A's were still down a run – and whacked a ball out toward the left field wall, where a truly bad outfielder, Riggs Stephenson, was playing. Dykes was only hoping for a sacrifice fly that (he thought) would tie the game.[81] He got much more. The ball went off Stephenson's finger tips for what was scored as a two run double, and now the A's led 10-8. Who cares that Malone struck out Boley and Burns to end the inning… the A's had gotten three extra outs (and 10 runs) in a single inning, and had Lefty Grove warming up in the bullpen. Old Mose struck out four of the six batters he faced, and, not for the last time, the Cubs were dead.

(What a lot of people don't know is that Malone came back and threw a shutout for eight innings the next day, and took a 2-0 lead into the bottom of the ninth, whereupon Bishop singled, Haas tied the game with a home run – this one over the right field wall – Simmons doubled and, after an intentional walk to Foxx, Miller ended the Series with another double.)

Hard to believe, isn't it? And, you know what? The events of Oct. 12, 1929 were not the only time a bizarre result in a penultimate postseason game snatched defeat from the jaws of victory through the slings and arrows of outrageous fortune (how's that for mixing metaphors?) and absolutely crushed the hopes and fortunes of its victim. Fact is, it happened three more times before bizarre fate struck on Oct. 14, 2003… on Oct. 5, 1941, on Oct. 26, 1985, and on Oct. 25, 1986… leaving us to postulate that a traumatic postseason loss that puts a team on the brink of extinction is also death for the victims' hopes in the next game.

The events of Oct. 5, 1941 have already been rehashed. So…. Oct. 26, 1985 was a day all good St. Louis Cardinal fans will remember as Don Denkinger's Myopic Moment… when he called a clearly "out" Jorge Orta "safe" at first base on the first play in the bottom of the ninth, leading not only to the Royals' two-run game-winning rally, but to the Cardinals completely falling apart from the moment Orta hit the bag. The score the next day… Royals 11, Cards 0, in one of the most gruesome sights ever seen in the World Series. In fact, the only more gruesome sight took place 364 days later, when Met Mookie Wilson's dribbler went through Red Sox Bill Buckner's legs, and gave the Mets an absurd extra inning win in game six. Game seven score: Mets 8, Red Sox (who blew a 3-0 lead – sound familiar?)5.

Item: October 1, 1949 and October 2, 1949 – Thanks largely to a home run from an unexpected source and a pop fly double, the Boston Red Sox blow two games in Yankee Stadium, thus losing the American League pennant to the Yankees.

Alright, now it's certainly time to cue the theme from the *Twilight Zone*. I still don't believe in curses, but, this is getting pretty strange. Maybe it is true that he who doesn't learn from history is doomed to repeat it. Just as the Cubs saw history repeat itself three nights ago, so too did the Red Sox last night. So, just maybe, the Bambino and Murphy the Goat are having a good laugh somewhere. (Of course, it doesn't help to have Grady Little deciding when and when not to change pitchers.)

Return to the closing days of the 1949 regular season. The Yankees had led the Sox all year, holding a 12 game lead in July. However, injuries and the Sox' two pitching aces, Mel Parnell and Ellis Kinder, closed the gap and Boston actually had a one game lead going into the final two games of the year which, as fate would have it, were at Yankee Stadium. Game one, on Oct. 1, put Allie Reynolds against Parnell. The Sox chased a wild Indian early in the game and took a 4-0 lead in the third inning. (When's the last time the Sox had a 4-0 lead early in a key game? Gee, seems like just yesterday.) However, the Sox' 25-game winner faltered a little in the middle innings, and manager Joe McCarthy (yes, the same Joe McCarthy who kept shuffling pitchers in and out on Oct. 12, 1929... I told you this was going to be weird...) pulled him in the fifth for Joe Dobson (whose ERA was more than a run higher than Parnell's) to get the platoon advantage and the Yankees tied it at 4. With two outs in the bottom of the eighth, the Yankees' fifth outfielder, Johnny Lindell, who would hit all of six dingers on the year, pulled a Dobson fastball down the left field line (where else?) for what would prove to be the game winner.[82] At least it wasn't a knuckleball. (In case you're interested, Aaron Boone hit six home runs for the Yankees during the regular season.)

It gets better. Or worse, if you're a Red Sox fan. The last game, on Oct. 2, with the two teams tied, pitted the Yankees' Vic Raschi (a pure power pitcher who liked to throw close to hitters… clearly, Roger Clemens was his stand-in) against the Sox' Ellis Kinder (who, although he could throw hard, was an excellent and deceptive slider/ change-up pitcher as well… and who liked to throw at hitters… hmmm, Pedro). Just two of the best pitchers in the AL going head-to-head with the season on the line, that's all. Kinder, trailing 1-0 in the top of the eighth, was lifted for a pinch hitter (by Joe McCarthy, of course), and the Yankees scored four times in the bottom half of the inning off of Parnell and Tex Hughson. The key blow? A bases-loaded pop fly double by Jerry Coleman that drove in three runs to make the score 5-0. (He picked up an extra RBI on Jorge Posada in the deal.) The Sox came back to score three times in the top of the ninth, but it was too late and the Yankees won 5-3.[83]

Well, it's probably still safe to say that the best team DID win in New York last night, just like the best team did win in New York on Oct. 2, 1949. So, what's going to happen in the World Series? After this year's National League playoffs, and as Lee Sinins has so astutely mentioned, the small sample size of games in a playoff series means that almost literally anything is possible. If you don't believe so, ask Hack Wilson, or Mickey Owen, or Jorge Orta and Bill Buckner. Having said that, we'll go out on a limb and pick the Yankees on the basic theory that the Marlins don't belong on the same field with them. Or, let's put it another way… who would you rather have in your rotation? Mussina/Pettite/Clemens/Wells or Beckett/Pavano/Willis/Redman? A 300 game winner is the Yankees' number three starter, for goodness sakes, and here's Marlins' manager Jack McKeon, afraid to let Brad Penney go near the mound. (And, he ought to be afraid to let Dontrelle Willis go there, too.) And then there's the Yankees' ace in the hole (and the bullpen), Mariano Rivera.

Now, Mike Lowell and Derrek Lee are pretty good in the infield for Florida, but don't you think that Giambi/Soriano/Jeter sort of outweigh them? And that's without even using Nick Johnson. And while Karim Garcia isn't much in right, the Yankees' Hideki Matsui and Bernie Williams are at worst the equal of Juan Juan and Juan Two (Pierre and Encarnacion), Jeff Conine and 20-year-old Miguel Cabrera. The catchers, we'll call that a wash.

Actually, looking at the big picture, it's a shame. This is exactly the wrong match up for baseball. Think of the possibilities in a Red Sox/ Cubs World Series. Think of the media blitz, the marketing potential, the PR... football gets shoved right to the back pages. Instead, we have possibly the most hated team in sports, and a team with only 10,000 real fans (the number that came out to their games regularly last year, when they were lousy... Howard Garson, this means you... take a bow.)

Oh well, that's baseball.

CHAPTER 46

October 27, 2003

Item: October 16, 1969 – The New York Mets defeat the Baltimore Orioles, 5-3, thus winning the 1969 World Series.

Depending on your point of view, baseball is either a funny game (Joe Garagiola), a great blessing (beisbol has been bery, bery good to me), frustrating – especially in conjunction with the postseason (Lee Sinins, et al), or inexplicable (see: Joaquin Andujar).

Joaquin's point of view may be the best. Certainly, there is no good explanation as to the Florida Marlins' 2003 World Series victory, especially if you try to analyze it from the point of view of either the personnel involved or the statistics generated. The Marlins' 1997 championship is pretty easy to explain. Just like the 2003 Yankees, the 1997 Marlins were the best team that money could buy (even though they didn't catch the Braves in the regular season that year). But, in 2003, not only were the Yankees' the best team (either bought or otherwise), the Marlins managed to go all the way by throwing away their limited fiscal resources on such sucker deals as paying Mike Hampton to pitch for the Braves. So, what's the story here? The answer doesn't exist, however, history does provide us with an answer, because, three times in the past – 1906, 1914 and 1969 – teams with very similar resumes to the 2003 Marlins walked off with shocking World Series titles. That is, three teams – the '06 White Sox, the '14 Braves and the '69 Mets – came from out of nowhere in the latter part of the season and flattened their competition all the way through the World Series like a steamroller driven by midget race car driver and Wild Hoss Pepper Martin.

The 1906 World Series was going to be a slam dunk. The Chicago Cubs were coming off a 116-win campaign that marks the 20th Century record for winning percentage (.763). The Chicago White Sox were notable only because they had the lowest batting average ever for championship team. Admittedly, this was just about the deadest of the Deadball Era, but still, the Sox hit .230 as a team and slugged .286. They put exactly one top-notch player on the field among their regular eight – future Hall of Famer George Davis at shortstop. However, something happened on the West side (where the Cubs played in that era) and South side of Chicago… and the White Sox won in six games… thanks largely to some hot, relatively young, pitchers (the Cubs hit .196 for the Series) and a major head of steam that started building in May 1906. In what Bill James characterized somewhat inaccurately in *The Politics of Glory* as "a perfect execution of the marathon runner's strategy," (top flight marathoners as often run from the front as from behind… for instance, Joan Benoit in the first women's Olympic Marathon in 1984) the Sox moved from seventh place in mid-May to sixth at the end of May to fifth an the end of June to fourth at the end of July. And then, they proceeded to tear off 19 straight wins, going into first on August 12.[84] Think they had a little momentum built up by the time October came around? Well, no one on the national scene thought so except ChiTown sportswriter Hugh Fullerton, who made his name by being the only pundit to predict a White Sox win in the Series. Maybe only Fullerton expected Nick Altrock (29) to go 1-1 with an ERA of 1.00, and Ed Walsh (25) to go 2-0 with an ERA of 1.20, and Doc White (27) to go 1-1 with a save and a 1.80 ERA against the mighty Cubs. They did, and thus was born the Legend of the Hitless Wonders.

Skip ahead eight years. The best team in baseball – in fact the best team in baseball pretty much since 1902 – is the Philadelphia Athletics. Only, this isn't the best team that money can buy… since Connie Mack didn't have much of that stuff. What he did have was a great system of informal scouts that made Mack the most successful team builder in the game in the era when winners were built by skill and strategy, and not by bucks. Well-established by 1914 as the American League's first dynasty, the A's had finished first in 1902, 05, 10, 11 and 13, and had played a significant role in the pennant races in every other year except 1901 (when they didn't get hot until too late in the year) and 1908 (when Mack was re-building.)

Then there were the Boston Braves. Led by a raging madman on the field, and a perfect Southern gentleman off the field – in both cases, George Stallings, the inventor of platooning – the Boston NL franchise had been the downtrodden of the earth since the heyday of the Frank Selee era ended in 1899, finishing last from 1909 to 1912, before pulling up all the way to fifth in 1913, 13 games under .500 and 31 ½ games out of first. Like the 1906 Sox, the 1914 Braves scared no one on the field, even though they did have two future Hall of Famers, Rabbit Maranville and Johnny Evers (both of whom got there for reasons other than their hitting… Maranville for his fielding and Evers for Tinker and Chance). The Braves' best hitter was one Joe Connolly (who?) at .306 with a .494 slugging mark. However, the Braves did have starters Dick Rudolph (26 years old, 27-10 and a 2.36 ERA) and Bill James (no, not THAT Bill James, this one was 22 in 1914 and went 26-7 with a 1.90 ERA), and, they split the four wins in the Braves' sweep between them, giving up just one earned run. Of course, it didn't hurt that the Braves were on a roll in October… so much so that Stallings was widely hailed as the "Miracle Man." Dead last as late as July 18, the Braves reached seventh on July 19, sixth on July 20 and fourth on July 21 (close race that year, huh?) They made .500 on August 1, second place on August 10 (still six-and-half-games behind the Giants) and then battled the McGrawmen for supremacy throughout early September, winning the pennant by 10 ½ games on the strength of going 34-10 over their last 44 games.

And, while the A's may have been the best team in baseball, individually they may also have been overconfident. For instance, Mack thought he had sent Chief Bender to scout the Braves in New York one day in September when the Chief wasn't pitching. When Mack bumped into Bender on the streets near Shibe Park, the future Hall of Famer told him he didn't see the need for scouting a bush league outfit.[85] Or, perhaps the Athletics were paying more attention during the Series to another pot of gold at the end of another rainbow... the dollars the Federal League was offering them for the 1915 season. Indeed, the Braves' four game sweep was such a shock that rumors that the A's threw the Series were around for years to come. That's not what happened – such talk was all rumors and no proof – and the sweep was enough to cement the Legend of the Miracle Man.

Now it's 1969. And while the Mets of 1962 to 1967 have widely been characterized as lovable losers, the honest fact is they were just plain losers, finishing 10th five times and ninth once and averaging 108 losses per year in the worst sustained stretch of baseball in history. Even though the 1968 team went 73-89 (whoopee!) they still only got back the ninth place. However, the '68 Mets had something the earlier Three Stooges versions didn't have... namely 23-year-old Tom Seaver, 25-year-old Jerry Koosman and 21-year-old Nolan Ryan. And, for 1969, they added 22-year-old rookie Gary Gentry and 24-year-old rookie Tug McGraw. They needed all those young guns, because the team they were putting on the field didn't have a best player. Tommie Agee hit 26 home runs and Cleon Jones hit .340, but neither one of them will ever be admitted to the Hall of Fame unless they buy a ticket. And, the Mets were facing a 109-win juggernaut in the World Series, the Baltimore Orioles, a team with two certifiable Hall of Famers in the field (the Robinsons), plus their leading home run hitter, Boog Powell, and three superlative young pitchers of their own – Dave McNally (26) 20-7, Pancakes Palmer (23) 16-4 and Tom Phoebus (24) 14-7. Plus they had a 32-year-old ace in Mike Cuellar (23-11).

Didn't matter one little bit. The Mets blew down the home stretch, going 38-11 after August 14 to demolish the faltering Cubs by eight games, and, after Cuellar beat Seaver 4-1 in game one, sweeping the next four contests 2-1, 5-0, 2-1 and 5-3. They were so dominant they didn't even need their relief ace (McGraw) and Ryan, who had hog-tied the Braves in the NLCS, was limited to an easy save in the 5-0 game three. Thus the Legend of the Miracle Mets entered the baseball lexicon. (Right after the Miracle Man, naturally.)

Same story, repeated three times. Carried by a young pitching staff, a previously mediocre team gets hot late in the season and, despite having a markedly inferior lineup to its opponent, rolls all the way to a World Series title.

So, it has happened three times before. However, there is a codicil to this too-simple explanation to the 2003 World Series… other teams have come into the World Series red hot, and fallen flat… notably the 1938 Cubs (who won 10 straight in late September) and the 1951 Giants (who won 16 in a row in late Summer), to say nothing of the Oakland Athletics over the past four seasons. Collectively, the best team in baseball over the second half of the 2000, 2001, 2002 and 2003 seasons, Oakland has yet to make the World Series in the 21st Century. Connie Mack would understand.

This, of course, is one reason why baseball is so frustrating to careful analysts. There's just no way, from an analytical viewpoint, that the Marlins should have won the World Series (see below). In fact, the Marlins shouldn't even have qualified for the Series. If indeed the post season is about excellence, then the Wild Card has to go.

Perhaps all the frustrated analysts will be comforted by what happened to the 1906 Cubs, the 1914 Braves and the 1969 Mets after their big years… all three largely went back to mediocre status, thus confirming their fluky World Series wins. Although the Sox were part of the dramatic 1908 three-team race, their next pennant came with a completely different team in 1917. The Braves fell even harder – second, third, sixth and seventh in the next four years. They didn't win another pennant until 1948. As for the Mets, they won 83, 83, 83 and 82 games over the next four years, reaching the World Series in the 82-win season (1973) with an awful 82-79 record in one of the biggest flukes of all time. They didn't get good again until the mid-80s.

Finally, a few specific observations on the 2003 Series.

As was the case with the 1969 Mets, the 2003 Marlins didn't have a best hitter, at least, not in the World Series. The much-discussed Juan Pierre, who is NOT the second coming of Rickey Henderson, did lead the team with an .890 OPS, but that meant very little in the box scores, since the Marlins' leadoff man only scored two runs in six games and was one for two in stealing bases. Just in case you're wondering, here are Pierre's career averages compared to Henderson's…

	On-base	**Slugging**	**OPS**
Pierre	.357	.372	.729
Henderson	.401	.419	.820

Alex Gonzalez did have a .500 slugging percentage, but he only drove in two runs and had zero walks, so, outside of his game four-winning home run, how big a factor was Mr. Gonzalez? More importantly, how big a factor for the Series as a whole were all the Marlins' hitters, collectively?

	AB	R	H	2B	3B	HR	RBI	BB	K	SB	BA	OBP	SLG	OPS
Marlins	203	17	47	8	0	2	17	14	48	2	.232	.281	.300	.581
Yankees	207	21	54	10	1	6	21	22	49	2	.261	.332	.406	.738

Rob Neyer, in his ESPN.com column, did the best mid-Series analysis, predicting that the team that hit the most home runs and drew the most walks would end up the winner… not the team with the best "small-ball" attack. (Why do so many baseball people and sportswriters… a lot of whom should know better… love small-ball so much? Is Ty Cobb down there somewhere ghostwriting?) Well, the Yankees scored more runs, hit with far more power (their Isolated Power was more than twice the Marlins'), including out-homering the Marlins 6-2, drew more walks (their Isolated Discipline was .022 higher), had a better K/W ratio (which also means that the Yankee pitchers had a better K/W ratio than the Marlins' pitchers), and, as a result, absolutely dominated in OPS. The Marlins' collective OPS, for goodness sakes, was below the Ordonez Line. Didn't matter one little bit. So, that leaves the pitching… As previously noted, young pitchers sometimes do ride a hot streak through the World Series. Certainly Josh Beckett (1-1, 1.10 ERA) and Brad Penny (2-0, 2.19) did just that. But, overall, the Yankees' team ERA (2.13) was still way better than the Marlins' (3.21), as was their K/W ratio and hits per inning.

So, how did the Marlins win? In one, simple, four letter word…

luck. And any other explanation is over-analyzing the outcome. The Flukes won the same way the Braves won in 1914 and the same way the Mets won in 1969 (the 1906 Series was more a matter of good pitching by the Sox)... by winning the one run games. As has been pretty conclusively proven by others far more knowledgeable than your humble scribe, success in one run games is largely a matter of luck... it doesn't even carry over from year-to-year, to say nothing of holding true in a four, five, six or seven game series... no matter how good (or bad) the teams involved may be. In 1914, the Braves were 2-0 in the Series' one-run games. In 1969, the Mets were 2-0 in that Series' one-run games. And, in 2003, the Marlins were 2-0 in games one and four – the one-run games. (In all fairness, they did have some help in game four when Yankees' manager Joe Torre insisted on leaving Mariano Rivera on the bench while waiting to get the lead.)

Sometimes, that's the way the rabbit's foot falls.

CHAPTER 47

November 3, 2003

Item: October 14, 1911 – The New York Giants come out for the first game of the World Series wearing black uniforms.

John J. McGraw, in addition to being one of the most successful managers in baseball history, was also an amateur psychologist, one who would look for any advantage to gain an edge for his team. Fortunately, the Fashion Police weren't around in the first two decades of the 20th Century, because McGraw's mind games and his love of winning led to the Giants being decked out in some pretty awful outfits, with the all-time stinker probably being the 1916 unis – a cross-hatched pattern with violet the predominant trim color. (McGraw liked NYU's colors.) You wear something like that today on a major league field, and you'd be laughed out of baseball.

McGraw first started playing around with psychology in outfitting his troops only six or seven decades before the Oakland Raiders decided they looked bad in black uniforms. Of course, "bad" has two meanings in this case, but that never stopped McGraw. The 1901 Baltimore Orioles help christen the first American League season with a road uniform that indicated Manager McGraw was willing to try anything… either that, or he was a bird-watcher on the side. That's because the O's uniforms were a direct copy of the coloring of their namesake – all black with orange trim, including black and orange striped socks and an orange "O" on the shirt front.[86] It's a shame the season in those days didn't last through the end of October… the O's would have been real popular at Halloween. Fortunately for Iron Man McGinnity, Wilbert Robinson, and the rest of the Orioles, the black uniforms went into the closet after one season. Can you imagine running around all summer, in that non-air conditioned era, dressed in black flannel?

Still, McGraw liked the black uniform idea, and he brought it back for the 1905 World Series. Having moved to the National League Giants in 1902, McGraw had an entirely new set of uniforms made up for the first official World Series – all black with a white capital "N" and a white capital "Y" on the chest. Did that make the Giants look evil? The early 20th Century version of Darth Vader? Well, that's what McGraw wanted… he typically went out of his way to paint his teams as the "bad guys," even to the point of sometimes demanding police protection for the Giants when they hit towns on the road. And, he undeniably got a thrill when the Giants came out for the Series in black… besides, he thought the new uniforms would give his team an edge over the A's, who were still wearing their old gray flannels from the regular season.

Actually, 1905 wasn't the first time the Giants wore black uniforms. Back in the late 1880s, Giants' Hall of Fame pitcher Tim Keefe designed an all-black uniform with raised white lettering (New York) and sold owner John Day on the idea that his team would look good in basic black. Keefe was, if nothing else, versatile.

Now, as to whether or not a new black uniform helped Christy Matthewson throw three shutouts in the 1905 Series… well, that's a matter of question. And, it seems even more unlikely that McGraw's uniforms caused Rube Waddell to wrestle Andy Coakley on a train platform in Providence, R.I., hurt his left shoulder, and subsequently miss the 1905 World Series altogether. However, the Giants did take the Series 4-1, and McGraw must have figured he'd hit on something. So, when the Giants made their next appearance in the Series in 1911 – once again against the Athletics – out came the black uniforms again, this time with the white NY on the sleeves. At least, that's the usual version of this story. It would seem, though, from a photo in Henry Thomas' excellent biography of his grandfather, *Walter Johnson*, that McGraw may have had black uniforms on his mind prior to the 1911 Series. Although Thomas does not remark on this revealing picture –

not surprising, since the book is about Johnson – he includes a shot of the two pitching icons of the early part of the 20th Century, Johnson and Christy Mathewson, shaking hands upon the occasion of their first meeting. The Big Six is wearing the black uniform with the white NY clearly visible on his left sleeve. What's interesting is that, according to Thomas' caption, the picture was taken in Atlanta during Spring Training 1911...[87] in other words, seven months before the Giants turned up in the World Series wearing the same all-black unis. Now, there would seem to be only two possible explanations for this. One, the picture was actually taken in Spring Training 1912, after the 1911 World Series, and McGraw was trying to get some additional use out of the once-worn black suits (remember, there was no sports memorabilia market back then... just imagine, though, what that black uniform of Matty's would bring today on the open market... can you say "six figures?") The other possibility is that Mac had the black uniforms already made up well before the 1911 Series, and was just waiting for another World Series to officially bring them out. There exists no record that I know of that the Giants used the black uniforms during the 1911 or 1912 regular season. However, given the uncertainty inherent in trying to judge colors in the black-and-white photography of the day, it's a little hard to say exactly what colors teams were wearing. There exist quite a few photos from the Deadball Era, mostly of the two New York and the two Chicago teams, where very dark colored uniforms are worn.

In any case, in October 1911 McGraw must have been thinking, hey, if it worked once against the Mackmen, it'll work a second time. Nope. The black unis clearly didn't bother Home Run Baker, whose two famous blasts – one against Matty and one against Rube Marquard – gave him his nickname and led Philadelphia to a 4-2 Series win... putting the all-black Giants World Series uniforms back in the closet for good.

But, as previously noted, basic black in baseball wasn't the sole province of John McGraw. In fact, 1905 and 1911 weren't even the only times black uniforms turned up in the World Series. Remember the 1979 World Series? The second American League version of the

Baltimore Orioles blew a 3-1 lead and lost to a Pittsburgh Pirates team that wore the most awful collection of uniforms ever seen on the planet… including an all-black version. (Recall the previously-mentioned all-yellow version that made Willie Stargell look like the largest squeeze bottle of mustard in the world.)

And, wouldn't you know it, in the World Series just concluded, the New York Yankees – who started life as those 1901 Baltimore Oriole-colored Baltimore Orioles (they moved to New York in 1903) – lost to yet another team wearing unbearably ugly black uniform (shirts, in this case)… the Florida Marlins. It is truly a wonder that the Fashion Police didn't invade the field at Yankee Stadium and haul Jack McKeon off for committing a first degree affront to good taste – especially in comparison to the Yankees' classic home pinstripes.

So, while the on-going regular season dominance of the Yankees and Braves may be bad for baseball, the Marlins' recent win presents a twin-edged sword for the sport. Yes, it shows that even the most downtrodden, anonymous teams can win, but, it also showcased some of the ugliest uniforms ever seen since John McGraw's days. Maybe New York teams–the Mets, f'rinstance – or former New York teams, like the now-San Francisco Giants, can get away with the black shirt look… but, in general, this has just got to be bad for baseball as well. Knowing that imitation is not only the sincerest form of flattery, but also one of the commonest phenomena in professional sports, can we then expect to see a proliferation of black shirts in baseball?

Sorry, but it's too late to worry about that, since the Devil Rays, Royals, Orioles (again?) and Pirates (ditto) as well as the Giants and Mets were also appearing in black shirts during 2003. At least the all-black look hasn't been seen for 20 years, when the Pirates finally stopped imitating a bag of the Licorice Sticks.

In case you're interested in exploring this subject at great length, the definitive work on baseball uniforms is Marc Okkonen's book, *Baseball Uniforms of the 20th Century*, the last word on just about every uniform iteration ever to take the field, compiled by the acknowledged expert on uniforms. Or, perhaps you want to do more than just research historic uniforms. If you want to *look* the part, go to www.mitchellandness.com, the web site for the oldest sporting goods company in Philadelphia. No, Mitchell & Ness doesn't have the actual 1908 Red Sox jersey with a red sock on the chest (although M&N has been around since 1904), but they do make replica jerseys of a wide variety of classic, vintage styles. Originally the biggest and best name in the standard sporting goods market in Philadelphia, Mitchell & Ness expanded out into making vintage replicas some 20 years ago, and now, as Mitchell and Ness Nostalgia Company, are THE name on the national scene in providing replicas that match the originals as closely as possible. Want a blue satin jersey like the Brooklyn Dodgers wore in 1944? This is place to get one. How about a Houston Colt 45s or a Seattle Pilots jersey? You go it. A 1903 Pirates road jersey like the one worn by Honus Wagner? Call 267-765-0663. They even have those awful mustard yellow and all-black jerseys that made Dave Parker look like something out of a low-budget horror movie (The Creature that Devoured Pittsburgh...) Of course, you can also go back to Okkonen's book, and find even more black uniforms... the Highlanders (1903, 1906) and Senators (1906)[88] both wore them, as did the Giants (at least only their jerseys were black then) from 1977 to 1982.[89] John McGraw would have loved it.

Actually, Okkonen's research and excellent illustrations also make it clear that tacky uniform designs have not been limited to basic black. The 1906 Giants[90] and the 1921 Indians[91] celebrated their World Series triumphs the previous year by coming out in uniforms that had "World's Champions" in bold lettering across the chest. Real modest. Then there were the 1936 Reds, under the direction of the brilliant, though sometimes erratic, Larry MacPhail. They sometimes showed up for home games looking like upside-down cherry parfaits... sporting white tops and bright red pants.[92] However, after that particular assault to good taste, boredom (or maybe sanity) prevailed pretty much until the advent of the Era of Bad Taste – the Seventies. The decade that gave us disco also produced such other atrocities (without even going back to mention the awful get-ups the Pirates appeared in) as...

The Orioles' 1971 bright orange tops – which made Boog Powell look like the Great Pumpkin…

The Braves' hideous softball-style uniforms – what a shame that Hank Aaron had to set the home run record dressed like a Sunday Beer League player…

The all-red '75 Indians' (poor Powell was on that team, too) and '79 Phillies' (ditto, Greg Luzinski… he looked a little bit like a very large blood clot, or a big grape) uniforms…

The Astros' gaudy and silly-looking orange, yellow and red horizontal striped tops…

The Padres' equally bad, though drab and not gaudy, mustard and chocolate outfits… (their recent military camouflage uniforms are in such bad taste that they won't even be mentioned in this discussion.)

And, finally, the few times in 1976 when Hall of Famer Bill Veeck persuaded his White Sox to take the field wearing black shorts. Hey guys… nice knees!

But wait, we've missed the last word in ugly uniforms. The only creations even worse than the Pirates' mix-and-match black, gold and striped combos. The outfits that really started the trend toward ugly uniform colors. That could only mean… the green and gold outfits first worn by the Kansas City A's in 1963. That sound is Connie Mack, spinning like a top.

CHAPTER 48

November 10, 2003

Item: November 15, 1968 – Pitcher and soon-to-be-author James Alan Bouton transcribes the first words,"I signed my contract today to play for the Seattle Pilots..."[93] of the book that will make him far more famous than his pitching... ***Ball Four.***

What is the greatest baseball book ever written? Is it *Ball Four*? *Shoeless Joe*? *The Great American Novel*? *The Long Season*? *The Boys of Summer*? *The Glory of Their Times*? *The Bill James Historical Baseball Abstract*? *The Macmillan Baseball Encyclopedia*? *The Natural*? *The Summer Game*? *Babe*? *Ty Cobb*? *The Southpaw*? *The Year the Yankees Lost the Pennant*? *Bums*? *The Giants of the Polo Grounds*? *Pitching in a Pinch*? *Even the Browns*? *Only the Ball was White*? *The Diamond Appraised*? *Eight Men Out*? *Win Shares*? *Total Baseball*? *The Baseball Cyclopedia*? *Fear Strikes Out*? *Beadle's Dime Base Ball Player*? *Judge Landis and Twenty-Five Years of Baseball*? *Bang the Drum Slowly*? *You Know Me, Al*? *Glory Fades Away*? *The Putnam Team History Series*? *The Fireside Book of Baseball* (all four of them)? *Veeck... as in Wreck*? *Moneyball*? Or none of the above?

And how do you categorize baseball books? Are we talking non-fiction or fiction? And, within non-fiction, what kind of non-fiction? History books? Current events books? Statistics books? What is the greatest of any or all of these?

Obviously, an unanswerable question. So, herewith are the Top 20 Baseball Books of All Time, starting with the five greatest; *Ball Four*, the *Macmillan Baseball Encyclopedia, The Bill James Historical Baseball Abstract, The Long Season* and *The Great American Novel*. (Long pause.) Sooooo... what are the criteria for answering the unanswerable? In the case of the first four named works, it's a larger definition of "great." In this case, great means an excellent book that in some very basic fashion, changed the way people look at baseball. Books that caused a paradigm shift. Books that went where no man has gone before (why do you think *Star Trek* is the greatest Sci Fi phenomenon of all time?) Books that, in some elemental way, shook baseball, and left the Great American Game a different game. It's a definition that can also be applied to the old chestnut, who's the greatest baseball (basketball, etc.) player of all time… a definition that, by the way, gives us George Herman Ruth and Wilton Norman Chamberlain as the greatest of their sports. (Sorry, no arguments allowed here… Wilt changed basketball as surely as the Babe changed baseball. Even more surely… Wilt caused several rules changes, something no one ever dreamed of doing for Michael Jordan.)

The fifth of the "Great Five" is admittedly a subjective choice, since it's a novel. But, if you've ever read Phillip Roth's tale of the Patriot League, Babylonian ace Gil Gamesh, Bob Yamm, O.K. Ockatur, Nickname Damur, Word Smith, General Douglas D. Oakhart, Hot Ptah, Roland Agni, Frenchy Astarte, Jolly Cholly Tuminikar, Bud Parusha, Luke Gofannon, Frank and Dubloon Mazuma, Big John Baal (and his predecessors, Spit and Base) and the Ruppert Mundys (Roth named most of his characters after mythological gods), you know it's certainly one the cleverest, most creative pieces of fiction ever created. For baseball fans, it is indeed the Great American Novel.

Besides, Roth clearly knows his baseball… and not just on the level of the average fan. One of his characters espouses the theory (in reality, as Roth notes in his "Acknowledgements," a theory first postulated by Earnshaw Cook in *Percentage Baseball* in 1966) that a lineup should be set up in descending order of run productivity[94] … maybe a theory that is no longer thought to be true, but, remember, Roth was writing this in 1973… sabrmetric didn't even exist then. Roth also knows his baseball history… he visited the Hall of Fame Library in Cooperstown while working on the novel and managed to weave fact in with his fiction, basing several of his characters on real people. For instance… Mundy Manager Ulysses Fairsmith is Connie Mack in disguise. One-armed outfielder Parusha owes a debt to Pete Gray. Yamm and Ockatur, like Eddie Gaedel, are both midgets. Gofannon is a fictional Lou Gehrig. And the Ruppert Mundys, having been made an all-road team by devious owners, clearly take a bow in the direction of Cleveland and the similarly homeless 1899 Spiders. In fact, Roth even knew that baseball teams were once named after their owners… in this case the Mundys owe their handle to the late Glorious Mundy.

How creative is Roth? Well, he created an entire third major league as the focal point of the story, even to the point of changing the names of seven American cities to make them the home of P-League franchises. Newark becomes Port Ruppert. Cheyenne, Wyoming is Terra Incognita, etc. Why did all these Great American Cities change their names? Well, it's for the same reason we've never heard of the Patriot League. That's part of the plot, too. And, believe me, "plot" is the right word. You see, according to the book's narrator, former sportswriter and alliterative ace "Word" Smith (the book's Melvillesque opening line is… "Call me Smitty")[95] the P-League fell apart in 1946 under the assault of those commies from Moscow… almost everyone in the P-League ends up being, if not a Red Agent, a pinko symp. Ultimately, the league folds and even its cities change their names to escape the red taint.

Most of the story revolves around the hapless 1943 Ruppert Mundys, who, thanks to the war and pinch-penny owners, disposed of all their real players and finished 34-120 with the most awful bunch of yahoos ever seen on the field, including a midget, the one-armed outfielder, a one-legged catcher, another outfielder who keeps running into the wall (hello, Pete Reiser), a slugger who can only hit home runs after he hits the bottle, a 14-year-old shortstop and a third baseman in his fifties who can't stay awake on the field. Along the way, the Mundys suffer some of the worst and most regular beatings in baseball history – while almost the entire team is desperately trying to get traded somewhere else – and record their only shutout before the last two weeks of the season in an exhibition against a team of inmates from an insane asylum (a piece so funny that it appeared in the Fourth *Fireside Book of Baseball*). They also ingest large quantities of altered

Wheaties, and, finally, kill their manager, the esteemed Mistah Fairsmith, who had previously survived cannibals in Africa, only to succumb to the Mundys' 31-0 loss in the last game of the season.

Along the way, Roth clearly has a lot of fun… even the name of the book pokes fun at the concept that every writer from Melville to Twain to Hemingway (all of whom Roth parodies) has chased for lo these many years… writing the Great American Novel. Of course, he pokes fun at almost everything else in the book – just about every aspect of baseball, the Red Scare and McCarthyism, the government, communism, capitalism, missionary work and religion, the disabled, Jews, prostitution, African-Americans, and every other writer who has ever dared to think he or she could write the Great American Novel. Sorry folks, it's already been done, by Phillip Roth.

What about the other four? Well, given our definition of "great," it's a tough call, but, give the nod to the Bulldog for *Ball Four* as the greatest non-fiction baseball book of all time. After Bouton's diary of the 1969 season came out in 1970, baseball journalism, which is to say, writing about baseball, would never be the same again. Never would those of us not directly involved with the game ever look at the players, managers, coaches, owners, umpires, etc., in the same way. For the first time, someone really told the truth about what goes on behind the scenes and, as a result, a lot of sportswriters got real mad at Bouton… mainly because they knew all this stuff already, but now, they'd actually have to go to work and write about it, because the word was out to the public. That, my friends, is changing baseball and the way it is perceived. Your classic paradigm shift.

In addition, Bouton provides an invaluable look at the dynamics, players and foibles of an expansion team. So, it's even a research book as well. However, clearly the most memorable character in the book has little scholarly value… because it's Pilots' manager Joe Schultz, whose main exhortation to his expansion team is, "pound that Budweiser." And, the second most memorable character, after Bouton himself, is someone who had already been written about ad infinitum by the time *Ball Four* was published. His name was Mickey Mantle, and Bouton's telling the truth about the Mick, was the other major reason the book stirred up the firestorm. Prior to *Ball Four*, no one, I mean, no one, had the "right" to tell the truth about the All American Boy.

Finally, Bouton cements his place in baseball history with the finest single line ever put in print about the game. The closing sentence to *Ball Four* is the one statement that best summarizes the hold baseball has on all of us who really care about the Great American Game…. and still gives goose bumps after more than 30 years…

"You see, you spend a good piece of your life gripping a baseball and in the end it turns out it was the other way around all the time."[96]

Among the other three of the Great Five, *The Long Season* is clearly the direct ancestor to *Ball Four*. Jim Brosnan's diary of the 1959 season didn't shake the foundation of the baseball world like Ball Four did, but, it is a most worthy candidate for its acclaim, in part because Brosnan actually wrote every word. (Bouton took notes throughout the year – either written or audio recorded – and had them transcribed and edited by Leonard Shecter.) In fact, it's fair to say that Brosnan is the best writer ever to play major league baseball. It is also true that *The Long Season* has been rightly noted as being the first book of its kind – an in-season diary that goes above the Frank Merriwell, gee whiz level to tell some hard truths. And, it's also true that Brosnan was the subject of some little controversy when this book came out in 1960, first because no one believed he actually wrote it himself, and second because it didn't pull many punches, giving honest opinions on a wide variety of subjects; Solly Hemus, sportswriters, race relations in baseball, religion, the English language, fans, etc. What's more, Brosnan was undeterred by the flak, and came back two years later with – to this writer's mind – an even better and more interesting book, *Pennant Race*, which told the story of the Cinderella 1961 Cincinnati Reds' drive to the National League pennant… still the best inside story of a pennant winner and, as such, also a valuable research tool as well. However, *The Long Season* was the first of its kind, and, as such is deserving of its ranking as one of the Five Great Books in Baseball.

Indeed, no less a sportswriter than Jimmy Cannon proclaimed that *The Long Season* was the greatest baseball book ever written.

The last two books are, in many ways, an entry somewhat in the fashion that *Ball Four* and *The Long Season* go together. It is not entirely unfair to say that the Macmillan *Baseball Encyclopedia*, as the first real attempt to systematically record every single major league players' basic statistics, made the Society for American Baseball Research, and the systematic, reasoned search for truths about the game, possible. And, that the revolution that "Mac" started, and that continues today, reached a key moment with the publication of the first *Bill James Historical Baseball Abstract* in 1985. If The *Baseball Encyclopedia* opened innumerable eyes to the fact that baseball had a codified history (especially prior to 1900), then James' first *Historical Abstract* brought that history to life as had never been done before. James was the first to do a painstakingly thorough job putting faces to many of the great names of the past while, at the same time, analyzing their performances to discover truths about their accomplishments. In other words, the *Historical Baseball Abstract* is the first systematic attempt to apply sabrmetric (which, of course, is a term James himself coined) to history on a broad scale.

Of course, along the way James, in his inimitable style, had almost as much fun as Phillip Roth… tossing in sidebars on remarkable minor league performances, uniform styles, platooning, blocking the plate, relief pitching, how the game was played, nicknames, great World Series, and the like. Most enjoyably, James didn't write about Babe Ruth, Chief Bender, Ty Cobb, Cy Young, and the like at great length. Everyone had done that before. He looks at Bender's brother John, Harry Krause, Henry Pulliam, Water Barbare, Bob Crues, Ed Reulbach, Jerry Denny, Bill Lange, Terry Larkin, Steve Gerkin, Ray Perry, Bill Thomas and many other, lesser-known lights. In short, James educates as well as entertains. All in all, a remarkable accomplishment, especially since James was, at the same time, putting out the yearly *Bill James Baseball Abstracts.*

And, while we're at it, let's not forget another remarkable chronicler of baseball history, the man behind *The Baseball Encyclopedia*, Hall of

Fame Librarian Lee Allen, who unfortunately died just before that remarkable volume saw print. Allen and James – two of the seminal figures in the study of baseball.

Over the years, many more great baseball books have hit the shelves, although it is true that the glory years of baseball publishing didn't really begin until the 1960s. Fortunately for those of us who love a great baseball book the way Billy Beane loves on-base percentage, we have a lot to choose from. Realizing that no one can possibly have read all the great baseball books ever written, here is one list of another 15 great books.

First, fiction. Most novels that have a baseball component may or may not be considered baseball books. For instance, although *The Natural* certainly revolves around a baseball player named Roy Hobbs, it's questionable as to whether or not it's a baseball book. A morality play that centers around Eddie Waitkus' unfortunate experience… maybe. But a baseball book? Not unless you're Robert Redford. However, here are three more superb novels written by authors with remarkable insight into the game. Of course, it doesn't hurt that all three are excellent stories as well.

Shoeless Joe by W.P. Kinsella – Probably the most famous piece of written baseball fiction, partly because of the Kevin Costner movie, *Field of Dreams* that came from it. However, if you've never read Bill Kinsella's original masterwork, it should be strongly noted that the book is even better than the movie – and the film was pretty good, especially the part about the way the game brings fathers and sons together (brought tears to my eyes, let me tell you.) Why is that? Because Kinsella didn't use a fictional author named Terrance Mann as Ray Kinsella's partner in his quest for truth, justice and Moonlight Graham… he used the most famous literary recluse of the 20th Century, Jerome David Salinger. Presumably, *Field of Dreams* didn't use J.D. Salinger (or even Seymour Glass) because the makers of the movie were afraid of getting their pants sued off by the New Hampshire Hermit. However, libel laws are apparently flexible enough that Kinsella was able to include Salinger in his original work… one of the truly brilliant strokes in American fiction of any kind that, by itself, ensures *Shoeless Joe* a spot in the pantheon of baseball literary greatness. Besides, how many pieces of baseball fiction have added a phrase to American pop culture… "if you build it, he will come."[97]

If I Never Get Back by Darryl Brock – A remarkable feat of research and a novel that blends fact with fiction. That is, an historical novel about the 1869 Cincinnati Red Stockings, Mark Twain, the IRA (the Irish Republican Army, not the financial vehicle) and a journalist who is definitely looking for love in all the wrong places… only in the case of hero Samuel Clemens Fowler, he's looking in the wrong century. In an improbable combination of a time travel novel, a tribute to Twain, and the story of the first professional baseball team, Brock has put together a book that somehow works, despite its rather far-fetched plot… a 20th Century San Francisco journalist gets off an Amtrak train outside of Cleveland (that was his first mistake) and somehow goes back to June 1869. Whereupon he falls in with the Red Stockings, meets his literary hero (who he happens to be named after), joins the Stockings as a substitute player/PR man (even though he hasn't played baseball in years) and runs afoul of the primordial version of the IRA, while winning the fair Irish hand of a teammate's sister. Whew. And, this is also an excellent source of information on early baseball and the '69 Reds, who, in case you're wondering, did actually have a substitute named Fowler.

The Universal Baseball Association, Inc., J. Henry Waugh, Prop, by Robert Coover – Maybe the record-holder for the baseball book with the longest title, this one is written by a college professor (Brock is one, too) who clearly played either APBA Baseball or Strat-O-Matic. The hero, a 56-year-old accountant named Henry Waugh, has invented a tabletop baseball game very similar to APBA or Strat-O-Matic, only he literally lives and dies by it. His Universal Baseball Association is not only more real to Waugh than "real" baseball, it's more real than reality. At this point, unless you've read the book, you're probably saying, "Get real!" Well, as one of the blurbs on the cover says, it's a dazzling gem of a novel about a man in a diamond-shaped world. A must-read, even if you're not an APBA player.

Of course, the real meat of baseball books is in the realm of non-fiction. As previously noted, there are essentially three kinds of non-fiction baseball books... history books, books on current events, and statistic-based books. As an historian, my personal preference is toward history books, and while a tip of the baseball cap MUST go to Lawrence Ritter's seminal *The Glory of Their Times*, his justly-famous oral history just misses making this list, mainly because oral histories tend to be notoriously inaccurate and more often dictated than written. For great baseball history books, we'll choose the written histories, like...

The New Bill James Historical Baseball Abstract by, who else? James' 2002 revision of the 1985 classic introduced his Win Shares concept of evaluating players, and was one of the most heavily-anticipated baseball books of many a year. Naturally, James did not disappoint, partly because the *New Abstract* is actually all three types of non-fiction baseball books rolled up into one – a history book, a statistics book, and a book on current players as well.

The Politics of Glory by, yes that's right, him again. Possibly James' best piece of pure writing is also the best systematic study of the Hall of Fame, as well as a history of the Hall of Fame. Want to know how and why players get into the Hall of Fame? Want to see careful analysis of some of the Hall of Fame controversies (both who is in and who should be in)? It's all here, along with some short bios and studies of some notable players... George Davis (*Politics*... certainly helped him get elected to the Hall), Phil Rizzuto (*Politics*... couldn't keep him out of the Hall... not that that was what James had in mind), Jerry Priddy, Joe Tinker, Don Drysdale, etc.

Baseball Dynasties and *Rob Neyer's Big Book of Baseball Lineups* by Rob Neyer. (...*Dynasties* was co-written with Eddie Epstein.) "Toto, we're not in Kansas anymore." No wait! Yes we are. Because Neyer was James' second research assistant on the edge of the Great Plains and is still a devoted Royals fan from growing up in the heyday of George Brett, et al. Now one of ESPN.Com's ace columnists (along with James' first research assistant, Jim Baker), Neyer is no longer following in the master's footsteps... he's blazing his own trail, putting out super baseball books every year. However, Neyer does have some things in common with James… the ability to create discussion about baseball with his books (their most valuable trait), a format that features sidebars interspaced throughout the regular text, and a blending of past, present and stats that works every time. They both are super writers as well.

Baseball as I Have Known It by Fred Lieb. A different kind of history book, this retrospective of 70 some years of baseball, and baseball journalism, was written when Lieb was holding Card #1 in the BBWAA and was pushing 90 years old… making him possibly the oldest sportswriter to complete a book. Now, Lieb's facts are sometimes a little shaky after all that time – for instance, he has an incorrect score for the Merkle Game – and, it's also true that he was known for sometimes not letting the facts get in the way of a good story. Nonetheless, this book defines the word "unique" for its perspective on baseball history… I mean, the man was THERE for most of it (and writing about it), from before 1910 to 1980.

Big-Time Baseball edited by Ben Olan. This is a completely idiosyncratic choice. This oversize paperback, published in 1960, was the first baseball history book I ever read – my dad bought it for me for, I think for Christmas when I was eight years old. A collection of historical anecdotes – some of which are even true – and accompanying cartoons, it fascinated me at the time, and really started my interest in baseball history. It might be added that the stories, and illustrations, were relevant enough that no less an author than John Thorn used a bunch of them in his 1974 book, *A Century of Baseball Lore.*

Then there are the books that are written about current events or still-active players, teams, executives, managers, etc. *The Long Season* may have changed the genre dramatically, but it was far from the first book of this type. Among the early books in this category was *Pitching in a Pinch*, published in 1912 under Christy Mathewson's by-line, although it was as actually ghostwritten by New York sportswriter Jack Wheeler. Either way, it is a fine early inside look at baseball in the dead ball era and gives invaluable insight to the game at the time, especially into Matty's basic theory of pitching… that, at a time when few batters posed a home run threat, a hurler could coast through the lineup, and would only have to bear down "in a pinch." However, even *Pitching in a Pinch* doesn't make this list of the top 20… there's just too much competition.

Pennant Race by Jim Brosnan does. Although maybe not as important a book as his earlier *The Long Season*, it is a more interesting book, since it tells the inside story of one of the few real "Cinderella" teams… the 1961 Reds who were picked by absolutely no one to win the National League. And yet, they did, thanks in part to a super season out of the bullpen by the author.

More Than Beards, Bellies and Biceps by Bob Gordon and Tom Burgoyne. Just as *Pennant Race* is an insider book about an unexpected pennant winner, so is *More Than B3*. Only in this case, it's the worst-to-first 1993 Phillies, and it's written in part by Phillies' employee Tom Burgoyne… who would become the full-time Phillie Phanatic in 1994. Thanks in part to the subject matter, a team that John Kruk had previously characterized as "25 Morons and a Mormon" (Dale Murphy, in 1991, in case you're interested) this is another highly entertaining story.

What about the statistical books, which can be said to have begun with Ernie Lanigan's *Baseball Cyclopedia* back in the game's Jurassic period? (No, there wasn't a team playing in Jurassic Park in those days…) These are essentially research books, although there exists no law that they can't make for interesting reading as well. After Macmillan's ground-breaking work following the 1968 season, a veritable plethora of encyclopedias, research and statistical works came forth, most notably *Total Baseball, The Sports Encyclopedia: Baseball* and *The Baseball Timeline*, all of which make the Top 20. Of the most note here is *Total Baseball*, which combines a thorough encyclopedia with some excellent editorial content, not the least of which is Joseph Overfield's excellent essay on shortened careers and tragedies, wherein we learn that, prior to the unfortunate Dernell Stenson, the last major league player to be murdered while still an active player was Lyman Bostock – also a shooting death in conjunction with a car – in 1978.

Now, if you've been keeping count thus far, you'll see we're up to

19 books. Number 20 is currently the hottest baseball book on the market, a review of the 2002 Oakland Athletics and the mad (as in angry) genius who runs them. A book that combines several notable attributes – it's part bio, part sabrmetric, part seasonal review – and has already been recognized as a milestone in the further establishment of the revolution in baseball thought that was launched by the *Bill James Baseball Abstract* series. (If we wanted to add some more titles to the list of great books, you could include add James' 1982 through 1988 *Abstracts*.)

Moneyball by Michael Lewis. It is possible, as time goes by, that *Moneyball* may push its way into the top five. That's because it has the potential to cause another paradigm shift… the general popularization of the sabrmetric approach to baseball. Of course, Pete Reiser had a world of potential, too, but he kept running into walls. Hopefully, Lewis' book will not suffer the same fate, because Lewis has the power to finally bring what could well be called the Bill James Approach to baseball into the mainstream. And why is that? Well, because Lewis is basically writing about A's GM Billy Beane, the foremost proponent inside baseball of Jamesian Theory. And, because Lewis IS in the mainstream of literature and culture – pop or otherwise. He's not just another stats geek writing about OPS, he's MICHAEL LEWIS, for goodness sakes. This is the guy who wrote best sellers about the 1996 presidential campaign, Silicon Valley and Wall Street. This is one of the best writers – not just the best sportswriters – in America, and, as such, he is far more likely to be taken seriously by, well, by everyone, not just those SABR geeks.

Although Lewis is ostensibly writing about the Athletics' 2002 season and Beane, what he's really writing about is the attempt – largely by Beane, but also by a few other brave souls – to bring reasoned analysis to jockdom, more specifically, to baseball. Let's face it, any form of intellectualism has traditionally been frowned upon by the game. Jim Bouton knew that… he wrote about it in *Ball Four* back in 1969[98] … he faced it himself. It's all part of an old baseball saying that Bouton quotes… "quit thinking, you're hurting the club."[99] And, things have changed very little in 30+ years, as we can see from Beane's battles with his more-traditionally-oriented scouts, coaches and managers… a war Lewis allows us to witness from the point of view of a fly on the wall in the A's draft room, locker room, video room, manager's office and clubhouse.

However, one of the things that makes *Moneyball* so intriguing is Beane himself. Although he comes directly from a traditional baseball background – he was just about the hottest prospect in baseball in 1980 – he has been able to overcome that background (notably an 80/11 strikeout/walk ratio and an ID of .027)… to transcend his own experiences, and to witness a new paradigm. In fact, Beane considers his experience as a player a hindrance he needs to overcome to succeed in his current job. Maybe that's why he can't always convince everyone else there IS a new paradigm.[100]

One other thing we learn right away in *Moneyball* is that Beane's battle with the Philistines is complicated by the little matter of his temperament. Usually, when you refer to someone as a "mad genius," you mean a brilliant thinker who sometimes has a long lead off third… back toward second. That's not Billy Beane. His genius is his ability to see beyond his personal athletic experiences (as noted, he had no plate discipline himself). However, he does get sort of angry, as in, he threw a chair through (not against, through) a wall when the A's drafted Jeremy Bonderman in the first round in 2001.[101] He's the guy, as Lewis notes, you don't want to sit next to on the bench after he strikes out.[102] In fact, once in high school, he bent a bat (aluminum, of course) at a right angle after such an event, and then insisted on still trying to hit with it.[103] Lewis postulates that Beane's failure to live up to his immense talent on the field is largely attributable to his failure to keep his emotions in check, both inside and outside the batter's box.[104] Certainly, Beane hasn't changed that much since his playing days… Lewis' story tells of a GM who is so worked up that he can't stand to watch his own team play… he claims because it will adversely affect his ability to be objective about the team and the players.[105] Whatever. Does that explain why he hits the A's weight room when the game starts? Why he'll sometimes drive around the Oakland Coliseum during a game, sneaking peeks at a little white box that reports wireless game scores? Why there are loud crashes in the A's clubhouse when things aren't going good for the green and gold? "Billy breaking things,"[106] is how Lewis describes his reaction to ill fate on the field.

In between trying to keep out of Beane's way during his tantrums, Lewis gives us a true insider's insight to the baseball draft and how the A's evaluate players, to the trading game, where Beane is a master partly because, as Lewis notes, he has the gift of making people like him,[107] and to a couple of key A's players that nobody else wanted – Scott Hatteberg and Chad Bradford, thus illustrating Beane's genius in identifying cheap labor that can play major league baseball at a high level… the ability that gives him "the art of winning an unfair game," as the cover notes. And, in fact, baseball, as it is currently structured – with free agency and without meaningful controls on the George Steinbrenners – IS an unfair game. Lewis and Beane clearly understand this, and so should the "Lords of Baseball." Of course, if a pig had wings, it could fly.

CHAPTER 49

November 17, 2003

Item: November 1947 – Jack Roosevelt Robinson is named to first official "Rookie of the Year" by the BBWAA.

Well, at least they got that one right. Of course, if there was one Rookie of the Year vote that was virtually goof proof, it was the first one. On the other hand… just because Jackie Robinson deserved the Rookie of the Century Award, those fine upstanding members of the Baseball Writers Association of America (BBWAA) could have still blown the 1947 Rookie of the Year vote. Even given the incredible hardships Robinson labored under, while playing a new position (first base) and while still leading the National League in steals and Power/ Speed number (and finishing in the top 10 in eight other offensive categories), don't assume that the BBWAA couldn't have given the award to, oh, Frankie Baumholtz (who was fifth in the voting). They've made some almost equally bad decisions in the past, and, after all, Robinson only got a 78% share of the vote, despite these numbers…

G	AB	R	H	2B	3B	HR	RBI	SB	BB	SO	BA	OBP	SLG	OPS
151	590	125	175	31	5	12	48	29	74	36	.297	.383	.427	.810

In reality, 1947 was a pretty good year for rookies, so Robinson was facing some stiff competition – there was only one ROY Award that year for the entire major leagues – from 21-game winner Larry Jansen (who was second) and Ferris Fain (who was fourth). In fact, Fain's numbers, compiled while also playing first base and with half his games in a tougher hitter's park (name o' Shibe), were overall pretty much as good as Robinson's, given he played fewer games.

G	AB	R	H	2B	3B	HR	RBI	SB	BB	SO	BA	OBP	SLG	OPS
136	461	70	134	28	6	7	71	4	95	34	.291	.414	.423	.837

Still, this is JACKIE ROBINSON we're talking about, and it is patently unfair to assume Robinson deserved the first ROY Award strictly based on his superficial numbers or the immense publicity that surrounded his year as the first African-American to play major league baseball since 1884. Clearly, the only person ever to have his number retired by an entire sport earned every honor he received.

A more relevant question in 2003 is... did Dontrelle Willis and Angel Berroa deserve the ROY honors they just received? Certainly, the BBWAA picked the right man in 1947. And, it is absolutely NOT true that they haven't made a correct choice since then. However, some of their poorer decisions (e.g.; Andre Dawson as NL MVP in 1987) do lead to a certain amount of uncertainty as to the accuracy of the post-season awards process. And, we can unquestionably add the 2003 Rookie of the Year choices to that already long list of bad votes... at least for the National League. Because, whoever voted the Marlins' Willis first was choosing hype over substance. Superficial stats (i.e., wins) over meaningful stats. In other words, they must have been on drugs (or at least on steroids... but that's another subject entirely.) You will recall that the voting went like this...

Willis – 118
Podsednik – 81
Webb – 73

Now comparing the two pitchers to outfielder Scott Podsednik is admittedly somewhat like comparing apples to oranges. So, leaving aside the Brewers' surprising candidate, let's compare the Marlins' Dontrelle Willis and the Diamondbacks' Brandon Webb...

	G	IP	W-L	H	HR	HR/9	W	K	K/W	K/9	ERA
Willis	27	161	14-6	148	13	.727	58	142	2.4/1	7.9	3.30
Webb	29	181	10-9	140	12	.597	68	172	2.5/1	8.6	2.84

Alright, so maybe it's not overwhelming, but, the ONLY category that Willis leads Webb in is wins and losses. Webb is simply better everywhere else, including both sabrmetric measures and the simple stuff that the BBWAA usually loves. Furthermore, he not only pitched better, he pitched more as well. And, it might be added, Webb didn't pitch half his games in the pitchers' heaven that is The House That Marino Built. Add to that the fact that, while Willis did help jump start the Marlins out of the cellar, he was basically a replacement-level pitcher in the second half of the year, going 9-1 with a 2.08 ERA before the All-Star Game and 5-5 with a 4.60 ERA afterwards. In fact, Willis flopped so bad late in the year that Manager Jack McKeon took him out of the starting rotation in the post-season. Wonder how many Rookies of the Year that has happened to before? Well, since you asked… there were 27 previous ROYs whose teams made it to the postseason… and NONE of them were demoted in October. For that matter, Joe Black of the 1952 Brooklyn Dodgers came out of the bullpen to throw three excellent starts (2.53 ERA) against the Yankees in the World Series.

But wait. Willis only had two unearned runs scored against him all year. So maybe his ERA should, given a few different scoring decisions, be lower. After all, Webb gave up eight unearned runs, which lowered his ERA. So maybe Willis really was better, at least according to ERA. Sorry, that doesn't wash, either, particularly if you follow the Voros McCracken theory of pitching. For those not familiar with Mr. McCracken's work, he postulates that the only statistics that pitchers truly have control over are their home runs and walks allowed, and the number of strikeouts they ring up. Everything else is a function of their team, park effects and/or luck.[108] Now, that theory may be a bit overstated, but it's worth noting that Webb also leads Willis by a significant margin in two of the McCracken stats – home runs per nine innings and strikeouts per nine innings, while holding a slight edge in K/W ratio. Hence, there is absolutely NO excuse – none, zero, zip, macchus – by using any measurement except for looking at those 14 wins and all the hype surrounding Willis in mid-season, for voting him ROY ahead of Webb.

As to the issue of where Podsednik fits in this continuum… that is harder to say. A situation like this begs for the creation of a Rookie Pitcher of the Year Award and a Rookie Hitter of the Year Award for the BBWAA. Certainly, Podsednik easily surpasses the offensive credentials of the fourth place finisher, Marlon Byrd. Besides, Podsednik is also a slightly better candidate to join the All Eye Chart Team.

	G	AB	R	H	2B	3B	HR	RBI	SB	W	K	BA	OBP	SA	OPS
Podsednik	154	558	100	175	29	8	9	58	43	56	91	.314	.379	.443	.822
Byrd	135	495	86	150	28	4	7	45	11	44	94	.303	.366	.418	.784

That's a no-brainer. Podsednik not only played more than Byrd, he surpassed him in every offensive category (although Byrd is probably a little better fielder). Podsednik had himself quite a year, so good a year that he probably should have finished second, behind Webb in the voting... at least, that would have been my vote. Pretty good for someone who wasn't even on the Rookie Radar Screen in the Spring. And this begs another question… why could the voters so clearly see that Podsednik was better than Byrd, but not see that Webb was equally better than Willis? Was it all in Willis' wins? Or was it in Willis' hype? Let's put it this way… why do you think that Barry Bonds is the favorite to win the NL MVP Award… maybe because he was on Sports Center every night? Well, so was Willis.

As to the American League ROY vote… well, this was one time I'm glad I didn't have a vote. This was a tough call, although it does seem strange that the top two finishers, Berroa (88) and Hideki Matsui (84), so easily outdistanced Rocco Baldelli (51) and Jody Gerut (20), because there's really not much to choose from between them…

	G	AB	R	H	2B	3B	HR	RBI	SB	W	K	BA	OBP	SA	OPS
Berroa	158	567	92	163	28	7	17	73	21	29	100	.287	.338	.451	.789
Matsui	163	623	82	179	42	1	16	106	2	63	86	.287	.353	.435	.788
Baldelli	156	637	89	184	32	8	11	78	27	30	128	.289	.326	.416	.742
Gerut	127	480	66	134	33	2	22	75	4	35	70	.279	.336	.494	.830

Three key factors need to be noted… first, their defensive positions. Although all of the bottom three are outfielders, Baldelli is a centerfielder, Gerut a right fielder and Matsui a leftfielder. Score two points for Rocco, one for Gerut and take one away from the latest Japanese import. Berroa, of course, is a shortstop, and a pretty good one. Secondly, Berroa played half his games in the best hitters' park in the American League. That's one strike against Berroa, devaluing his offensive stats. Thirdly, as you can see, Gerut played significantly less than the other three (why, oh Eric the Wedge?), otherwise, the prize in question would have clearly belonged at Jacobs Field, since his power (and, as a result, his OPS) is better than the other three. Balance it all out, and you have a very close race. The most valuable defensive players (Berroa and Baldelli) are also the least valuable offensive players, Berroa largely because of park effects and Baldelli largely due to his awful .037 ID. And while Matsui may or may not be the best offensive threat – partly due to his greater playing time, and partly due to the fact he's the only one who'll take a walk – Gerut is more valuable defensively in right field, and, his OPS is still more than 40 points higher than Matsui.

Now, it's right about here where the subject of Matsui's eligibility has to be tackled… after all, it was THE hot topic in this year's ROY award voting after two voters left him off the ballot entirely. Actually, as the rules now stand, it's very simple. The voting rules state something to the effect that anyone who has surpassed an established threshold of at bats or innings pitched in what are euphemistically called the major leagues is eligible for the award. Matsui, having never played in the American majors prior to 2003, clearly had not surpassed that threshold. Hence, he was eligible for the ROY. What's not simple is what needs to be done to rectify the situation caused this year by

Matsui and by various of his countrymen in previous years. It's especially complicated because no one should argue that the caliber of Japanese professional baseball at its highest point is equal to the caliber of play in the major leagues… the same also being true of professional baseball in Korea, Taiwan, Mexico, Italy, Venezuela, Sri Lanka, Burkina Faso, Kazakhstan (actually, they play kokpar there… it's sort of like polo, only played with a headless goat instead of a ball) and every other country you care to mention. So, what to do? Eliminate all first-year foreign professionals who played at the "major league" level overseas from ROY voting? Maybe. Or, in the immortal words of the Dutchman, Norm Van Brocklin, when he was asked what to do about soccer style kickers in football, indicated in no uncertain terms that he was in favor of tightening the immigration laws.

Anyway, this year's AL vote was a very tough call, and any voting arrangement of the top four can be logically defended. If forced to choose, I'd rank them Gerut, Berroa, Matsui and Baldelli.

Before leaving the first round of awards, a briefer visit to the Cy Young voting is necessary. Briefer because this year's awards were much less interesting than the ROY, mainly because they were less controversial. About the only issue to come up revolves around the value of a relief pitcher versus as starter… to wit (as opposed to Ernie Whitt), did reliever Eric Gagne deserve the Cy Young over starters Jason Schmidt and Mark Prior? Let's look at just a couple of key stats…

	IP	HR	W	K	ERA
Gagne	82	2	20	137	1.20
Schmidt	208	14	46	208	2.34
Prior	211	15	50	245	2.43

Wow! Gagne's numbers, to say nothing of his 55 saves in 55 chances headline stat, are mind-boggling. Even better than Schmidt's and Prior's superb seasons. Although one important factor that isn't immediately obvious is the fact that Prior's home games were in cozy Wrigley Field and that Gagne and Schmidt called the two best pitcher's parks in the league – Dodger Stadium and the Big Phone Booth – home. However, pretty much by every measure, the winner of the Billy Goats Gruff Look-Alike Contest was a superior pitcher. Every measure but one… both Schmidt and Prior threw two-and-half times as many innings than Gagne. Is that significant? Well, ask yourself this… who won the ERA crown? Schmidt (Prior was third), and not Gagne… because you have to pitch at least 162 innings to qualify. Obviously, THAT qualifier, either rightly or wrongly, places more importance on starters than on relievers. Yes, it's true that, overall, a closer's innings have more concentrated importance than a starter's… but, two-and-half times more important? That's harder to say. Who, in fact can say exactly?

However, it is interesting to note that Gagne got a decision (a win or a save) in 57 games the Dodgers won. Prior got a win in 18 games the Cubs won, and Schmidt picked up a "W" in 17 games for the Giants. Big difference, right? However, Gagne only pitched 38.9 percent as many innings as Prior. Does that mean that we could, or should, assign a similarly proportional importance to Gagne's results? In other words, since his innings were only 38.9 percent of Prior's, can you consider his decisions to be 38.9 percent of Prior's in value? If you multiply 57 by .389, you get 22, and that's getting pretty close to Prior's 18 or Schmidt's 17. Like the AL ROY, it's a tough call. If I had a vote, I'd have been tempted to place them… Prior, Schmidt, Gagne.

(Another one of those asides you've hopefully grown to love… the issue of the value of a reliever vs. a starter was also raised by the first big trade of the off-season. No, not the daring daylight heist the Twins pulled on the Giants – getting Joe Nathan AND Boof Bonser for a catcher with little power, who doesn't walk, and who has a career .788 OPS isn't a trade, it's a steal – we're talking about the Phillies/Astros deal that saw one of the three best closers in the NL head east for three young starters. Is 32-year-old closer Billy Wagner worth no less than three young starters? Under these circumstances, the answer is "yes." Even though the last time the Phillies made such a deal – the 2001 trade of young starters Bruce Chen and Adam Walker for old relievers Turk Wendell and Dennis Cook – it blew up in their faces, this was a trade they had to make. By November 2003, the Phillies' bullpen was exactly… Rheal Cormier and Carlos Silva, and they had young starters to spare. In this case, Brandon Duckworth, who had regressed in each of his three years in the majors, Taylor Buchholz, who was only their third best prospect, and a 24-year-old who hadn't pitched above Single A. In this case, at least, a 32-year-old closer was certainly worth that price.)

The American League Cy Young Award voting, on the other hand, looks to be pretty simple. (Hey, they unquestionably got one out of four right… that's a .250 BA for the BBWAA!) Although Roy Halladay's and Esteban Loaiza's numbers are pretty similar, there's no denying that Loaiza's failure in those two key September starts against the Twins cost him dearly.

	IP	W-L	HR	W	SO	ERA
Halladay	266	22-7	26	32	204	3.25
Loaiza	226	21-9	17	56	207	2.90

Halladay threw 40 more innings, and had a better won-loss record and a better K/W ratio. On the other hand, Loaiza gave up fewer home runs, led the AL in Ks, and had a better ERA. On the surface, that doesn't add up to a 136-63 difference in the voting. Ah, but return with us now to those Thrilling Days of Yesteryear (no, wait, that's the Lone Ranger, not the Lo Aiza). Let's make that the days of September, when the Sox and the Twins were in a virtual dead heat (f'rinstance, they were tied on both the 7th and the 14th of the month), battling it out for the right to lose to the Yankees in the ALDS. The Pale Hose went with their ace, and maybe at the time the favorite in the Cy Young balloting, against the one team they had to beat – remember that the Royals were falling out of the race by this point. On both Sept. 11 and Sept. 16, Loaiza goes against the Twins. Here's what happened…

	IP	H	R	ER	W	K
9/11	7	7	5	5	1	9
9/16	2.1	4	4	4	5	1

While Loaiza wasn't awful in the Sept. 11 game, he also didn't get the job done, like an ace is supposed to when the chips are down (oops, that's a gambling term… can't use that.) And, he WAS awful in the Sept. 16 game. The Sox lost them both, 5-2, and Loaiza very well may have lost his chance at the Cy Young at the same time.

CHAPTER 50

November 24, 2003

Item: November 1947 – Joe DiMaggio is voted the American League MVP.

First of all, somebody, anybody – the BBWAA, the Commissioner's Office, the Hall of Fame, Billy Beane, Bill James, Webster, Roget, Ken Hirdt, John Thorn, Rob Neyer, Jim Baker, Dick Young (oops, like Webster and Roget, he's dead), Fred Lieb (ditto), Ford Frick, Michael Lewis, Rich Lally, Bill Chuck, Lee Sinins, David Halberstam, Jim Hardy, Pete DeCoursey, Theo Epstein, Bill Deane, Howard Garson, Ted Taylor, George Will, somebody – has just got to define the world valuable.

You see, that's the basic problem with the Most Valuable Player Award. No one… no one in the BBWAA really knows what they're voting for. The best player? The best player on the best team? The guy who leads the league in RBIS? The guy who leads the league in OPS? The runs created leader? The most heavily-promoted player? The player who had the biggest impact on a pennant race? (This has been a popular one over the years.) The guy who was on Sports Center the most times? The player who made the biggest difference to his team? The most indispensable player? The highest-paid player? (Don't laugh, the very first definition in Webster's pertains to "having material value." The second states, "of great merit, use, or service.") Lacking such guidelines, there are basically two ways to view controversial MVP choices… which means almost every choice since Henry Chadwick declared George Wright the most valuable Red Stocking in 1869. First, in terms of why the vote came down like it did. And, second, from a statistical viewpoint, who did the most to help his team win.

In 1947, the BBWAA did indeed pick the right man, Jackie Robinson, for Rookie of the Year. However, they balanced that off with probably the most controversial MVP choice ever, giving Joe DiMaggio a one point win over Ted Williams. And, probably, their biggest voting faux pas as well. First, the voting was, to put it politely, weird… and not just because five different people got first place votes (after all, 10 players picked up first place votes in the 2003 AL election.) DiMaggio did get the most firsts with eight, but Yankee relief pitcher Joe Page, who was fourth overall in the voting, was second with seven firsts. Here are the top six…

	1st Place	Total
Joe DiMaggio (NY)	8	202
Ted Williams (BOS)	3	201
Lou Boudreau (CLEV)	1	168
Joe Page (NY)	7	167
George Kell (DET)	0	132
George McQuinn (NY)	3	77

Now, Williams had a lousy relationship with most sportswriters. As a result, it appears as if one of them left him off the ballot entirely in 1947. Exactly who that was is something of a mystery… many sources say it was Boston writer Mel Webb (Williams thought it was him), however, MVP voting expert Deane calls that story a myth, and notes that the contemporary Boston press blamed it on someone in the Midwest. Either way, what is true is that two BBWAA members left DiMaggio – who really had a mediocre Joe DiMaggio season – off their ballots as well. Just as odd was the split of the New York vote… three different Yankees got first place votes, including first baseman George McQuinn, who got as many firsts as Teddy Ballgame. On the surface, this is absurd… as we can see by running the stats…

	G	AB	R	H	2B	3B	HR	RB	W	K	BA	OPB	SLG	OPS
DiMaggio	141	534	97	168	31	10	20	97	64	32	.315	.391	.522	.913
Williams	156	528	125	181	40	9	32	114	162	47	.343	.499	.634	1.133
McQuinn	144	517	84	157	24	3	13	80	78	66	.304	.395	.437	.832

Williams not only won the Triple Crown in 1947, he played more than DiMaggio or McQuinn and led the other two in every meaningful offensive category (except for trailing DiMag 10-9 in triples). Yes, DiMaggio was a better outfielder than Williams, but, it would take a whole lot of defense to make up that big a difference. And, you can't blame it on park effects either (not that the BBWAA would have paid much attention to that in 1947), since both superstars were playing in parks that were ill-suited to their offensive talents. McQuinn? This was the only time he appeared in the top 10 MVP vote, and he was out of baseball after the 1948 season.

Boudreau's figures weren't as good as McQuinn's, Kell's OPS was below .800, and Page was the first relief pitcher to ever make an impression on the MVP voters… Otis Crandall didn't, Wilcy Moore didn't, Firpo Marberry didn't, Johnny Murphy didn't, Ace Adams didn't, etc. Hence, his presence in the top five was something of a fluke. In other words, Williams should have run away with the MVP voting, with DiMaggio a distant second and no one else, except maybe Page, in the ballpark. But, it didn't happen that way. So, the moral of the story most likely is that Teddy Ballgame should have cultivated the media a little bit more – maybe not calling them "Knights of the Keyboard" might have helped – at least, he should have if he wanted to do better in the MVP voting.

On the other hand, the logic behind the 2003 National League MVP voting is crystal clear. For the first time in his entire career, Barry Bonds became a sympathetic figure, thanks to the death of his father, Bobby Bonds. That, combined with Bonds' recent past history (the 2001 and 2002 awards), his superficially impressive numbers, and his constant promotion by ESPN ("All Barry, All the Time" ought to be their motto) and other media outlets, gave him a huge boost among the electorate. So, a salute is due to Hal McCoy (*Dayton Daily News*), Don

Ketchum (*Arizona Republic*), Bill Zack (Morris News Service) and Joe Strauss (*St. Louis Post Dispatch*) for giving a first place vote to someone else.

	G	AB	R	H	2B	3B	HR	RBI	W	K	BA	OPB	SLG	OPS
Bonds	130	390	111	133	22	1	45	90	148	58	.341	.529	.749	1.278
Pujols	157	591	137	212	51	1	43	124	79	65	.359	.439	.667	1.106

There's no denying that Bonds put up impressive numbers. But, there's also no denying that, for a variety of reasons, most admittedly not under his control, he just didn't have as many opportunities to help his team win. Yes, his walks do have value, but remember that 61of those walks aren't his, they belong to opposing managers. There's no getting around it, Bonds didn't play enough to be number one. He played significantly fewer games and had many less at bats than his closest competitor. Hence, he does not deserve the first place votes or the MVP award. Albert Pujols does. One statistic not seen above is the basic runs created, which does, by the way, count walks, both intentional and unintentional. Because of bereavement leave, managers' Bondsaphobia and various injuries, Bonds created an estimated 152.5 runs. Pujols created 171. Hence, Pujols did more to help his team to win, by creating more of the game's basic currency – runs. Is this fair? No, but life isn't fair, and neither is baseball. Pete Reiser almost certainly would have been MVP in 1942 if he hadn't run into the wall at Sportsman's Park on July 19 of that year. Does that mean he deserved the award? (Incredibly, he still finished sixth, despite hardly being able to stand up the rest of the year.) No. And neither did Bonds.

Then there are times when no one knows what to do, or what should be done, with the voting. Like this year's AL MVP election. Without any of the top teams having a player having an outstanding year – and let's face it, that's who wins the MVP most of the time, assuming someone fits that description – it's anybody's ball game. It's under these circumstances that it is most likely that the outcome will be one that will raise a howl that some dog had gotten the MVP... most notably, someone who had the nerve to play for a LOSING team. Horrors! If course, there's nothing in the rules that says that you don't have value just because your teammates do not.

So, it's not totally off the wall to make some kind of case for ANY of the 10 individuals who garnered first place votes; Alex Rodriguez, Carlos Degaldo, Jorge Posada, Shannon Stewart (well, that might be a bit of a stretch), David Ortiz (the "Half-a-Year Award," he only played 128 games), Manny Ramirez, Nomar Garciparra, Vernon Wells, Miguel Tejada (the carry-over vote from 2002, when he didn't deserve the award, either) and Jason Giambi. How close is this 10-pack? Except for Giambi, they all had batting averages between .278 and .325. Except for Nomar and Miggy, they all had on-base averages between .359 and .429. And, except for Stewart and Tejada, they all had slugging percentages between .518 and .600.

A-Rod's MVP really should be popular among the Knights of the CRT, and the fans. He is, after all, the best player is baseball (You gotta a problem with that? He's led the majors in home runs each of the last two years, and he's a shortstop, for goodness sakes… a shortstop with two Gold Gloves in the past two years... although he may have won them partly with his bat.) And, the "best player" designation is one that typically attracts MVP voters. And, he's never won an MVP before, so maybe this is a make-up call. If so, it's a good one, under the circumstances.

Item: November 1987 – *Sports Illustrated* fires the poor schlump who picked the Cleveland Indians to finish first in the magazine's 1987 Baseball Preview issue.

The Indians were coming off an 84-78 season in 1986, a remarkable accomplishment for the Tribe in those days. And, *SI* came out with what would become either one of the most famous bad predictions in sports history, or one of the outstanding examples of the Jinx of Time, Inc., also known as the Curse of the Cover. Because, the 1987 Indians, picked by *SI* to be the best team in baseball, finished 61-101, the worst record in baseball. Now, *SI* isn't the only publication that makes predictions, either directly or indirectly. *Baseball: 1862 to 2003* has made a few over the course of the 2003 season as well, so it seems only fair to wrap things up by reviewing what happened to some of the year's headline players and stories. Remember, there are only three possible outcomes in baseball... you win a few, you lose a few, and the rest get rained out.

Pete Rose – He's still in the news. By one reporting, there were 27 major Pete Rose stories from January 2003 to November 2003. Actually, Rose has seldom been out of the news since December 1978 – almost 25 years ago – when he signed that big free agent contract. At this writing, it looks more likely than not that he will be re-instated by Bud.com, and, as a result, will be elected – as he deserves – to the Hall of Fame. A second, ultimately less-important question... will Pete ever manage again... is very much a matter of question, and speculation. However, if the unexpected does happen, and, for instance, the Cincinnati Reds decide to go with popular opinion (at least in Cincy), and re-hire the Prodigal Hilljack, well, that will make one of the biggest single sports stories of 2004. One of the Reds' first series in 2004 happens to be the opening game in the new ballpark in the other city that still loves Pete, Philadelphia. Just in case, you might want to mark Apr. 12, 2004 on your calendar for a major hype explosion.

Rickey Henderson – No, Billy Beane didn't sign Rickey for a fifth trip to Oakland. He opened the year at Port Ruppert (oops, they changed the name to Newark a few years back) in the independent Atlantic League, before the Dodgers picked him up for the stretch drive. Well, neither Rickey nor the Dodgers made much of a stretch, the Bums and their weenie offense finishing second and Rickey showing he's pretty much finished.

G	AB	R	H	2B	3B	HR	RBI	SB	CS	W	K	BA	OBA	SLG
30	72	7	15	1	0	2	5	3	0	11	16	.208	.321	.306

Still, it's pretty remarkable that a 44-year-old can steal three bases without getting caught, and still have an ID above .100.

Kevin Millwood and Johnny Estrada – After going 7-1 with a no-hitter in the early going for the Phillies, Millwood cooled off considerably, finishing 14-12 with an adjusted ERA of just 103, although he did lead the National League in shutouts with three. However, he failed to lead the Phillies into the playoffs and is now a free agent, asking for a five-year contract. Anyone who gives a pitcher a five-year contract gets what they deserve. Johnny Estrada, on the other hand, played all of 16 games for the Braves, compiling a fairly typical (for him) .665 OPS. With Javy Lopez a free agent, the Braves have been making noises about Estrada being their regular catcher next year. Lotsa luck, Bobby.

The New York Mets – Picked for third place on the basis of having an old and overpaid team, they managed to finish dead last, as almost ALL their old and overpaid players – Mo Vaughn, Roberto Alomar, David Cone, Roger Cedeno, Jay Bell, etc., etc. – did exactly as predicted. They flopped, or got hurt. Or both. Count this one as a win for *Baseball: 1862 to 2003*.

A-Rod – As previously noted, he won the MVP, and hence took another step toward the peak… Honus Wagner. He's not there yet, but, at this point, the two things A-Rod needs to move Wagner off the mountain as the Greatest Shortstop of all Time are staying power and staying at short.

Brooks Kieschnick – Although he didn't become the first two-way player since Wonderful Willie Smith and Mel Queen – he only played three games in the outfield – he actually had a pretty good year, at least at the plate.

G	AB	R	H	2B	3B	HR	RBI	W	K	BA	OBA	SLG
69	70	12	21	1	0	7	12	6	13	.300	.355	.614

G	W-L	IP	H	HR	W	K	ERA	ERA+
42	1-1	53	66	5	13	39	5.26	83

It's a small sample, but seven home runs in 70 at bats is pretty good. Even his plate discipline, though not great, improved. On the mound, except for his strikeout/walk ratio, he'd be better off going back to the field. The jury's still out, so we'll say Brooks was rained out.

The Chicago Cubs – Much to the surprise of many people, including a lot of Cardinals' fans, the Cubbies went 19-8 in September, and took the NL Central pennant away from the stumbling Redbirds and Astros. Given the Cubs' long-term grisly history of poor play in September… they've never had a winning record in September in three straight years since before World War II…can we expect a Fall Flop in 2004? However, having also predicted, at various times, that either the Cards or the Astros would take the NL Central, this one is clearly a loss for the Cards, Astros and *Baseball: 1862 to 2003.*

The Pennant Races – Maybe better off forgotten. The Phillies, Cardinals and Diamondbacks did not win their respective NL divisions, in part due to pitching problems. The AL was a little better, with the Yankees (the AL East, for the sixth straight year, finished in the same order… what are the odds against that?) and Athletics coming through, although the White Sox fell flat on their faces against the Twins in September. Two out of six is a .333 batting average, but, that still isn't very good in the predictions game. Another loss.

Barry Bonds/Sammy Sosa/Ken Griffey – The chase for Henry Aaron's record continues, with the increasingly-injured Junior dropping from the hunt – he only hit 13, and stands at 481 career homers at age 34. Bonds hit 45, to move up to 658, and Sosa 40 to reach 539. Also note that Sammy's production didn't suffer after breaking his corked bat, re-affirming that his mid-career explosion (with the bat, not of the bat) is a function of his rare improved plate discipline, and not cork or (maybe) drugs. Bill James' Favorite Toy now gives Bonds a 26.5 percent chance of reaching 756, and Sosa a 15 percent chance of breaking Aaron's mark. Of course, if the current steroid investigation really kicks in… This one is still up in the air, a rain-out.

Rick Ankiel – The numbers from his year in Double A are not pretty…

G	W-L	IP	H	HR	K	W	ERA
20	2-6	54	45	5	64	49	6.29

And that's in Double A, and it doesn't even take into account his six hit batters and 10 wild pitches. Sorry, Cardinal fans, he still has Steve Blass disease, and there still is no cure. A win for *Baseball: 1862 to 2003*, however.

Curt Schilling/Randy Johnson/Greg Maddux/Tom Glavine – Are any of these four "losing it?" Judgment on Schilling and Johnson will have to be reserved, since, due to injuries, they combined for less than 300 innings. However. Johnson's knee injury would seem to be the more serious issue. However, we'll wait till next year on these two. Maddux struggled terribly at times, as both his home runs allowed and ERA went up, and his adjusted ERA went down, to barely above (105) the league average. However, he still won 16 games (thanks, Braves' offense) and his strikeout to walk ratio was still good (124/33), so some team will certainly give him (and Scott Boras) large, vulgar sums of money to continue his quest for 300 wins. And Glavine, well he was just awful…

W-L	IP	H	HR	K	W	ERA	ERA+
9-14	183	205	21	82	66	4.52	94

His innings pitched went down, his hits allowed went up, as did his home runs allowed, walks and ERA. Meanwhile, he barely struck out more than he walked, and his adjusted ERA dropped below the league average (94). And, he was pitching half his games in a pitcher's park. If this was anyone other than Tom Glavine and his Huge, Four-Year Contract, he might be out of work right now. Although one bad year does not by any means necessarily signal the end, the Mets have to be worried.

The Kansas City Royals and the Detroit Tigers – The former were expected to fade after their hot start, and the latter were expected to continue their awful start. Well, the Royals, to the surprise of almost everyone, stayed in the AL Central pennant race until their badly beaten up pitching staff finally crumpled around Labor Day. Los Tigres came within one game of matching the 1962 Mets' modern-day (i.e., post 19th Century) record of 120 losses. That's bad, but we'll call it a rain out, since the Royals, thanks to some creative deals that brought them Brian Anderson and Jose Lima Bean, among others, hung on a lot longer than expected.

The Atlanta Braves – A loss for *Baseball: 1862 to 2003*, a win for the Braves, who somehow continued their torrid hitting all year long… until the postseason, that is, when they became the first team in 95 years to lose a postseason series to the Cubs. Rumors that Mr. Applegate was seen hanging around the Braves' clubhouse and talking to Javy Lopez, Vinny Castilla, Rafael Furcal and Marcus Giles, though entertaining, are, at this point, unfounded. However, there's no denying that the Braves, totally unexpectedly, finished second in the majors in runs scored and OPS, and third in home runs, in each case leading the National League in those categories.

Rocco Baldelli – Finished third in the AL ROY voting, and continued to make a name for himself as a mini-folk hero in Tampa where, heaven only knows, that franchise needs some heroes – despite the fact that he really wasn't a very good hitter. A .742 OPS isn't going to scare anybody who knows anything. However, Baldelli, your classic, speedy, high average, little power and no ID player, just turned 22 in September, and could still improve. But, if he doesn't improve his plate discipline and/or his ID, he's unlikely to be really valuable. This is one prediction that still looks pretty good.

Roger Clemens – Continued to pitch remarkably well for a 40-year-old following his incredible double of reaching 300 wins and 4000 strikeouts in the same game… a feat of such rarity that only history will really be able to judge it adequately.

W-L	IP	H	HR	K	W	ERA	ERA+
17-9	212	199	24	190	58	3.91	112

A remarkable season for a pitcher who swears he has retired. If he does hang it up with 310 wins and 4099 strikeouts, he will also have left his mark among the legion of 300 game winners as having gone out with by far the best finishing season of the modern era among that clan. (Eddie Plank posted a 1.79 ERA, but only went 5-6 in 131 innings.)

And, maybe that's the real reason why he will retire… to seal his place in history.

The Ordonez Line – Two players who played enough to qualify for the batting title (i.e., 502 plate appearances) fell below the Ordonez Line. Dodgers shortstop Cesar Izturis posted .282/.315/.597 numbers and Astros catcher Brad Ausmus managed to bottom that, with .303/.291/.594. Reports that Ausmus, who will be 35 just after Opening Day 2004, subsequently signed a new, two-year deal with the Astros are either fiction, or an indication that the Astros will once again fall short in 2004.

Pat Burrell/Paul Konerko/Jermaine Dye – All managed to finish the season standing, and in the major leagues, but it wasn't easy, given these numbers…

	AB	R	H	2B	3B	HR	RBI	W	K	BA	OPB	SLG	OPS
Burrell	522	67	109	31	4	21	64	72	142	.209	.309	.404	.713
Konerko	444	49	104	19	0	18	65	43	50	.234	.305	.399	.704
Dye	221	28	38	6	0	4	20	25	42	.172	.261	.253	.514

As bad as Burrell was, he wasn't as bad as the other two, at least by The Rule of 10. Both his extra base hits and his walks were within 10 percent of his at bats, making him, by this measure, an average hitter. Now, no one, least of all Philly sportswriters, will be claiming that Burrell had an average season. And yet, his strikeout to walk ratio wasn't too far off what it was in 2002 (153/89) and it was better than it was in 2001 (162/70). He just wasn't hitting as many singles or home runs as he was in past seasons. Dye, on the other hand, wasn't hitting anything in an historically bad season that even his injured shoulder couldn't explain.

The Worthless 48 – Congratulations, Jermaine Dye. By coming back from your shoulder injury, you managed to play enough to be considered the Athletics' regular right fielder, and thus, you've made this grouping The Worthless 49. And, it was an historic year. Only Ray Oyler and Don "Hulk Hogan" Zimmer ever posted a lower batting average as a regular for a pennant winner. And only Oyler and

Fettuccine Alfredo Griffin have ever come in below Dye's OPS as a regular for a pennant winner. In fact, Dye's Death March was actually somewhat similar to Oyler's unbelievable 1968 season.

	AB	R	H	2B	3B	HR	RBI	W	K	BA	OBA	SLG	OPS
Oyler	215	13	29	6	1	1	12	20	59	.135	.212	.186	.398
Dye	221	28	38	6	0	4	20	25	42	.172	.261	.253	.514

Recall, though, that Oyler did this in the Year of the Pitcher, while Dye was playing in the Rocketball Era, making his year truly one for the record books… at least for all baseball fans who cherish the extreme, at either end of the accomplishment spectrum. So, to Jermaine Dye, Mike Maroth (didn't mention him previously… partly to save him further embarrassment, but he did end up 9-21) and the entire Detroit Tigers… thanks guys, you helped make 2003 special in your own unique way.

BIBLIOGRAPHY

____________. *STATS All-Time Major League Handbook.* Morton Grove, IL: STATS Publishing, 2000

____________. *The Baseball Encyclopedia.* New York: Macmillan, 1969

____________. *Baseball America 2000 Almanac.* Durham, NC: Baseball America, 1999

Alexander, Charles. *John McGraw.* New York: Viking Penguin, 1988

Alexander, Charles. *Ty Cobb.* New York: Oxford University Press, 1984

Angell, Roger. *Once More Around the Park.* New York: Ballantine Books, 1991

Asinof, Eliot. *Eight Men Out.* New York: Ace Publishing Co., 1963

Bilovsky, Frank and Westcott, Rich. *The Phillies Encyclopedia.* New York: Leisure Press, 1984

Bouton, Jim. *Ball Four.* Cleveland: World Publishing, 1970

Brock, Darryl. *If I Never Get Back.* New York: Crown Publishers, 1990

Brosnan, Jim. *The Long Season.* New York: Grosset and Dunlap, 1960

Brosnan, Jim. *Pennant Race.* New York: Harper & Row, 1962

Bryson, Michael. *The Twenty-Four-Inch Home Run.* Chicago: Contemporary Books, 1990

Cohen, Stanley. *Dodgers! The First 100 Years.* New York: Carol Publishing Group, 1990

Cohen, Richard and Neft, David. *The World Series.* New York: The Dial Press, 1979

Coover, Robert. *The Universal Baseball Association, Inc. J. Henry Waugh, Prop.* New York: New American Library, 1969

Davids, L. Robert, editor. *Insider's Baseball.* New York: Charles Scribner's Sons, 1983

Dewey, Donald and Acocella, Nicholas. *Encyclopedia of Major League Baseball Teams.* New York: HarperCollins Publishers, 1993

Dickey, Glenn. *The History of the American League.* New York: Stein and Day, 1982

Einstein, Charles, editor. *The Fireside Book of Baseball (fourth edition),* New York: Simon & Schuster, 1987

Fleming, G.H. *The Unforgettable Season.* New York: Holt, Rinehart and Winston, 1981

Frommer, Harvey. *Primitive Baseball.* New York: Antheneum, 1988

Golenbock, Peter. *Bums.* New York: Simon & Schuster, 1984

Gordon, Robert and Burgoyne, Tom. *More Than Beards, Bellies and Biceps.* Champaign, IL: Sports Publishing L.L.C., 2002

Halberstam, David. *Summer of '49.* New York: Avon Books, 1989

Hynd, Noel. *The Giants of the Polo Grounds.* New York: Doubleday, 1988

James, Bill. *The Politics of Glory.* New York: Macmillan, 1994

James, Bill. *The Bill James Historical Baseball Abstract.* New York, Villard Books, 1985

James, Bill. *The New Bill James Historical Baseball Abstract.* New York: The Free Press, 2001

James, Bill. *The Bill James Baseball Abstract.* New York: Villard Books, 1982-1988

James, Bill. *The Baseball Book.* New York: Villard Books, 1990-1992

Jordan, David. *The Athletics of Philadelphia.* Jefferson, N.C.: McFarland & Co., 1999

Kaese, Harold and Lynch, R.G. *The Milwaukee Braves.* New York: G.P. Putnam, 1954

Kahn, Roger. *The Boys of Summer.* New York: Harper & Row, 1973

Kinsella, W.P. *Shoeless Joe.* New York: Ballantine Books, 1982

Lansche, Jerry. *Glory Fades Away.* Dallas: Taylor Publishing, 1991

Levy, Alan. *Rube Waddell.* Jefferson, N.C.: McFarland & Co., 2000

Lewis, Michael. *Moneyball*. New York: W.W. Norton, 2003

Lieb, Frederick. *Connie Mack Grand Old Man of Baseball*. New York: G.P. Putnam, 1945

Lieb, Frederick. *Baseball As I Have Known It*. New York: Grosset & Dunlap, 1977

Lowry, Philip. *Green Cathedrals*. Manhattan, KS: AG Press, 1986

Neft, David and Cohen, Richard. *The Sports Encyclopedia Baseball (Sixth Edition)*. New York: St. Martin's Press, 1985

Neyer, Rob. *Rob Neyer's Big Book Of Baseball Lineups*. New York: Simon & Schuster, 2003

Neyer, Rob and Epstein, Eddie. *Baseball Dynasties*. New York: W.W. Norton, 2000

Olan, Ben. *Big-Time Baseball*. New York: Hart Publishing, 1960

Okkonen, Marc. *Baseball Uniforms of the 20th Century*. New York: Sterling Publishing, 1991

Okrent, Daniel and Wulf, Steve. *Baseball Anecdotes*. New York: Oxford Press, 1989

Reichler, Joseph. *The Baseball Trade Register*. New York, Macmillan, 1984

Ritter, Lawrence and Honig, Donald. *The Image Of Their Greatness*. New York: Crown Publishers, 1979

Roberts, Robin with C. Paul Rogers, III. *My Life in Baseball*. Chicago: Triumph Books, 2003

Robinson, George and Salzberg, Charles. *On A Clear Day They Could See Seventh Place*. New York: Dell Publishing, 1991

Robinson, Ray. *Matty, An American Hero*. New York: Oxford Press, 1993

Roth, Philip. *The Great American Novel*. New York: Holt, Rinehart and Winston, 1973

Salin, Tony. *Baseball's Forgotten Heroes*. Chicago: Masters Press, 1999

Scymour, Harold. *Baseball The Early Years*. New York: Oxford University Press, 1960

Scymour, Harold. *Baseball The Golden Age*. New York: Oxford University Press, 1971

Shatzkin, Mike and Charlton, Jim. *The Ballplayers*. New York: William Morrow, 1990

Solomon, Burt. *The Baseball Timeline*. New York: DK Publishing, 2001

Sowell, Mike. *The Pitch That Killed*. New York: Macmillan, 1989

Stark, Benton. *The Year They Called Off The World Series*. Garden City Park, NY: Avery Publishing, 1991

Thomas, Henry. *Walter Johnson*. Lincoln, NB: University of Nebraska Press, 1995

Thorn, John. *A Century of Baseball Lore*. New York: Galahad Books, 1980

Thorn, John, editor. *The National Pastime*. New York: Warner Books, 1987

Thorn, John and Palmer, Pete. *The Hidden Game of Baseball*. Garden City, NY: Doubleday & Co., 1985

Thorn, John and Palmer, Pete. *Total Baseball (fourth edition)*. New York: Warner Books, 1995

Thorn, John and Holway, John. *The Pitcher*. New York: Prentice Hall Press, 1987

Tiemann, Robert and Rucker, Mark. *Nineteenth Century Stars*. Kansas City, MO: Society for American Baseball Research, 1989

Veeck, Bill. *Veeck – as in Wreck*. New York: Ballantine Books, 1962

Westcott, Rich. *Philadelphia's Old Ballparks*. Philadelphia: Temple University Press, 1996

Websites/Electronic Format:

All Baseball
www.all-baseball.com

Atlanta Journal-Constitution
www.accessatlanta.com/ajc

Baseball Almanac
www.baseball-almanac.com

Baseball Archive
www.baseball1.com

Baseball Immortals
http://totk.com/baseballimmortals

Baseball Index
www.baseballindex.org

Baseball Library
www.baseballlibrary.com

Baseball Primer
www.baseballprimer.com

Baseball Prospectus
www.baseballprospectus.com

Baseball Reference
www.baseball-reference.com

Billy-Ball
www.billy-ball.com

ESPN
http://msn.espn.go.com

Historical Society of Pennsylvania
www.hsp.org

Major League Baseball
http://mlb.com

Mudville Magazine
www.mudvillemagazine.com

National Baseball Hall of Fame
http://baseballhalloffame.org

Neyer, Rob
www.robneyer.com

Philadelphia Inquirer
www.phillynews.com

Philadelphia Phillies
http://phillies.mlb.com

Retrosheet
www.retrosheet.org

Sabrmetric Baseball Encyclopedia
www.baseball-encyclopedia.com

Society for American Baseball Research
www.sabr.org

Sports Illustrated
www.sportsillustrated.cnn.com

The Sporting News
www.sportingnews.com

USA Today
www.usatoday.com/sports

Sinins, Lee. *Sabrmetric Encyclopedia of Baseball*. Livingston, NJ:
Lee Sinins, 2002

Newspapers:

Atlanta Journal-Constitution
Cincinnati Times-Star
Philadelphia Inquirer
Pittsburgh Post-Gazette
The Sporting News

ENDNOTES

1   Bill James, *The New Bill James Historical Baseball Abstract* (New York: The Free Press, 2001) p. 788.

2   Fred Lieb, *Connie Mack Grand Old Man of Baseball* (New York: G.P. Putnam's Sons, 1945) p. 174.

3   Bill James, *The New Bill James Historical Baseball Abstract* (New York: The Free Press, 2001) p. 486.

4   Ibid, p. 490.

5   Charles Alexander, *Ty Cobb* (New York: Oxford University Press, 1984) p. 185-186.

6   Ibid, p. 186.

7   Ibid, p. 187.

8   Ibid, p. 194.

9   Fred Lieb, *Baseball As I Have Known It* (New York: Grosset & Dunlap, 1977) p. 62.

10   Charles Alexander, *Ty Cobb* (New York: Oxford University Press, 1984) p. 188.

11   Ibid, p. 188.

12   Ibid, p. 226.

13   Bill James, *The Bill James Baseball Abstract 1987* (New York: Ballantine Books, 1987) p. 299.

14   Bill James, *The New Bill James Historical Baseball Abstract* (New York: The Free Press, 2001) p. 592.

15   Ibid, p. 358.

16   Burt Solomon, *Baseball Timeline* (New York: DK Publishing, 2001) p. 110.

17   Bill James, *The Bill James Baseball Abstract 1986* (New York: Ballantine Books, 1986) p. 187.

[18] Bill James, *The Bill James Baseball Abstract 1983* (New York: Ballantine Books, 1983) p. 220.

[19] Bill James, *The Bill James Baseball Abstract 1985* (New York: Ballantine Books, 1985) p. 300.

[20] Bill James, *The Bill James Baseball Abstract 1988* (New York: Ballantine Books, 1988) p. 229.

[21] John Thorn and Pete Palmer, editors, *Total Baseball, Fourth Edition* (New York, Viking, 1995) p. 172.

[22] Peter Golenbock, *Bums* (New York: Simon & Schuster, 1984) p. 34, 35.

[23] Ibid, p. 34

[24] Ibid, p. 79

[25] Ibid, p. 204, 205

[26] Ibid, p. 79

[27] Roger Angell, *Once More Around the Park* (New York: Ballantine Books, 1991) p. 58.

[28] Ibid, p. 63.

[29] Ibid, p. 66.

[30] Robin Roberts, with C. Paul Rogers, III, *My Life in Baseball* (Chicago: Triumph Books, 2003) p. 173.

[31] Bill Veeck, with Ed Linn, *Veeck... as in Wreck* (New York: Ballantine Books, 1976) p. 143.

[32] Bill James, *The Bill James Baseball Abstract 1985* (New York: Ballantine Books, 1985) p. 300.

[33] Bill James, *The New Bill James Historical Baseball Abstract* (New York: The Free Press, 2001) p. 686.

[34] Ibid, p. 686.

[35] Ibid, p. 686.

[36] Peter Golenbock, *Bums* (New York: Simon & Schuster, 1984) p. 29.

[37] Jim Bouton, *Ball Four* (Cleveland: World Publishing, 1970) p. 326.

[38] David Jordan, *The Athletics of Philadelphia* (Jefferson, N.C.: McFarland & Company, Inc., 1999) p. 21.

[39] Philadelphia Inquirer, April 25, 1901.

[40] Bill James, *The New Bill James Historical Baseball Abstract* (New York: The Free Press, 2001) p. 558.

[41] Ibid, p. 538.

[42] W.P. Kinsella, *Shoeless Joe* (New York: Ballantine Books, 1982) p. 3.

[43] Bill James, *The Bill James Baseball Abstract 1983* (New York, Ballantine Books, 1983) p. 7.

[44] Bill James, *The Politics of Glory* (New York, Macmillan Publishing, 1994) p. 122

[45] Bill James, *The Bill James Historical Baseball Abstract* (New York: Villard Books, 1988) p. 225.

[46] Ibid, p. 227.

[47] The Sporting News, February 27, 1913.

[48] Jim Brosnan, *Pennant Race* (New York, Dell Publishing, 1962) p. 158.

[49] Bill Veeck, with Ed Linn, *Veeck... as in Wreck* (New York: Ballantine Books, 1976) p. 248.

[50] Ibid, p. 174.

[51] Peter Golenbock, *Bums* (New York: Simon & Schuster, 1984) p. 140.

[52] Bill Veeck, with Ed Linn, *Veeck... as in Wreck* (New York: Ballantine Books, 1976) p. 119.

[53] Robert Gordon and Tom Burgoyne, *More than Beards, Bellies and Biceps* (Champaign, Il.: Sports Publishing, 2002) p. 5.

[54] Ibid, p. 125.

[55] Ibid, p. 181.

[56] Ibid, p. 232.

[57] Bill James, *The New Bill James Historical Baseball Abstract* (New York: The Free Press, 2001) p. 784, 785.

[58] G. H. Fleming, *The Unforgettable Season* (New York: Simon & Schuster, 1981) p. 184.

[59] John Thorn, Editor, *The National Pastime* (New York, Warner Books, 1982) p. 273.

[60] Ibid, p. 276.

[61] Bill James, *The Bill James Historical Baseball Abstract* (New York: Villard Books, 1986) p. 71.

[62] Bill James, *The Politics of Glory* (New York: Macmillan

Publishing, 1994) p. 200.

[63] G. H. Fleming, *The Unforgettable Season* (New York: Simon & Schuster, 1981) p. 244.

[64] Ibid, p. 207.

[65] Ibid, p. 245.

[66] Ibid, p. 245.

[67] Ibid, p. 249.

[68] Ibid, p. 245.

[69] Ibid, p. 293.

[70] Ibid, p. 266.

[71] Ibid, p. 287.

[72] Philip J. Lowry, *Green Cathedrals* (Manhattan, KS: AG Press, 1986) p. 36.

[73] Fred Lieb, *Baseball As I Have Known It* (New York: Grosset & Dunlap, 1977) p. 5.

[74] Peter Golenbock, *Bums* (New York: Simon & Schuster, 1984) p. 44.

[75] Ibid, p. 41.

[76] Ibid, p. 47.

[77] Jerry Lansche, *Glory Fades Away* (Dallas, TX: Taylor Publishing, 1991) p. 28, 29.

[78] Roger Kahn, *The Boys of Summer* (New York: The New American Library, 1973) p. 179.

[79] Fred Lieb, *Connie Mack Grand Old Man of Baseball* (New York: G.P. Putnam's Sons, 1945) p. 227.

[80] Philip J. Lowry, *Green Cathedrals* (Manhattan, KS: AG Press, 1986) p. 70.

[81] Fred Lieb, *Connie Mack Grand Old Man of Baseball* (New York: G.P. Putnam's Sons, 1945) p. 228.

[82] David Halberstam, *Summer of '49* (New York: William Morrow and Company, 1989) p. 256-260.

[83] Ibid, p. 267-272.

[84] Bill James, *The Politics of Glory* (New York: Macmillan Publishing, 1994) p. 192.

[85] Fred Lieb, *Connie Mack Grand Old Man of Baseball* (New York: G.P. Putnam's Sons, 1945) p. 177.

86 Marc Okkonen, *Baseball Uniforms of the 20th Century* (New York: Sterling Publishing, 1991) p. 90.

87 Henry W. Thomas, *Walter Johnson* (Lincoln, NB: University of Nebraska Press, 1995) p. 90m.

88 Marc Okkonen, *Baseball Uniforms of the 20th Century* (New York: Sterling Publishing, 1991) p. 94, 100.

89 Ibid, p. 243, 253.

90 Ibid, p. 101.

91 Ibid, p. 130.

92 Ibid, p. 161.

93 Jim Bouton, *Ball Four* (Cleveland: World Publishing, 1970) p. 2.

94 Philip Roth, *The Great American Novel* (New York: Holt, Reinhart & Winston, 1973) p. 280.

95 Ibid, p. 1.

96 Jim Bouton, *Ball Four* (Cleveland: World Publishing, 1970) p. 398.

97 W.P. Kinsella, *Shoeless Joe* (New York: Ballantine Books, 1982) p. 4.

98 Jim Bouton, *Ball Four* (Cleveland: World Publishing, 1970) p. 242

99 Ibid, p. 22.

100 Michael Lewis, *Moneyball* (New York: W.W. Norton & Company, 2003) p. 24.

101 Ibid, p. 17.

102 Ibid, p. 9.

103 Ibid, p. 9.

104 Ibid, p. 198.

105 Ibid, p. 244.

106 Ibid, p. 152.

107 Ibid, p. 198.

108 Bill James, *The New Bill James Historical Baseball Abstract* (New York: The Free Press, 2001) p. 885.

Printed in the United States
22960LVS00008B/94-123

9 781413 742763